D.B. COOPER & ME

PRINCIPIA
MEDIA

GRAND RAPIDS, MI
2018

by CARL LAURIN
as told to Lisa McNeilley

D.B. COOPER & ME

A CRIMINAL

A SPY

MY BEST FRIEND

D.B. Cooper & Me: A Criminal, A Spy, My Best Friend

© 2018 Carl Laurin

Published in the United States by Principia Media, LLC

Principia Media, LLC
678 Front Avenue NW Suite 256
Grand Rapids, MI 49504 www.principiamedia.com

ISBN 978-1-61485-325-1

Cover Design: Nicole Fadden of The Buffalo Works
Interior Design: Frank Gutbrod
Digital Imaging: Sherry Baribeau
Editing: Patricia Waldygo

Photos courtesy of Carl and Loretta Laurin, Lisa Story, Jim McCusker, Julie Hurley, Jeff Osiadacz, Sherry Baribeau and Dirk Wierenga

19 18 17 16 15 14 7 6 5 4 3 2 1
Printed in the United States of America

CONTENTS

PREFACE

The clock gets wound only once for all of us, and we don't know when it will stop. Some choose to set the clock and let it tick their time away, and others do not.

Casual observers would think we had a death wish, but not so. Ex-paratroopers all, some of us became mercenaries, bush pilots, diamond smugglers, assassins for various governments. One became involved with the notorious Barry Seal in a plot to overthrow Castro's Cuba. Yet another became the hijacker D.B. Cooper.

CHAPTER 1

THE MICHIGAN PARACHUTE CLUB

November 25, 1971—*In a crime that shocked the world, a lone man hijacked Northwest Orient Flight 305 over Washington State, parachuted out of the plane with a ransom of $200,000, and disappeared. No one knew whether he'd survived the jump or died in the mountain wilderness.*

As news about the "D.B. Cooper" hijacking flashed on TV, I turned to my wife, Loretta. "What the hell did Walt just do?"

She looked over in surprise. "You really think it was him?"

Of course, I had no proof. Yet ever since Art Lussier and I had taught our friend Walt how to free-fall, he'd talked about using a parachute to commit a crime.

I hadn't seen much of Walt Peca since 1965, when he was in jail for the Big Boy robbery. Walt was a complicated man who lived a complicated life. He'd been a member of our Michigan Parachute Club—or Team, as we often called it—a ragtag bunch of guys with nothing to worry about, except how one bad plan might lead us to another adventure. Guys who lived somewhere just off to the side of a "normal" life.

Back then, we considered life a huge laugh and a chance to beat the odds. Every time we jumped in the snow or a storm, in the dark,

Walt geared up and ready to jump

from a plane that wasn't fit to fly, or over woods or neighborhoods, and we didn't die, we felt the euphoria of surviving. We were young, and we had cheated death.

We had all been U.S. Army paratroopers at various points in our lives. Art, Bill (a.k.a. Colonel Parker), and I had formed the club in 1957. That same year Walt read an article about us in the *Detroit Free Press* and drove to Flint, Michigan, to investigate.

Our team took the burgeoning sport of parachute jumping to new levels. We felt like the original adventurers and innovators, doing batwing jumps, loops, and suicide spins with jubilation and not much discipline.

This was the group Walt joined in 1957 at age twenty-four, where he learned to embrace danger, take chances, and act on a whim with only the slightest of plans. Our philosophy was "One bad idea deserves another."

Yet the jumps we did were not just dangerous, they were nearly suicidal. Today, modern parachutes open gently, with minimal bounce after they inflate. The modern parachutist goes from free fall to a steerable, controllable descent with a soft landing. Back in 1957, the round chutes couldn't be steered. They opened with a vicious jerk upward, then we landed very hard and were often dragged

Today's parachutes are steerable

Yesterday's round parachute

hundreds of yards by the wind. We jumped out of the plane at 800 feet, free-fell for 3 seconds, and then opened the chute hopefully a few feet above the ground.

Now parachutists jump from 13,500 feet, open the canopy at 5,000 feet, and the reserve chute automatically opens at 2,500 feet. We jumped from as low as 800 feet and as high as 9,000 feet, leaving little margin for error. None of us should have lived through five jumps, but for some reason we survived hundreds. My most dangerous jump was opening at 40 feet in a blinding snowstorm.

In the 1950s, the Russians got into parachuting much more than Americans did. Leo Valentin, a Frenchman, experimented with batwings. Who knows what he might have achieved if he hadn't been killed in 1956 when one batwing hit the plane as he exited? He spun to the ground below, tangled in his chute. When we heard about that, we decided we'd find a way to do successful batwing jumps.

Amazingly, the most we suffered was a few broken bones. We did those batwing jumps in suits we made ourselves. When 85 percent of batmen were getting killed, we survived, even though we didn't know what we were doing. We just made it all up as we went along, without testing anything for safety.

Reunion at the Billabog

Fast-forward thirty-eight years. The idea of a team reunion was Art's. He was a genuine daredevil and everyone's best friend. He called me in the fall of 1997, when he lived in Michigan, and I lived near Daytona Beach, Florida.

"Damn, Art, it's thirteen hundred miles from there to here," I said, hoping he'd change his mind.

"Not here to there," he said. "There to here: my place. I'm alone now. We got all kinds of room." The kids were on their own, and his wife, Patty, had left him.

Batwing

The reunion Art was talking about had nothing to do with growing up or growing old. It was about a special time in our lives that very few men had lived through; great battles, as in World War II, come to mind. The difference was, we did things for fun, not because we had to, yet the end result was close to the same. Death was just a whisker away, but death never came. Why? Perhaps now that all of us were older, someone had figured it out. I hadn't, and, as it turned out, no one else had either.

Art told me he had located most of the Michigan Parachute Club, and I was to call them and fix a date most suitable. We would meet at Art's place, which I soon dubbed the Billabog.

May 5, 1998

The Billabog was not a resort. It was a 44-acre swampy bog with Art's cabin sitting on an acre of fill at its farthest point from Bay Gladwin Road in Pinconning, Michigan. The drive into the Billabog was sand and would only support cars on good days, four-wheel drive on most days, and Fed Ex and UPS never. Art loved it that way, but before he died, he would rue never updating that driveway with a solid surface.

On May 5, 1998, the day of our first Billabog, all the cars made it through the swamp on Art's trail of sand and ended up at his cabin. My doubts about the treacherous drive faded with the cheers, the handshakes, and the ring of gunshots. I had to admit it felt pretty good to hear my nickname, Charlie Brown, again. Especially from this crew.

I was as happy that day as I had ever been, and it only got better. Soon we'd be telling old stories of when we met and formed the team in the fall of 1957—the air shows, the batwing jumps, Alaska, and Las Vegas. And there would be new stories, covering the thirty-eight years between 1960 and now.

On the second day of the Billabog, as morning turned to noon, then noon turned to evening, Art ingested an enormous amount of booze—one-half gallon, maybe. He collapsed on his living room floor near the potbelly stove.

"I'm a swagman!" he yelled. He raised his bottle over his head, spilling its contents all over himself. Then he tried to sing.

"Once a jolly swagman," Art wailed,

. . . camped by a billabong,
Under the shade of a coolibah tree.
He sang and he watched and waited 'til his billy boiled,
"You'll come a-waltzing, Matilda, with me."

"What the fuck is that?" Walt said.

"It's the only fucking song I know all the words to," Art said.

He had learned the song in a saloon with a couple of Aussies, all of them tanked. He felt good when he sang it, so we egged him on by attempting to sing along with him. It was a song made for drunks. It sounded so bad, it was good—at least, if you were drunk, I think it sounded good.

But we never sang the chorus—"Matilda, my darlin'" was too schmaltzy for us.

Parker said, "Your place is a billabong, if I ever saw one."

"No, it's a billa-*bog*," I said.

The name stuck, and we started calling Art's place the Billabog.

By this time, the shooting was over. We did that in the afternoon. We were pretty good shots, too, if we had something to rest our guns on. Walt and Parker had brought the guns. Apparently, Walt had an arsenal at home.

Walt made a delicious meal, lasagna—the best I'd ever had. We all downed it with a few more beers, even me. The Billabog became a time in our lives for reflection, good and bad—for storytelling, for things we wished we'd done better. For me, each Billabog was a window into the lives of my friends.

I was struck by how we'd all stayed the same. Everybody looked and acted the same—that is, if you went from 1960 until now and skipped the thirty-eight years in between.

Yet I remembered a period of time when Walt had seemed different. It was around 1975—August, I think. Walt's ex-wife Joni had called to say he was in town from the Middle East and invited Loretta and me for a visit. We drove to Westland to Joni's apartment and parked in her drive behind a new black Cadillac that at the time I didn't know was bulletproof.

Walt answered the door, his blond crew cut replaced by long dark hair, his casual dress by a custom-made suit. I did a double-take at his changed appearance, but he didn't explain anything.

"Hi, Charlie . . . Hi, Loretta," he said. "Come on in."

Walt and Joni seemed to be back together again. We talked about the old days and watched a poorly focused movie of his diamond mine in Sierra Leone. Yet despite our shared history and long friendship, Walt seemed distant, as if he had a lot on his mind.

On our drive home, I remember saying, "Walt has become really serious, don't you think?"

"He wore a suit," Loretta said. "Maybe he had someplace to go later."

We let it go at that but were in full agreement that he was not the old Walt, laughing and full of fun.

Now, at our first Billabog, the old Walt was back. The crew cut, the blond hair, the smile, the "How you doin', Charlie? Good to see you."

Since then, I have learned so much about Walt's time in the Middle East and why my old friend hadn't been smiling . . . it was because he couldn't.

Great Stories and Lifetime Memories

On the final night of the first Billabog, we stayed up for hours telling stories, gathered around Art's potbellied stove for warmth. Though Walt never sang, the rest of us belted out a few more rounds of "Waltzing Matilda," led by Art.

I drank my coffee, while the others downed a few beers, until everyone got tired and fell asleep in various rooms and corners.

I turned out the light and curled up on the hard floor. But sleep doesn't come easy when you're sixty, need a new hip, and are wrapped up in a sleeping bag on a wooden floor, so I had time to think. Being together with these guys made me feel young again. I didn't exactly long for the old days, but maybe I longed for a time when we were all together.

After forming the Michigan Parachute Team more than forty years ago, we'd stayed in contact only intermittently over the years. Still, we had a unique bond based on our lives hanging in one another's hands, and we had survived.

Our escapades faded into stories and memories, as work and families and responsibilities took over. We weren't jumping out of airplanes or flying across the world anymore, but tonight we were together with all those memories to share.

The next morning, we'd all go back to our separate lives. Most nights, before I went to sleep, I thought about how lucky I was, and that night I felt it more than ever. I would go back to a great life—my wife, Loretta; my farm; my golden retriever Minnie; and my pet goat Beauty. My two kids were grown and happy.

Yet there was something special about the time I had with my friends, and I wanted to hold onto it, if I could. As I drifted off, I kept thinking that the way these guys were putting away the booze, they would die and take all of their stories and years of experience to their graves. They meant too much for me to let that happen.

After I left the first Billabog, I felt determined to recapture those early years. So in my free time, I sat at a table and wrote down things we had done. I wanted to reconstruct the past, as I remembered it, and our friendships and the thrill of being young.

In my writing, I briefly mentioned my suspicion that Walt was D.B. Cooper. Loretta had hatched the plan of putting this in the manuscript, as a way of drawing Walt out.

The Second Billabog: Confronting Cooper

At the end of the first Billabog, we decided to meet every two years, but McCusker came up to me and said, "These guys aren't going to make it two more years. We better do this every year, or we'll never see half of them again." So from then on, we gathered every May at Art's cabin. When it was time to go home, we looked forward to the next Billabog. I don't know how, but it fell to me to plan everything.

It reminded me of the times when we used to go someplace together, and as we left, McCusker would say, "Pay 'em Charlie," and I would. McCusker would use this line for drinks or food, but Art said it even when we bought cars or airplanes. Somehow I usually ended up paying.

Out of all of us, I was the responsible one, so I planned the Billabogs, and each year after that, we met in May.

Up at Art's place again in May 1999, we all fell into our regular patterns, talking, laughing, drinking. This time even Walt's old friend Willard showed up, looking round and puffy from the vodka. In the evenings, Walt cooked dinner, and we sat around reminiscing.

We got into a discussion about the pretty girls we had known, the ones we had loved, and the ones who walked away. Walt had the most experience here, but he had the least to say about it.

Parker said to Mike, one of Art's little brothers, "Michigan's Youngest Parachutist."

When Mike the Kid was thirteen, we let him jump. We thought he might be the youngest parachutist in the United States or maybe the world.

"What was that, February?" Parker asked.

"It was, and freezing," Mike said. "Winds at thirty miles per hour."

"We got up to twenty-five hundred feet in that little three-seater," I said, "and Art tapped you on the shoulder, and out you went."

"You should have seen him down below," Parker said. "That chute was blowing like crazy. It nearly took him to the farm next to the airport."

We all laughed at the idea of Mike being blown away. He was tall and solid now.

Art was about thirty pounds lighter than Mike and had thinning gray hair. His face was lined and reddened from too much time in the sun, and in spite of the drink, he still had ropy muscles. It was funny to see this man play the big brother role. After that, Art started us on a drunken rendition of "Waltzing Matilda."

The next morning, I had a gift for everyone. Loretta had taken my stories and had them typed up. We'd added some photos, then had the book Xeroxed and bound at a copy shop. The cover was a collage of some of our best pictures and the title *The Last Barnstormers*. Everybody loved it.

Strangely enough, those stories led me to begin this project. A few months before the second Billabog, Loretta and I had watched a television special about D.B. Cooper, the hijacker. The show described what he said to the stewardesses, which cigarettes he smoked, and a few other things.

Back in the seventies, we'd seen the FBI's composite sketch, and we didn't think it looked anything like Walt. Yet after watching this TV special, I revisited the possibility that Walt was the hijacker.

Cover of Carl Laurin's book about the Michigan
Parachute Team

I remembered the Big Boy holdup and the way the robber was always so polite. I couldn't get that out of my mind.

I later heard that the same night when Loretta and I first saw the news about the hijacking, Willard's father, Zephie Stahl, had said the same thing we did: "Did you hear what Walt did?" Yet none of us had known Walt was in Washington State at the time.

For weeks, I examined what I knew about my friend: his need for money, his daredevil attitude, and that he seemed to disappear in the seventies, popping up from time to time with outrageous stories about where he had been or with no explanation at all, just a phone call to say, "I'm still alive. Are you?" We never let go of the bond that tied us together, but sometimes it stretched pretty thin.

I felt pretty sure Walt was the guy, so at the second Billabog, I said to him, "You son of a bitch, you're D.B. Cooper."

"No, I'm not," he said.

A couple of times when we were talking, I called him D.B., just to see his reaction. Each time, he looked at me kind of funny and said, "No, no, Charlie, I'm not."

Then when I asked him again, he started hemming and hawing, but he didn't deny it.

Once Art interrupted our conversation and said, "You know what you should write about, Charlie? Ask Walt about the time he spent in Sierra Leone with the diamonds."

Art pulled out some paper and a pen and handed them to me.

We had all heard bits and pieces of Walt's escapades. Maybe getting him to talk about Africa might make him confess to what I believed was the truth.

"How'd you hear about the diamonds in Sierra Leone?" I asked Walt.

"I was on a fucking oil platform, when I met a man who worked in a commercial diamond mine in Sierra Leone." Walt said. "We got to talking, and he told me all about it."

"How did you smuggle the diamonds out?"

"I dressed up as a priest, so they let me through the checkpoints."

"Were you afraid when you crossed the border?"

"I was afraid of dying in a foreign land, Charlie. Those borders are rough. If they suspect something, those bastards will shoot you or hang you on the spot. If they did, nobody would know where I was or what happened to me."

I could tell this would be a typical story from Walt's life, full of excitement and craziness.

"Was anybody with you?"

"One time Joni came along. That was after I got back with her and after she lived with me and Carla. She posed as a journalist for *National Geographic of Canada*, right there."

"When did you decide to hijack a plane, D.B.?" I threw in, hoping to catch him off guard.

"I never decided nothing, Charlie," Walt said.

This conversation was one of many during our second Billabog.

Never knowing for sure about Walt might have driven me crazy, but the way things happened, it almost felt like it was meant to be.

Walt's denials about being D.B. Cooper didn't surprise me. He had a lot of secrets. None of us knew what he'd been up to for all those years. Yet after I got back home from the second Billabog, I kept hearing news or conversations that reminded me of D.B. Cooper.

I seriously began to suspect Walt when a friend gave me a copy of the book *D.B. Cooper: The Real McCoy*, written by two retired FBI agents.[1] They revealed new facts about the hijacking—for example, that the hijacker offered money to one of the stewardesses, saying, "This is for your troubles." That got me thinking about how Walt had done the same thing when he robbed the Big Boy. So I kept asking him more questions about the hijacking.

---

1   Bernie Rhodes and Russell Calame, *D.B. Cooper: The Real McCoy* (Salt Lake City, Utah: University of Utah Press, 1991).

The bombshell came when Walt said, "At least, the waitress took the money."

"Tell My Story, Charlie . . . after I Die"

The more I thought about it, I felt sure Walt was D.B. Cooper, and I couldn't resist piecing the story together. I imagined Walt getting on the plane, holding the briefcase, talking to the stewardess.

Sitting at my kitchen table in the spring of 2000, I wrote it all down. I had written a shorter story about Walt in the Xeroxed book I gave the Billabog group in 1999, but this was an expanded version. Loretta typed up my story of the hijacking, and I mailed it to Walt in late 1999 or early 2000.

When I called later to ask him about it, Walt said, "You give me too much credit, Charlie. There was no planning."

That was the first time he admitted anything—almost.

Then, in a 2008 phone conversation, Walt told me, "You know, I've had a lot of jobs. I've traveled around the world, right there. In some ways, it's been a good life. In others, things have just gone wrong, I don't know why. Some of my best memories are the days when we were young, flying, jumping, having a great time."

"Yeah, I remember," I said, wondering what this was all about.

"I've never told anybody about everything I've done, but I'm gonna tell you. You just got to promise me that you'll wait until I die, and then you can tell everyone."

"Who am I gonna tell?"

"I've got some papers and stuff to go through," Walt said, "and I'll send you some things. I'm trusting you with this."

No More Lying

It wasn't until Thanksgiving of that year, 2008, that he finally called and said the words, "I am D.B. Cooper."

Walt's confession to me came like a small boy telling his father he had taken a dollar out of his dad's pants pocket. His voice was soft and apologetic and unlike Walt. It came one month after the last time he'd denied his involvement in the hijacking.

I stood stone cold. "I'm not surprised. On the night we saw the news report, Loretta and I looked at each other and said it seemed like something you'd do."

Walt laughed his old laugh, the one that showed he was up for anything. "You weren't wrong. I don't want to lie to you anymore."

So Loretta's plan—of me writing about Walt as D.B. Cooper—had worked because at each Billabog from 1999 on, when we were away from the others, Walt confided more details about his life. Yet it wasn't until I mailed him the longer story I'd written in 2008 that our intensive phone calls began, and Walt agreed to be audiotaped. So our crude plan gradually got Walt talking. He also had some health scares later that year, and I think he realized it was time to fess up.

Months later, after we'd discussed the hijacking in detail, I asked about his motives. "You said the reason you did this thing was more for your kids than yourself, because you never wanted them to go through the hunger that you did."

"I wanted a future for them," Walt said. "They turned it all down. I got them a car. I paid for them to go to school. They didn't want none of it."

Walt's Story Slowly Emerges

Beginning that Thanksgiving Day 2008, during a series of phone conversations for the next six years, the story of Walt's life unfolded. We talked nearly every day and sometimes made two or three calls on the same day, while Loretta listened in. I recorded about four months of these conversations on an audiotape hooked up to my daughter's telephone in her home (all with Walt's permission). Because I couldn't figure out how to record on my own home phone, calls made to and from my house were not recorded.

I asked for and received permission to write the story of Walt's life, and he signed a permission agreement.

It always amazed me how many people knew about the Cooper hijacking and had an opinion. The thing they asked the most often was, "What kind of person would have the skill and the knowledge to pull it off? Who would have the nerve?"

As I pulled together stories about our skydiving days, Walt's childhood, his time on the run, and his work with the Teamsters, I was pretty sure I knew the answer. Walt's phone calls just filled in the details.

It was like a puzzle coming together. The bits and pieces I picked up from our conversations added up to a story as true as a story can get.

CHAPTER 2

WALT PECA, THE EARLY YEARS

To learn what drove Walt to hijack Northwest Orient Airlines Flight 305, we need to understand the winding, often perilous course of his life.

Walter R. Peca was born on September 20, 1933. He had vivid memories of his early days in the Church. If you were Polish growing up in Detroit, you were with the unions, and you were Catholic.

Before his father died, his entire family went to mass together each Sunday. His sister, his mother and father, and his grandparents sat in the pews at the front of the church. The priest said mass in Latin, and Walt learned a little of it in his brief service as an altar boy.

After mass, they would have a big dinner, as much as they could afford that week, and his grandparents would say in Polish, "*Pewnego dnia będziesz księdzem.*" ("Someday you will be a priest.")

He had believed them enough to stick with the Church until he was an altar boy, to marry Joni in a Catholic Church, and to pray every day. Yet he also had to make a living however he could, to help his mom and his sister. Then, later in life, all he wanted to do was try to make money for Joni and the kids and then Carla and the kids.[2] All of his mistakes had really been motivated by a desire to take care of his family.

---

2   "Carla" is a pseudonym for the woman Walt became involved with after Joni.

Young Walt with his mom and sister

Tragedy Strikes

I remembered the stories Walt told me about his childhood. His dad had died in 1939 when Walt was just six years old. The entire family lived in an apartment building owned by Walt's grandparents. All of their hopes were pinned on Walt's father, Big Walt; the grandparents were putting him through medical college. One day Big Walt went to the coal yard to get coal for the stove. The basement floor of the coal yard had flooded from melted snow, and when he plugged in the conveyer belt for the coal, he was electrocuted.

After that, Walt had told me, they pinned all of their hopes on a big lawyer, who told the family they should be compensated for their loss. He promised them riches, and Walt's mom went to court to testify. The lawyer won the case, but the family received only a small payment. It was enough to buy a junk car, and the lawyer shafted them for the rest. By the time Walt was ten, he already knew that the big guys had all the power, and the only thing the little guys could do was fight for whatever they could grab for themselves. Almost everything he did in his life came from this overriding belief.

Almost everything *I* did was because I thought it would be fun. That showed how different we were. Yet my life could have been a lot like Walt's, if not for the amazing people who adopted me. My parents made me the luckiest guy in the world. They told me that I had come to them like a gift.

Once when I was a kid, an older person said to me, "You're an orphan, aren't you?"

And I said, "Yes, I guess I am—or, at least, I was."

The man then said, "How lucky you are . . . you were chosen."

I went dead silent. I couldn't believe I'd never thought about it that way, and then he said it again, "You were chosen."

During that entire day, the man's words stuck with me. *Wow*, I thought, *it's a great day for me. A great day for being an orphan or whatever my friends think about me.* I didn't care anymore because I knew that unlike most of them, I was chosen and I could do anything.

The Pay Phone Scam

In 1943, the Great Pay Phone Scam landed Walt, just ten years old, in the hallowed walls of a big brick building on the corner of Forest and Revard—Juvie Hall. Usually, young Walt could talk his way out of such things, but this complaint came directly from the telephone company to the chief of police. Although it involved only forty or fifty phones at that point, they wanted to nip it in the bud before the tactic went nationwide. For sure, Walt got his information from an older boy with a well-established route. Walt already had plans to expand his own route, so you can see how something that provided free money like this could spread like wildfire.

Sam Hat, a little foreign man with his market just off Woodward, often gave Walt old eggs, four for a nickel. Walt would use them to set his phone traps to collect dimes at the end of the day. Here's how it worked: Walt put raw egg in the coin return of every phone on his route, and because callers didn't want to put their fingers in the slimy goo to retrieve their dimes, they'd move on to the next pay phone. Walt would then fish out the dimes using a popsicle stick.

Phone Number One paid off with two shiny dimes, and Walt walked down Woodward to Phone Number Two, next to a building that had a side door beside the phone. It couldn't have been a more perfect hiding place for the police detective peering through the door's peephole.

While Walt fished in the coin slot with a secondhand popsicle stick, he heard a voice say, "Looking for these?" The detective held two dimes between his fingers.

"Oh, no," Walt said, "I have my own dimes. I was going to call my mom and tell her I'll be late for supper."

"Tell her you'll also be late for breakfast, maybe lunch, too—depending on whether the judge lets you out or keeps you."

Walt turned around and looked up at the big man. Except for that day two years ago when his mom said, "Your father won't be coming home this evening, children. He's been electrocuted," this was the next-worst day of Walt's life so far.

Walt and his father

In a nanosecond, everything that was good vanished: the priesthood, his job as altar boy, his ability to contribute to his mom and his sister, Sandy, and to be a big brother. For the first time in his life, he wouldn't be going home. He was going to Juvie Hall. Some of his friends called it jail for little kids.

Busted: A Gravelly Voice in the Darkness

The glow of street lamps through mesh-covered windows and a dim bulb in the ceiling showed a room lined with cots, full of sniveling boys. Walt couldn't believe he was one of them. He sipped warm milk through a straw, trying to choke down dry bologna between two slices of bread.

Then he heard a voice in the darkness that would change his life forever: "Hey, Bed 29. Who the hell are ya?"

Walt made out the form of the gravel-voiced kid lying on his back, legs up and crossed at the knees, as if he were at the beach.

"Who the hell wants to know?" Walt said.

"Tough guy, huh? Name's Stahl . . . Willard Stahl. Been here before. Ya know that?"

"I didn't know that," Walt said. "How many times an' that there?"

"Oh, seven or eight times, maybe. They call me Willard, not Bed 28. Pretty good, huh? When all the dicks know ya by yer first name. What ya in for?"

"Robbery." After that, Walt's words fell off to a soft-spoken, "an' that there."

"Who'd you rob?" Willard said it like a statement, not a question.

"I didn't rob anyone. I got money from a telephone booth."

"Ya robbed a phone booth, huh? What did you say? Stick 'em up, phone booth? Put your mouthpiece an' speaker over yer head."

Walt kept still then, as did the kid in Bed 28.

For the longest time, Walt lay with his eyes closed, listening to the barracks sound out the misery of the night. Sometime between then and daylight, sleep came.

At seven o'clock sharp, the barracks sprang to life. A man in a gray union suit walked between the cots, rattling two broomsticks between the rails of the metal beds. After making a short speech, he turned toward the door and left.

Then the guy in Bed 28 said, "I probably shouldn't say this, but I will anyway. Yer kind of a smartass, 29, but at least you never kept me awake all night crying. I'm giving you my address, so after we get sprung, you can look me up. You'll be after me in line to see the judge. Say what I say, even if it chokes you. 'I'm sorry, Yer Honor. I won't do it again.' We'll be out of here before noon. The dumb asses, the judge keeps . . . ya know that?"

"I do now," Walt said, probably thinking the Stahl kid expected an answer and not yet realizing he said, "Ya know that?" as a matter of habit, not as a question.

The next seven years of Walt's life were probably more painful for me to write about than they were for him to live. I am speaking from an orphan's point of view. It was almost always one mistake after another, followed by a whole slew of new mistakes. Orphans are the world's greatest risk takers because they seldom learn from their mistakes. If that one didn't kill them, neither would the next one.

On Walt's deathbed, his favorite niece, Lisa, said to him, "You sure did live an exciting life."

Walt responded, "Maybe it wasn't as exciting as it was filled with bad decisions."

Because they grew up unsupervised, mistakes were routine for the Stahl gang in 1943. Walt was ten, Willard was twelve, and his brother Weldon, ten, at the gang's formation. Individually, they were not necessarily bad. The gang joined the Boy Scouts for a while. At the suggestion of Sam Hat, the local merchant they routinely stole from, they took to shining shoes and being ball boys at the stadium where the Detroit Tigers played, but they still had sticky fingers.

Once at Willard's house, when they were kids, Walt somehow got hold of a buffalo gun. One thing led to another, and he shot a hole through a wall into the bathroom, where the bullet shattered the toilet. Walt always did love guns.

I've tried to picture myself at ten years old. What would I have done?

By now, Regina, Walt's mother, had found work in the war effort, driving trucks from Detroit defense factories to Baltimore for shipment overseas. This required leaving Walt and his sister at home while she traveled. Although she wasn't the best mother, Sandy and Walt really loved her. At the suggestion of the Stahl boys' father, Zephie, Walt moved in with the Stahl family in his early teens.

The Stahl Gang

The Stahl gang had a reputation that often went unchallenged. Willard, no larger than the ten-year-olds, had a roundhouse right that connected on the face of an opponent like the kick of a mule. Fights with other gangs often ended with one punch. That left Weldon and Walt more spare time for shenanigans.

By nature, Willard was not a thief. He would make the rounds through the neighborhood with the young ones, stealing beer from apple crates nailed to first-floor windowsills. The taste of warm beer was too much temptation for a boy who loved to fight but otherwise had righteous ways.

The boys' favorite movies were the gangster type, and their favorite actors were the tough guys—for example, James Cagney as the gangster boss trapped up on a gasoline storage tank, yelling, "Look, Ma . . . top of the world!" just before the tank explodes, blowing the guy into a billion pieces. Soon the Stahl gang began emulating their gangster heroes.

They got to the tops of buildings by climbing fire escapes or shimmying up drainpipes. Then Willard would take charge in "follow the leader" style, running and jumping the gaps from one building to the next, until they got to a gap too wide.

That's what happened one day in 1944. Willard had made it across by the skin of his toes, and he dared his young charges to follow.

"Chicken, ya know that?" he said several times, then again, "Chicken."

The young boys weren't buying it. They had seen their leader slip and almost fall six stories below to an alley filled with junk barrels.

Weldon, who normally ran second, flatly said he wasn't going to do it. Not until Walt did.

"Someone better do it!" Willard shouted back. "I'm getting tired of being a one-man gang. What if I get tired of fighting for ya? Ya know that?"

Walt retreated to the far side of the building, turned, then took off for all he was worth. Halfway through the leap, he knew he would come up short. When he hit the far wall, the toes of his shoes were on the top ledge, but his body began falling backward. Alert, Willard tackled him around his knees. Neither knew what the other was going to do.

Walt pleaded, "Don't let go."

Willard, who had squatted down, shouted, "We're both going over!"

Across the gap, Weldon screamed, "See what I told ya!"

Then Walt got a hand on the ledge and scrambled to the top and over. He fell half on the roof and half on a breathless Willard.

"That was too close. . . . Ya know that?"

"I already know that," Walt said, ". . . an' that there."

By 1947, the gang had begun to look for bigger targets. On Cass Street stood a building with an open window that Weldon had had his eye on for some time. "It's ten or twelve feet off the ground, too small for a man to get through."

"I suppose *you* could," Willard said.

"If I had a boost."

"That's the showmen's building, ya know that? There wouldn't be any money."

"What about it, Walt?"

"Sure."

"You assholes are gonna trash a building for no money and chance going to jail?" Willard said. "I'm out."

Later that night, the Stahl gang entered an abandoned alley next to the showmen's club. The two younger ones talked Willard into helping boost Weldon to the sill, after which he could go home. That was their agreement. You can see how the younger ones manipulated the older boy. When Weldon dropped to the floor inside, he quickly went to the back door and shouted for Walt, who said, "Come on . . . an' that there." Willard tagged along.

The flicker of Willard's Ronson lighter bouncing off block walls was eerie but not bright at all. An old table appeared in the darkness, piled high with envelopes containing donations for charity. Walt opened one.

"Money!" he shouted.

Sticky fingers stuffed envelopes down shirts and in pockets and held as many as they could.

"Who's down there?" yelled a gigantic figure at the top landing.

Willard, his adrenaline boiling, bolted for the figure standing between him and freedom, followed by his two henchmen.

The grappling and shoving at the top of the stairs were only overpowered by the screams of adolescent boys and a dowdy middle-aged woman. Willard was too strong for her to stop him, but Weldon and Walt would have gotten caught in her grasp had they not been so scared. The gang of hoodlums ran, envelopes sailing behind, until Willard's raspy voice commanded that they stop and seek shelter in a vacant lot overrun with high weeds.

"That's it," Willard said. "I'll fight with ya, but I won't rob with ya."

However, some things don't end just because you want them to. The boys had left a trail, not completely home but close enough that the police could figure out who'd probably done it.

Willard, trying to keep ahead, finally caught his breath. He cautioned his young charges to whisper. "Noise travels farther on a still night," he said. "And something else . . . did you guys drop any envelopes?"

When both of them said they did, Willard told them, "We gotta leave this place before sunup because the cops are gonna search this field."

"How do you know that?" Weldon asked.

"Because the trail of envelopes stops here. So we're gonna quietly take out the money, then find something to hide the envelopes in and drop them in a sewer. Then walk the back streets until we get home, where we go to bed as if nothing happened."

"You really sure they'll come?" Weldon asked.

"Pretty sure. If they think the Stahls are involved. They always do, ya know that."

When the boys woke the next morning, Willard's mom was in the front yard talking to the police. She told them the boys had gone to bed at 11 p.m. and were just now waking up.

Willard's plan was to take his share of the money from the showmen's club and buy a one-way ticket to Kentucky, where he had relatives, and stay there until the money ran out.

Walt in Detroit's Cass Corridor

Weldon and Walt went in halves on a four-man rubber raft from an army surplus store and escaped across the Detroit River, heading for Canada. They were picked up halfway across by a U.S. Coast Guard cutter, then turned over to the police in Detroit. They were released for lack of evidence, after neither boy would tell the police anything.

Walt quit school after eighth grade. I would have quit early, too, but I honored my adoptive parents' wishes and graduated from high school.

Walt had learned English in St. Linus Catholic School, to complement the Polish and Russian he'd learned as a toddler. But Walt's real education began at age eight, after his father was accidentally electrocuted. Streetwise beyond his years, he ran the Cass Corridor in Detroit, dealing with Mafia figures, pimps, and prostitutes.

Walt told me, "As with most gangs, we took oaths. One of which was to join the paratroopers on our seventeenth birthday. I would describe my time in the Eleventh Airborne as uneventful."

Walt enlisted in the army as a paratrooper on February 5, 1951. He was stationed in Germany and honorably discharged from the army on January 6, 1954.

Although Willard didn't consider his army career a life-changing experience, he distinguished himself by repelling several North Korean charges.

On Weldon's fifth jump, he won his wings and broke his back. He did return home, where he and Walt resumed their life of crime, until a car wreck ended Weldon's life.

The same year that he left the army—1954—Walt went to barber school under the GI Bill and became a barber in Royal Oak, Michigan. He served in the National Guard from March 8, 1954, through March 7, 1957.

Later in life, he and Willard went on to run numbers for the mob and get caught up in various cons, until Willard got married and went somewhat legit.

In *Birdmen, Batmen and Skyflyers*, Michael Abrams uncovers the whys of, and reasons for, risky behavior—and, oddly, orphans take far more risks than most people.[3] Walt and I had a lot in common. I was an orphan, and a couple in Michigan adopted me as an eight-day-old baby. Walt was as well, after his father died.[4]

---

3   *Birdmen, Batmen, and Skyflyers: Wingsuits and the Pioneers Who Flew in Them, Fell in Them, and Perfected Them,* Michael Abrams (Harmony Books, 2006; Amazon Kindle edition 2007).
4   *Webster's Dictionary* defines *orphan* as "a child deprived by death by one or usually both parents."

CHAPTER 3

THE PARACHUTE GANG—FRIENDS FOR LIFE

Carl: My Years at Fort Bragg

J ump school at Fort Bragg was supposed to test us, but back in 1954 I was already in pretty good shape. Before joining the army, I had worked in a lumberyard, and I lifted weights. I never smoked or drank, and I loved being out in the sun and the heat. Climbing the tower and simulating jumps were new experiences, but I just told myself that if the guy in front of me could do it, so could I.

Over time, the jumps all seemed to merge together. I couldn't remember much about any specific one, only black nights somewhere over North Carolina and vomit from the first-timers rolling down the aisle of the C-119 transport that carried us to the drop zone. The hold was stifling hot, and the equipment weighed about a hundred pounds, tightly strapped around my middle, making each breath difficult.

When the green light came on, the jumpmaster said, "Stand up and hook up." We lined up to jump, the drone of the engine fading to a dead calm.

I had no memory of jumping, just the sudden realization of floating in total blackness. The adrenaline jolt of fear faded away.

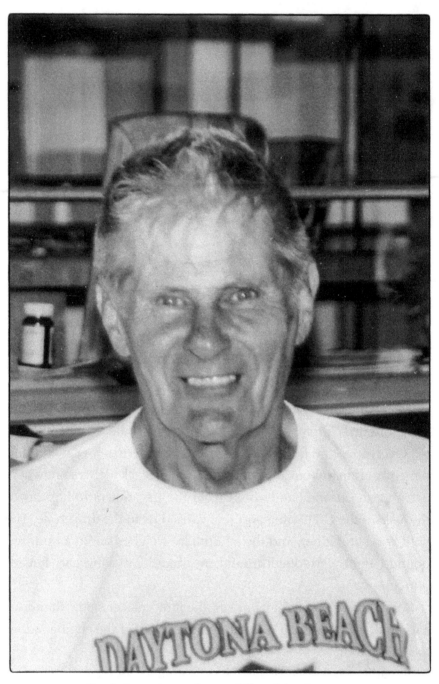

Carl Laurin a.k.a. "Charlie Brown"

After all, there was no enemy below, waiting to shoot when we landed, like the guys who did this for real in Normandy. But in 1954, transporting paratroopers and parachuting were not an exact science. We just aimed for the drop zone and hoped for the best.

Once, as I came down, I searched for the ground in complete blackness. I couldn't see it, until a tree came into focus, and I prepared for a tree landing. Then KA-BOOM, I was on the ground, wondering what the hell had happened. I saw the tree, which was actually a bush, and realized the darkness had played a trick on me. I spit some dirt out of my mouth, gathered up the old T-10, and checked to see if anything was broken. My legs and arms worked fine, and my head was attached the same as always, so I caught up with a couple other guys and hustled over for pickup.

When I went through that gate at Fort Bragg in January 1956, I knew it was the last day I expected to ever serve in that army. I never expected to parachute again either or to invade some other guy's country. That's what parachutes were used for in those days. As I reflect back on my time spent in the army, I wonder, *Was it my fault or theirs that my time wasn't put to better use?*

Back to Civilian Life

They call me Charlie Brown. It's not my real name. With these guys, almost all of us have a nickname. When I got out of the army in January 1956, I started hanging around the Flint Airport, meeting the other pilots and trying to get ready for my GI Bill training in avionics.

About that time, the comic strip *Charlie Brown* came out in the newspapers. I read it in the mornings before heading to the airport. When I ran into one of the guys around the tower or the hangar, I usually asked, "Did you see that *Charlie Brown* today?"

Pretty soon, the guys would see me coming and say, "Hey, Charlie Brown, kicked any footballs today?" And we'd have a laugh. The name stuck, and pretty soon, I don't know if anybody knew my real name—or even cared.

Within one year of being discharged from the army, I had my commercial pilot's license and was a multi-engine land and sea instructor. I had every license short of airline transport rating, which I got later. I didn't get all of those licenses for any particular reason; I just enjoyed the challenge.

Art: Taunting the FAA

In the spring of 1957, I met Art Lussier, and we began rebuilding an old wooden army trainer we found in a field, a PT 19. It resembled a Flying Tiger from World War II, but the fabric covering the fuselage hung in strips. Both wings had bushel-basket size holes, and I could stand through them, feet on the ground. The wings didn't appear to have enough surface to create a lift, yet she flew like a dream. The wood propeller was split, as if hit by lightning. But we only saw the possibilities in her. We checked the oil and brought it up to level, then poured in five gallons of gas. The odds of the engine starting were slim to none, but I looked for the crank that plugged into a hole in the cowling and found it.

Art gave the inertial starter two revs, and the engine sprang to life. It sounded beautiful. After she warmed up a bit, I ran her up and did a mag check.

"It sounds fucking perfect," Art called to me. "Why don't you taxi her down the field to see what she feels like?"

I hopped into the cockpit, which was in surprisingly good shape for sitting out in the Michigan rain and snow for so many years. I turned south and taxied for about 600 feet before turning around. I didn't have a seat belt on or a takeoff plan or a route to fly. I never expected the plane to go airborne, but it did. It rose off the grass like a swan taking flight off a pond. Fabric from the fuselage flapped in the breeze.

Not a single person would have risked taking off in that plane, but I did it without planning to. Once in the air, I had time to wonder if the wings would stay on. Had wood rot weakened the wood-and-fabric plane? Would the cracked propeller split apart, or would the engine, which had sat idle for years, just quit?

I looked through a hole in the plane's body at the crowd gathered below. I circled the airport and brought her in for a perfect landing, then taxied to the ramp. Everybody at the airport came out to see this plane. I patted her on the wing.

Later I had to examine in my own mind the theory of flight: What makes airplanes fly? This airplane defied every rule in the book. It was in worse shape than anyone could imagine.

Life was different then. Nobody ever talked about safety. *Safety* was a word for candy-asses. Danger was everywhere.

But the Federal Aviation Administration felt differently about safety. It had started to oversee the small aircraft and goings on at little airports like Flint. Once word reached Detroit about my flight, the FAA dispatched Mr. Ruby to check out what we were doing.

Ruby went around looking for whoever piloted the plane, but nobody ratted me out. And I never admitted to being the pilot because it would have cost me my license.

I later heard that when Ruby first saw the plane, he said, "How the hell did he [meaning me] get that off the ground?"

I thought, *I don't know, but it did fly. Get over it.*

But Ruby never did.

From then on, Ruby pursued me in everything I did. That never stopped me. Hell, it made everything more fun.

Parker: His First Jump

In the summer of 1957, Art saw a tall, dumb-looking guy walking around the airport, looking for someone who would take him up for a parachute jump.

"Colonel" Bill Parker was dressed in full military combat gear, professionally pressed, and shined boots. He carried a World War I bayonet, belt included, a first-aid pouch, and a canteen. His T-10 parachute was modified to accept a ripcord and a reserve parachute. And oh, yes, an army .45, which I assumed to be loaded with one in the chamber.

Using a rope, Art pulled over his Taylorcraft BC 12D, a small side-by-side two-seater. I loved doing aerobatics with it, but it was tiny, and its engine was worn out and lacked power. It had no electrical system, so Art had rigged his own setup to let us fly at night. He'd painted the lenses of three battery-operated flashlights and attached the red and the green ones to the plane's two wing tips and the white light to its tail.

Colonel Parker's expression said it all: *How in hell does he expect me to get into that airplane?*

Art and I then proceeded to take off the two doors and dismantle everything unnecessary from the plane. We stripped Parker of his weapons and military gear and crammed him in.

Art, the pilot, straddled the doorjamb with his butt, while both legs were in the plane, held in by his seat belt. Parker also sat sidesaddle, with his main chute backed up to Art's right side. His left foot was on the airplane step, and his right leg swung free in the breeze. Both hands held the airplane strut.

I swung the prop, and a well-worn cylinder caught hold. After a mag check at the runway's end, they were off in a puff of smoke.

From every corner of the airport, people watched. The tail wheel lifted, but nothing happened. The little airplane carrying two morons rolled on for another quarter mile, and still nothing happened.

Finally, the plane cleared the 4-foot fence at the end of the runway but rose no higher. Then that plane became a dot in the distance, now in the air thirty feet or so, and finally she flew out of sight to even the best pair of eyes.

When the airplane finally returned, along with the chase car carrying Parker, we learned that Parker had jumped from about 400 feet. His chute had opened, then closed, and when he hit the ground, he bounced a few feet into the air.

"Three more feet lower, and I'd be dead," Parker said.

That was the night we started the team and the beginning of the low bomb-in—opening our chutes so low, it seemed impossible. That little Taylorcraft got the engine overhaul she so badly needed, and we finished that PT 19 we had in the hangar, and what a beauty she was!

Walt: Meet the New Guy

As I look back now, everything just magically fell into place. No wonder we thought we couldn't fail. We kept doing the crazy things we did, and more opportunities just came our way. We had the young man's belief that we could show life just who was in charge.

In May 1957, Art told me that a barber from Royal Oak, Michigan, had called him, and Art asked the guy how many jumps he had and where he went to jump school. The guy replied that he'd been a paratrooper in Germany, with more than thirty jumps.

Walt Peca, the new guy, seemed ordinary, but if you were to judge this book by its cover, you'd be wrong—as wrong as I was about predicting our future relationship. If someone would have told me that by the time Walt and I reached eighty, we'd be best friends, I'd have said, "Nobody here will ever see eighty."

When we were paratroopers, that had failed to kill us. Yet it seemed we were bent on killing ourselves now, especially Art. I don't know where we got the idea that we were invincible when it came to parachuting, but we had it.

The new guy, Walt, didn't know that yet, but if he didn't pick up on that idea, he wouldn't last long with us. I'm not sure whether we were bad teachers or good teachers, but something about us inspired confidence, and confidence is everything.

Art found a guy, Ward Seeley, with a Cessna 170 up in Saginaw, Michigan. Ward wasn't afraid of getting into trouble, so he let us use the plane whenever we wanted. Ward was the manager of what is now the H. W. Browne Municipal Airport in Saginaw, Michigan—an average-size grass strip airport thirty minutes' drive north of Flint. Ward was also a top mechanic who mentored several of our club members and gave us a place to jump.

When we picked up Walt in Detroit to take him to the airport, keep in mind that Saginaw was roughly a hundred miles away from Walt's apartment off Eight Mile Road in Detroit. This was quite a jaunt back in the day, prior to interstate highways, taking around two hours each way—the point being that we had to drive a long distance to get to an airport willing to let us jump. This was before sport parachuting existed. We were young guys who had jumped in the military and wanted to keep jumping, but in a way that required far more skills than military static line jumping.

We were out there every Sunday, jumping, putting on a performance for whoever showed up, and gathering a following. Over time, we tried different styles of jumps at various heights to experiment and learn how to control the parachutes. We knew we were taking risks, but it was the only way we could learn what worked and what didn't.

The risks didn't bother us. Once Ward asked Art, "Do you think you'll make it past twenty?"

"Who wants to live forever?" Art said.

Saginaw Airport

We all laughed, and it became a kind of slogan. Part of our dispassionate attitude toward death came from being the children of massive death. In World War II, millions died in major battles and concentration camps. As army paratroopers, we were constantly lambasted by our superiors: "You SOBs are going to die, anyway." After a while, people's threats went in one ear and out the other. We figured that if we hadn't died all the times we were supposed to, then we couldn't die even when we did other crazy things.

How and why did our team of parachute jumpers come about? We were rudderless ships, discharged from an army without going to war (the Korean ceasefire happened in July 1953). We weren't students; we had too much energy for that. We were tired of taking unproductive orders in the military, nor did we care to give them, should we be in that position. We were men of action by nature.

Back then, in addition to me, Art, and Walt, the team consisted of the following members:

43

Bill Parker, or "Colonel Parker," a gun-loving eccentric.

Jim McCusker, a preppy-looking kid from St. Clair Shores, age nineteen. While reading the *Detroit News*, he'd noticed an article about some crazy guys jumping out of planes. The interview featured a barber named Walt Peca. Jim looked up his phone number, called him, and accepted an invitation to join the team for a weekend jump.

Art's little brother Mike Lussier—the youngest parachutist in the world, I believe—who did his first jump at age thirteen.

Steeplejack Clapp ("Jack"), a steeplejack by trade, who was fearless and made from scrap iron, as tough as they come. He made his first jump on his seventy-third birthday.

Suicide Slim, who wasn't fearless, just stupid. He could have been a double for movie actor Jimmy Stewart.

The new kid, Walt—boy, was I right that you couldn't judge a book by its cover. We all went to Saginaw when he made his first free-fall jump.

That Sunday was crisp and clear. Winter had settled early in Saginaw, and the lack of snow on the ground meant it would be frozen hard with no cushion. The west wind blew across the sugar beet fields of the Michigan thumb, combining with the hard landing to make a sport jumper's nightmare.

"Tell you what," Art said. "Me and Parker will go first. We'll probably go out at five thousand and open at eight hundred. You ride along and watch, then you can jump with Charlie on the second trip. That way, you can see how we exit the airplane. That's the easy part. You ever free-fallen before?"

"No," said Walt.

"The most important thing is not to forget to pull your ripcord. And hold onto it. Replacing them gets expensive."

"You've now been through our entire parachute training course," I said, trying to sound official. "After you complete your first jump, if you're still alive, that means you passed."

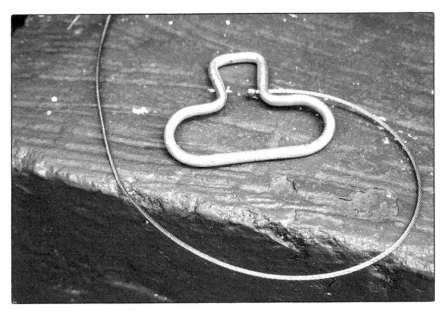

Ripcord—Be sure to pull it!

Everybody laughed, especially Art's younger brothers, Mike and Raymond.

We returned to Parker's car and took a couple of backpacks out of the trunk.

"Where'd you get these?" Walt asked.

"We had them made up at Novi, right down by your house," said Art. "Parker's a master rigger, you know. He actually had to show the guy how to do it."

Parker put on his regular pack and a reserve pack. Art left his reserve in the trunk.

"Don't you have a reserve?" Walt asked.

"Sure," said Art, "but I usually open so low, it wouldn't do me any good if my main fails."

"How low do you open?" Walt asked.

"Real low," Mike answered for Art. "Last Sunday his feet were within ten feet of the ground when his chute blossomed."

"I don't think it ever came down," Parker said. "Maybe it will when it freezes. I'll tell you one thing, when we hit the ground, we're going for a ride today."

We all knew what it was like to jump in this kind of weather. The open chute would act like a sail being pushed by strong winds. Sometimes we would be dragged across the ground at speeds of 40 miles per hour.

A month ago, in April 1957, with Ward's permission, we'd altered the Cessna to make it better for jumping. We had taken out the copilot's seat and removed the door on that side. I hopped into the pilot's seat, and Art kneeled where the copilot's seat had been. Walt sat behind me, and Parker climbed in next to him, behind Art, ready to follow Art out of the plane.

I kicked over the starter, and the engine came to life. We taxied out to the runway.

Down the runway, I put the power to the engine. A dusting of light powdered snow drifted down and blew into streams of gray. Cold air blasted through the missing door hole during takeoff. As always, when I was behind the wheel, I felt confident and cocky. Art and Parker looked like they felt the same. Walt would come to feel this way if he joined us. For now, I just heard his heavy breathing in the seat behind me.

"I'm on the final pass over the drop site," I said.

Art didn't say a word, simply got out of the plane and held onto the wing strut. Parker edged up to the position Art had vacated, and I cut the power to the engine. All of a sudden, Art disappeared and Parker dropped right behind him. I banked the airplane to the right, so Walt could see them careening to the ground. First, Parker's chute opened and billowed around him. But Art waited. He seemed to keep going and going, hurtling to the ground. Then, at the last second, his chute burst open.

"Boy, that was really something," Walt said. "This is better than I expected."

"I'll get this crate on the ground. Then we'll have to listen to their war stories."

When we landed, Parker walked back carrying his chute with a half grin, half sneer.

"The wind took me for a ride for more than half a mile. That's enough for me," he said. "I think I'll just sit and watch."

"Man, that ground is hard," Art said. "That's my jump for today."

He was usually game for several jumps, and he hadn't fared as bad as Parker, so I knew what we were in for.

"We'll go in the hangar and pack up for you and Walt," Art said. "After you two jump, we'll go get some beer. There'll be better days to do this."

In the hangar, Parker walked Art through the rigors of repacking his chute for Walt. Parker was an absolute perfectionist, and Art wasn't bad when he decided he wanted to do something. They were probably trying to show the new guy that no matter what else might go wrong, his chute would not fail him.

Art carefully helped Walt get into his chute, while I put mine on.

"You'll be all right," Art said to Walt, as we boarded the plane. "Just follow Charlie out and let yourself fall four or five seconds before you pull. And don't forget to hold onto your ripcord. You can try a longer free fall next time, when the weather's better. We'll just go to three thousand this time. God only knows where the wind will blow you if you open up too high. I know you've made jumps before, but probably never in wind like this."

Walt made the sign of the cross—and we soon found out that no matter what he did, his Catholic upbringing would show through. Later in life, Walt said that he still prayed every day. That was another thing we had in common. My dad, being a preacher, had instilled in me the need to pray—no matter how my religious beliefs changed.

I kneeled in the copilot's seat this time, and Art piloted the Cessna. I could hear Walt behind me breathing again, ready to take my place. When we reached 3,000 feet, I stepped out onto the strut and jumped. Looking up, I saw Walt right behind me. He seemed to tumble upside-down and pulled his ripcord before me. The chute gave him a heck of a jolt when it opened, then I opened mine and drifted on the wind to the ground. A strong gust blew me along the frozen field a little bit, but someone, probably Parker, managed to grab my chute and dump the air out of it.

Above me, the wind took Walt on a direct collision course with the hangar. He tried to steer, with no luck. He slammed into the steel hangar door about 10 feet from the ground and slid down onto the cold pavement below. I ran over to where he landed, but the spectators surrounded him, helped him up, and brushed him off.

"I'm okay," he slurred, as I approached. He shook his head as if his brain might be rattling around in there. I wondered whether he really was all right.

"Man, that was neat!" Raymond said.

As Walt gathered up his chute with a giddy grin, I nodded, thinking he was now one of us.

Then he wanted to go up again. So he did, and his second jump was much better. I could tell he had little regard for pain. He soon became part of our team, participating in air shows. Technically, he would never be a great jumper. Walt was a street fighter who never lost that mentality, so he parachuted the same way. He never jumped with batwings, but other than that, he would do *anything*.

"Let's head to my place. Mom will have dinner," Art called. He had turned around and landed the plane while we focused on Walt.

Soon we piled into my car and went to Art's house. His mom fed us beans and bread and beer.

Raymond said, "You should have seen it, Mom. Walt came down with his chute open, headed right to the hangar. Then, bam! Just like Roadrunner, he hit at the top and slid to the ground."

The story was getting old, but Walt was a good sport.

"Thank you for this fine dinner, Mrs. Lussier," Walt said, as Art's mom cleared away our bowls.

"You're always welcome here," she said, walking toward the kitchen.

It must have been nice for Walt to be in a home and have a meal. His life wasn't like that at all. The next time we drove down to get him— he still didn't have a car—we went into his apartment above the barbershop where he worked. He had rigged up an extension cord that ran from the barbershop below through a window to power his overhead light, apparently because he couldn't afford to pay for electricity. His furniture consisted of a three-legged table and a chair. It looked like he slept in a pile of blankets on the floor—maybe he had some kind of mattress under there, but I couldn't see one. None of us was rich, but it seemed kind of odd that even though he worked, Walt had so little. Maybe he burned all his money on beer and cigarettes; he smoked four packs a day, and even at a quarter a pack, that had to add up. Or maybe he sent money to his mom and sister. He had always felt he had to take care of them.

The truth was, it was a different time. Jobs were so plentiful when we were growing up, due to the post–World War II boom, you could get five jobs a day—good jobs with health benefits and retirement, not that you wanted to work in a factory. Most of the other guys worked for a while and then quit after saving up a bit of money. Then, when they ran out, they just got a new job. Walt didn't seem to have that luxury and appeared as if he'd do anything for money. He often said that he never wanted to be as poor as he was growing up.

It's Only a Fracture

One vicious night in January, we all managed to be at the field at the same time. The wind whipped through the hangar, cold seeped into our bones, and the field of the drop zone had frozen as hard as concrete. We gathered in the dark, packing our chutes, wondering who would go first and who wouldn't go at all. For once, Jack said he'd meet us in the bar afterward. (Though Steeplejack Clapp was a lot older than the rest of us, he was normally up for anything. But not tonight.)

Art and Walt took the first jump, and I flew the plane. The night was so clear and crisp, I could see their chutes collapse on the ground below as I flew back to the runway. When I landed, they still hadn't made it back to the hangar, so I went to the drop spot to see what had happened. In that cold air, moving was better than standing still, anyway. Art was hovering over Walt, whose left arm dangled at his side in zigzags. They were trying to get him into the car and wrap someone's scarf over his shoulder like a sling.

"I'll be fine," Walt said, grimacing.

"I'm pretty sure it's broken," Art said.

"We'll go to the hospital when we're done," Walt said. "I can make one more jump. I only need my right hand to pull the ripcord, and it's got to be better than jumping with a broken leg."

Walt took one more jump, and after Jimmy McCusker and Parker went, we put Walt in the car.

"We have to stop and tell Jack, or he'll be waiting for us," Parker said, but when he and Jimmy ran into the bar, they didn't come back out. Art, Mike, and I took Walt to the hospital.

"Why does this stuff always happen to me?" Walt asked.

If we knew it was because he always did things without planning or thinking about the next hour or the next day, we didn't say. After all, the rest of us were pretty much the same.

Walt's arm had been broken in five places and he had to wear a cast for almost three months. But as soon as he was able, Walt got back out there.

Two Broken Legs in One Day

On another night, Walt decided to teach two new guys to jump. The wind gauge in Ward's hangar reported steady winds from the west at 45 miles per hour. Skydiving in those heavy wind gusts would be madness. Yet somehow Walt got a pilot to agree to this. Sissler was in the Air Force Reserves, but he planned to quit and transfer to become an army Ranger. He wanted to enlist in the war in Vietnam and get a medal of honor, so he was determined to learn to jump at night. (In death, Sissler actually was awarded the nation's highest medal of honor. He'd undertaken a bayonet charge alone to save his remaining Rangers in Vietnam.)

Ziggler, a friend of Sissler's, had decided to come along. After Walt, Sissler, and Ziggler each completed two jumps, everyone piled into Ziggler's car and went to a tavern.

As they sat around the table drinking beer and talking about how great night jumps were, Walt felt warm blood in his boot. When he held out his leg, they all could see his bones showing.

Sissler said, "You're done for the night. Ziggler and I will make one more jump, then we'll take you to the hospital."

"If you're going up for another jump, so am I," Walt insisted, repeating what he'd said when he broke his arm. This time, though, it was a compound fracture of his leg, so Sissler and Ziggler had to help him walk to the car and get onto the plane. On that jump he favored his good leg and, of course, broke it.

Joni, Walt's girlfriend, and her friend Loretta (my future wife) took him to Garden City Hospital at three in the morning. He didn't have insurance, so the doctor told him to take a couple of aspirins and see his own doctor in the morning.

Paratrooper vs. Parachutist

What's the difference between a paratrooper and a parachutist? For those old enough to remember, on the day before D-Day 1944, the invasion to free Europe, 17,000 paratroopers (mostly American, Canadian, British, and Polish) were dropped behind German lines. Their orders were to take no prisoners, disrupt, destroy, and pave the way for the largest land invasion ever. For those who died in that attempt, it was the last jump they would ever make. For those who survived, it was also, in all likelihood, the last jump they would ever make because, back then, there were so few sports parachutists, you could almost count them on your fingers. Traveling air shows, like the Bowmans and others, sometimes had a parachutist. Now and then, some nutty guy would try to fly with wooden or homemade wings, and he often had a parachute as a backup, but it usually ended up in a heap, until another guy thought he had a better idea, which only ended up in a better heap.

Parachutes of the day were round, opened with a bang, and ended with a crash, but people made developments, nevertheless. Parachutists had evolved from being hooked to a line, as they were in the paratroopers, to falling free, sometimes more than two miles, before pulling a ripcord. More than a few military paratroopers had also become part of the new breed of parachutists and enjoyed the freedom of falling for longer and longer distances before opening the chute. Those who had learned simple techniques taught other people how to be stable and fall a couple of miles without spinning out of control.

That is what Art and I did for Walt. We taught Walt what we knew in 1957, and Walt in turn taught others. We were risk takers. Art and I were the worst, as the batmen and the low bomb-in guys.

Walt never wanted to do a batman—a wing suit, they call them today—or a low bomb-in, when you open the chute within twenty feet of the ground or sometimes lower. I can't explain my own behavior. I certainly knew it was unsustainable.

Today we have wind tunnels and ram air parachutes. Our military, which formerly used parachutes only to drop a force behind enemy lines, now still does it but with GPS and modern equipment. Modern parachutists can hit a needle in a haystack, all due to folks who busted a leg or two to develop the modern parachute.

I prefer the old days myself, and even though I'm both a paratrooper and a parachutist, my son says, "You're a paratrooper through and through and always will be." Fact is, today most people in the military are both. Yet some are still paratroopers, meaning they don't free-fall, and some free-fallers aren't paratroopers. Either way, they both have one thing in common: having fun.

CHAPTER 4

THE THIRD BILLABOG REUNION

I n the spring of 2000, the old gang got together again at Art's place.
Here in this cabin in the Michigan woods, our informal group consisted of men who had trained as paratroopers for the military, who had innovated the sport of parachute jumping, who had collectively flown around the earth five thousand times, and who had saved many lives in far-off places like South America, Poland, and Africa. And the FBI considered one of us to be among the most elusive criminal masterminds in its history—though most of us didn't realize this at the time.

We stayed up late that first night, catching up on the previous year, until everyone passed out from either booze or exhaustion.

Breakfast Toasts

As first light streamed in through the window, I woke to the smell of fresh coffee and bacon and eggs. In the kitchen, I found Walt standing over the stove, flipping the last of the eggs. He hadn't changed much, except for his gut, which he said was all due to his own cooking. Over the years, he would gain more weight and suffer from congestive heart failure.

"How did you manage to get out of bed before me?" I asked.

"I didn't want to waste the day," Walt said.

"Breakfast," he called to the crew, banging the spatula against a pot.

He turned back to me. "Anyway, you guys are my family. If there's one thing I learned from all the stupid, crazy shit I done, it's that you gotta take care of family."

Jimmy McCusker came in first, stretching his arms over his head. "Smells good," he said, rubbing his small potbelly. Other than that, he was in pretty good shape for a guy in his sixties. He'd just retired as a pilot for a major airline.

Mike the Kid came plodding in. We still called him that because he was ten years younger than the rest of us. He had a desk job and had gotten soft around the middle—well, soft all over, truth be told. He had gone to college to become a packaging engineer. We teased him that he was the guy we all swore at every time we got a package in the mail and had to fight like hell to get it open.

Behind him came Parker, who drank too much but still managed to look pretty much the same.

Fat Willard shuffled in next. He was a lifelong friend to Walt, after they met in juvie as kids. Fat Willard never got fat until age sixty-five. He was a double for W.C. Fields. He'd jumped a few times with the team but never became an official member. He worked at GM for thirty years and became more of a family man than the other guys. When his wife died, he moved to Oscoda, Michigan. Walt later bought a house near him in Oscoda. Willard knew most of the guys, so it was okay with them that he came to the Billabogs.

Art was the last one up, another heavy drinker. He tried to counter the drinking by lifting weights, but he looked the oldest and most worn out of the bunch.

Art stood up to give a breakfast toast. He had already given several the night before, but chances were, he didn't remember much of them, so we let him talk.

The team in later years (joined by Carl's son, David, far left, and then left to right—Col. Bill Parker, Carl, Art, Jim McCusker, and Walt)

"Here's to the Michigan Parachute Team reunion," he said. "Here's to Charlie the storyteller, Mike the Kid, Parker the Colonel, Jimmy the Captain, and Walt the Pollack."

Walt added, "And let's have a moment of silence for Steeplejack Clapp and Suicide Slim, right there. May they be jumping off clouds in a blue sky."

We all raised our cups in the air. As we scarfed down our eggs and bacon, we made plans for the day. They were pretty simple. Go for a walk in the woods, fire at some targets, sit around and have a few beers, and shoot the shit.

Art, the Mastermind

Art was my feisty little buddy. At least, everybody thought Art was feisty. Actually, his big brother, Hank, the pro boxer, ruled the roost in Flint. Hank used Art for his sparring partner. Art could fight and win with people his own size, but he knew better than to pick a fight when he came up against a tough big man. Instead, he sometimes volunteered me or Walt.

One time we were far from home in our airplane when our prop came apart. We made a deal with a mechanic to buy a used prop for $10. That prop wouldn't work either, but the guy wouldn't give us our money back. Art took a quarter out of his pocket and flipped it.

The guy, who towered above Art and me, said, "What the fuck was that about?"

Art said, "I just wanted to see which of us is gonna beat your ass and get our money back. Take him, Charlie."

Art's appearance hadn't changed much. He still had his chipmunk cheeks. He drank more, lots more, and still had his blasé attitude when it came to others. He always refused to go to funerals because they weren't fun. "Nothing we can do to help them now," he'd say.

Yet Art had been the best bush pilot South America ever had, a mercenary in the Biafran war, and up over his head as a pilot for the infamous Barry Seal in the attempted overthrow of Cuba, orchestrated by the Mafia and our own CIA. As a parachutist, he was a batwing jumper and survived more low bomb-ins than anyone I know.

I wonder how far any of us could have gone if we'd had direction. We had raw talent aplenty and absolutely no fear of anything. Would we have listened to reason or anyone much smarter than we were? I'm sure we wouldn't have.

After dinner, we settled around the potbelly stove, and the tall tales began.

"Charlie, did you ever get that FAA guy off your ass?" Parker said.

"You mean Mr. Ruby?" I asked. "No, it turned into a cat-and-mouse game. Right after your first jump was when we started faking plane crashes. That near drove Ruby crazy."

Everyone laughed and raised a bottle to me and Art.

"What year was that?" Mike asked.

"Fifty-seven," I said.

"That always drew a good crowd," Walt said, reminiscing.

I figured everyone remembered the stunt but maybe not the details, so I embellished the story for them.

"Now that the law was after us, it felt like a new challenge. Remember how every Sunday we all went to Saginaw to jump? We first tried the fake airplane crash one Sunday in September. We flew south of town to a wooded area with two small hills and gunned the engine, then cut it off, to make it seem like we had engine trouble. Once we drew the attention of the people on the ground, Art bailed out, and I put the plane into a flat spin. The Taylorcraft could spin like nothing else in the air. I spun down below the tree line to about two hundred feet off the dirt, but from where the crowd stood, it looked like I'd crashed behind the second hill. The first Sunday we did this, people called the police to report a plane crash.

"After a few weeks, the cops refused to come out, even though the callers argued with them, assuring them it was a real crash. Mr. Ruby was called in, but, of course, he never found the crash site. If he could have seen the humor in it, he'd have realized we were giving him job security."

"Damn right," Art said with an evil grin. "But he saw us as archenemies."

I remembered back in the day before the whole airline industry got regulated. Ruby's hands were tied because until 1963, there were no laws on parachute jumping. Nobody thought jumpers would be crazy enough to jump at night or into unknown places or with possibly unsafe airplanes just for fun.

We got really good at jumping, taking almost any dare. In paratrooper training, we learned the reserve chutes could save our lives if our main chutes didn't open. But reserve chutes took time and cost money. Plus, we were opening our main chutes so low to the ground that if they failed, it would have been too late to pull the reserve chute anyway. We stopped using them because they were useless.

A few times, in our rush to cram in as many jumps as possible during our Sunday shows, we didn't even bother to let Parker pack up our parachutes. We just gathered the wadded canopy and risers in our arms and stuffed them back into the pack. We also tried an experiment of opening the chute in the airplane and holding the silk in our arms. Then when we leaped out the door and threw the parachute in the air, it would open right before we hit the ground.

Crowds gathered to watch the jumps

We could jump at very low altitudes and still survive, though nobody should ever try this—it's usually a sure death, and we were just lucky.

I finally convinced Art that we couldn't free-fall that way because the chutes would open the second we let them go, possibly even in the airplane. But any new idea was worth trying once—and more than once, if it was especially crazy.

I took another sip of coffee, and a voice broke into my reverie.

"So, what do you think we as a team added to the sport of parachuting?" Walt lay sprawled on the couch, a "devil's advocate" gleam in his eye.

"Nothing," I said.

He brought up the time in 1957 when I'd jumped with a 24-foot silk chute that blew up into a million pieces and left me plummeting from half a mile above ground with no main parachute. What Walt called an *invention*, I called a near-death experience. So this is how it happened, and I'll let you be the judge.

Art got the idea of driving to every airport within fifty miles of Flint and buying any parachute they had for sale. Our first airport was Flushing, home to three small airplanes in an old red cow barn that served as its only hangar. An eighteen-year-old kid in charge of operations told us they had a chute "up in the hay mow, unless someone carried it off."

We waded through two feet of old hay and found the oldest parachute I'd ever seen—a 24-foot silk round, late World War I vintage with no D-rings. I handed the kid ten bucks for a 40-year-old parachute that might never have been used.

So I put it on and went up for a jump.

I have no explanation for what happened next, other than to say how stupid I was. I had the pilot take me up about a mile, and as we made our run over the airport, I jumped out. The best thing I could have done then would have been to pull my ripcord while I was falling only 60 miles per hour. Instead, I went spread-eagled and increased my rate of fall to 176 feet per second and fell another half-mile before I pulled.

I never got a hard jerk to show my canopy had opened.

I looked up and saw only sky. My canopy had disintegrated.[5]

People say, "What did you expect?" and my answer is, "Not total disintegration. I was hoping for something less radical."

Worse yet, the ground was frozen rock hard. It was as if I had devised my own unique way to die.

I hit so hard, I split several teeth vertically but felt no pain. Parker, Walt, and Art stood around me, talking.

"Did you see that chute turn?" Parker said.

It felt good to lie on the ground, cold and frozen. I couldn't believe I was still alive. I tried my legs, feet first, and then moved arms and other body parts, and they responded.

"We'll cut out one gore at a time," I heard Parker tell Art and Walt.

Then Art said, "Get up, Charlie. We got things to do."

That would have been the time for me to rethink who my friends were. Not one of them asked, "Are you hurt?"

I didn't rethink the situation, and once again that was my fault. I feel good now knowing I got to piss on all of their graves, but did my unconstrained fall add very much to parachuting? Damn little.

This experience tells me more about the endurance of the human body than it does about aerodynamics, but we did develop blank gores and other stuff from that. Yet in the end, someone else got the credit.

Not long after my fall from space, a guy named Sherm Reed showed up with a new invention none of us had seen before. The

---

5   There were 30 panels, or gores, in the parachute. None were fully intact, and they ranged from completely gone to half gone, leaving enough material to keep him from a complete dead fall.

sleeve, he called it. As simple as it was, it had possibilities. It was nothing more than a bed sheet sewn together at its sides, which slipped over the canopy with a pilot sheet on top of that. As that pilot sheet pulled off the sleeve, it eliminated a quick opening shock when the chute opened.

I didn't much like it because it was just one more thing to go wrong. For example, if the pilot chute broke away, there was no way for the main chute to open, and since I had quit using a reserve chute, I didn't need that to happen again. The upside to the slow-opening chute was that if you were flying 200 miles per hour—in 727, for example—something akin to the sleeve would be in order.

Walt got up off the couch and replenished the snacks. Art brought another round of beers from the fridge and gave everyone a bottle.

Art glanced at me. "Remember that time we went up with Parker piloting a rented 172 Cessna? We were looking for a field or something, but we ended up jumping over a populated area with houses and yards and cars below us."

I burst out laughing. "And we couldn't steer the chutes, so I floated down, hoping I wouldn't hit a house or a car. When I got to about two hundred feet, I collapsed one riser and fell straight down. In three seconds, I landed and started pulling in my chute."

Art said, "I landed in someone's front yard, you came down in the back."

"Yep," I said. "I hit the ground about ten feet away from a little boy playing in the snow. He calmly stood up, brushed the snow from his knees, and ran to the back door. His mother came out and asked, 'What's going on?' 'Hey, there,' I said. 'I just fell out of a plane. Don't worry, everything's okay, and I'll be out of here in a second.'"

Art cracked up at the memory.

McCusker's Trial by Fire

Jimmy McCusker looked over at Parker and said, "You had it easy with your first jump. I had my first flight with these guys, and it wasn't fun."

We all laughed, thinking about when Jimmy joined the group.

"Yeah, but it led to you being a pilot with United Airlines," Art said. "Give us some credit for your distinguished career."

"I bet the rest of your flights were boring compared to that one," I said. "There's nothing more exciting than flying in emergency situations."

Everyone agreed with that. Normal flying was just like driving a car from one place to another. The best times were when something wild happened, when you knew your life was in jeopardy and every decision you made was vital.

We didn't intend Jim McCusker's flight to be anything special. That would have required planning, which we never did.

It was March 1958, and we'd gathered at the airport in Saginaw. I was flying, and Art and Jim got ready to jump. When we reached 8,000 feet, Art said, "It's been a while since you and I have jumped together, Charlie."

"That's because one of us always has to fly," I said. None of the other guys except Parker were pilots, and so far, we hadn't even considered having a civilian fly a plane.

"Jim, take off your chute and give it to Charlie."

"But I don't know how to fly," Jim said, "and I've never seen anyone land a plane. I always jump out before that happens."

"You've seen us take off, though, right?"

"Yeah, I guess." Jim knew where this was going.

"Well, just do everything we did to get up here, only backwards," Art said.

His confidence seemed to rub off on Jim, who handed me his chute and took my seat. He might have been about to ask for more instructions, but we never heard him.

Art and I jumped together and had a clean landing in a field near the airport. Looking up, we could see Jim trying to master the Cessna. It wasn't pretty, but he kept it right side up and took it down on the runway with just a few bumps. When we met him at the hangar, his face was red and his eyes the size of bowling balls, but he looked excited.

"I'd do that again in a heartbeat," Jim said.

We clapped him on the back and reloaded our chutes for another run.

It was past 2 a.m., and I could see some of the guys getting drowsy. But I had drunk coffee all night—I never cared much for booze. All year long, I'd looked forward to our third Billabog reunion, and I didn't want the night to end.

To jump-start the conversation, I threw out a challenge. "If you ask me, nothing we did ever topped the Great Caro Air Show."

Art perked up, and the others murmured agreement.

Walt said, "Charlie, you're the only one who can do justice to the story. Start at the beginning."

July 1958: The Great Caro Air Show

One Sunday in May 1958, we were doing some of our regular jumps with Ward's plane in Saginaw.

"I'm going to fly up to five thousand feet," Art said. "And I think everybody can jump. If we go one at a time about every thirty seconds, it will look really spectacular."

"Okay, let's make this a great show," Jack said. He was the toughest one of us, given his age. He was dauntless.

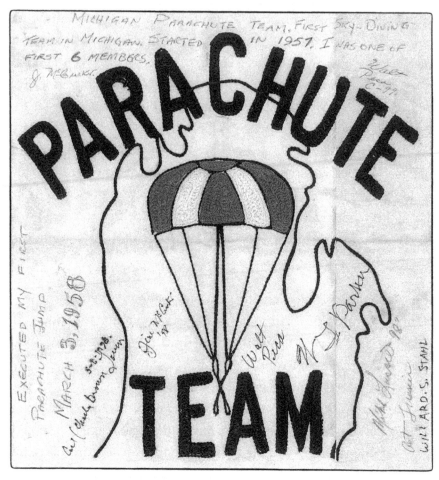

The team's patch

We started to advertise that at every show we would have a thirteen-year-old, a seventy-three-year-old, and a spectator jumping. Our team even bought matching white coveralls as a uniform. We took untrained people from the audience up and threw them out of the plane, laughing and telling them, "Don't forget to pull the ripcord."

One day a group of old guys from the Rotary Club, in Caro, Michigan, approached us. They had seen our daredevil parachuting in Saginaw and wanted us to put on a show for the people of Caro.

"Well, I guess professionals like us know how to plan a show," Art said. The word *professionals* rolled off his tongue with a hint of sarcasm. Although we thought of ourselves as great pilots and parachute jumpers, we were mainly entertainers. We weren't great businessmen, either. In all of the shows we did, we barely made any money, and at times we even lost some.

Just before what we came to call the Great Caro Air Show, we had another opportunity, the only one we ever turned down. Some guy wanted to film us flying an airplane into a barn—right through the open doors—and crashing. Art really wanted to do it, but I convinced him that the $200 the guy offered wouldn't even cover the cost of the airplane we would destroy. The guy assured us that if we filled the barn with hay and went through doors smaller than the wingspan, then the wings would hit the walls and peel off slowly, letting the plane crash softly in the hay. I pointed out that hay in barns burns really fast, especially when doused with fuel from a crashed plane. That was how I became the voice of reason for the Michigan Parachute Club, and when the voice of reason is someone who pushes spectators out of planes, you know you're in trouble.

"What we need is some beer," Walt said, always good at getting the fun started.

"Let's head to my house," Art said. "Mom will have dinner, and we can pick up beer on the way."

We sat in the parlor of Art's house, eating beans and drinking beer while we planned. The thing about a plan is that we knew we wouldn't follow it. We hated writing anything down, so we just committed it to memory, and if we happened to forget the plan and do something that seemed more fun, who could complain about that?

"I know a guy who has an old bi-wing Meyers open cockpit," I said. "He can do a loop and a roll."

"That sounds good," said Parker. "Then you can do your thing, and I'll do mine."

"Sounds like a plan," Walt said. "Let's get more beer."

They all agreed that they needed beer, lots of beer.

We stayed in all night, laughing and talking at Art's house. They decided to have more planning sessions just like that one, but I couldn't make it to the others because I had to work.

While we dreamed up stunts for the Caro show, another daredevil opportunity came our way. On July 4 of that same year, 1958, Art agreed to parachute into Flat Rock Speedway during the races that weekend. Art, in a batwing suit, jumped from 5,000 feet and opened the chute at only 300 feet.

The Great Caro Air Show was held on a beautiful July morning. When we showed up at the field, crowds had already gathered, spreading their picnic blankets on the grass. The field had the air of a festival with banners and balloons, stands selling hot dogs and soda pop, and a bandstand where the town band played "Yankee Doodle Dandy." They even had a first-aid tent. In the middle of the field, next to the bandstand, was a stage with a podium in front of a few rows of chairs, probably for the VIPs. The Sugar Beet Queen sat there with her crown and her velvet cape.

"Whoa, those Rotary guys really put this thing together," Art said.

"The whole town must be here," Mike said, his eyes wide with excitement and pride—something we all felt, but since we weren't ankle biters, we didn't show it like him.

I had driven the Buick over with our equipment. Art brought the Cessna as the jump plane with his truck. As we drove to the hangar to set up our tables and get our gear together, we could see that only the runway was clear. The whole show felt like Mardi Gras, with all the excitement and daring. We were having a good time before we even started.

AIR SHOW

presented by the MICHIGAN PARACHUTE TEAM
at the SAGINAW MUNICIPAL AIRPORT
3 miles East of Saginaw on Janes rd.

World's only living Batman
Art Lussier

SEE:

✳ A Parachutist falling over a mile before opening his parachute

✳ The Free-Fall contest, the most daring & dangerous contest ever conceived by man

✳ A mass parachute jump

✳ A man jumping an untested experimental parachute

✳ All the stunts ever attempted by parachutists

✳ Sixteen parachute jumps in ninety minutes

World's youngest Parachutist
14 year old - Mike Lussier

FREE

Every 100th paid admission wins a free airplane ride

Every 500th paid admission wins a free flying lesson

ADMISSION   Adults 75¢   Children 35¢

Sunday Aug. 17

2:00 P.M.

Air show poster

Caro was a farming community, and farmers are practical and no-nonsense, but clearly even they enjoyed this. Air shows were very rare in the 1950s. The days of the barnstormers in the Roaring

Twenties were over. That was the time of Al Capone and speakeasies, one of the most glorious ages the world has ever seen. After World War I, when America had a huge surplus of leftover airplanes and pilots, they took to the skies in small air shows. In the early 1930s, Bowman barnstormed in the South with his mom, a wing walker. Wimpy Wiseman, the Human Bullet, was the parachutist. It was pure genius how they captivated the crowds.

By the time we started parachuting, airline flying for the general public had started to catch on, and the field of aviation worked to establish an aura of *safety* and *professionalism*, two words we pretty much avoided. We weren't trying to undermine airlines, we just wanted to have fun, and the more smoke and mirrors, the more daring and risky we were, the more the crowd got excited, and the more fun we had. We wanted to emulate the early barnstormers, trying low bomb-ins, replacing wing walkers, using cutaways. We had larger-than-life imaginations and the balls to try anything.

In the spirit of that showmanship, the announcer called to the crowd from the stage. "In this first jump, you will see the youngest parachute jumper in the world, thirteen-year-old Mike Lussier, jumping out of a plane piloted by his brother Art. Following him is the oldest parachutist, Steeplejack Clapp, who is still jumping at age seventy-three. He probably has more guts than all of us put together."

The crowd roared.

When we were ready, Art piloted the Cessna along the runway and took off to reach 2,000 feet. Mike and then Jack fell from the plane, one at a time, and at around 800 feet, each pulled the ripcord. Out billowed their white chutes against the blue summer sky. On the ground, the crowd applauded, awed by their performance. The farmers, the salt of the earth, appreciated everything we did. We couldn't help but love them, and I thought about my uncles and how much they would have enjoyed a show like this.

Once Art landed, Parker took the pilot's seat, and I pulled on my parachute up on the stage. "Art Lussier and Carl Laurin will be performing bomb-in jumps," the announcer shouted to the spectators. "This is a kind of competition among friends, and we'll see who will wait the longest to open his parachute. If one of them crashes to the ground, he wins!"

This got a laugh, but the truth was, we had come pretty close to crashing. During our practice run in Saginaw, both Art and I had waited until we were just six feet above the ground. If Parker had been standing there, I could have kicked him in the head before our chutes deployed. Our chutes barely had time to swell open before we hit the ground.

This time we pulled the ripcords at about 400 feet, but that was close enough for the people below, who probably felt like we were about to fall on top of them. They were mesmerized, and we had actually stuck to a plan that worked for once.

Parker landed, and Art and I got our stuff together.

"You're in for a real treat, folks," the announcer said. "Art is going to pilot, while Charlie and Suicide Slim do a precision jump. That means from over five thousand feet above, they will jump and land on the mark."

I walked over and handed the Rotary guys my mother's bed sheet, thinking, *Boy, she'd be mad if she knew what we were using her clean sheet for.* We found a few rocks to anchor it, and then Walt and Slim and I paced around the field, looking for the exact right spot. Walt held his hand in the air to check the wind direction, and Slim shielded his eyes from the sun, as if checking the windsock. Actually, we didn't plan to hit the sheet, but we knew how to put on a show.

Or, at least, Walt and I did. Suicide Slim never seemed to realize just how foolish our stunts were. This guy would do just about anything. The previous winter, he and a friend had offered to put an addition onto Slim's mother's house. The ground was frozen solid, so they decided the only way to proceed was with dynamite. They carefully laid a trail on the ground where the foundation would be and then lit the dynamite. When the smoke cleared, all the windows in the neighborhood had been smashed in, and the entire side of his mother's house was gone. In the spring, when the snow melted, every basement in the neighborhood leaked. To Slim, that's just how life was. How could we not like this guy?

Art took the little Cessna with Slim and me up to 5,000 feet above our exit spot in Caro. I jumped first. As we exited the aircraft, I planned to free-fall only a short distance before pulling the ripcord and guiding myself close to the spot on the field. That's what the crowd was led to believe when the announcer explained the stunt, but instead we pulled off a modern take on the old cut-away trick from the barnstorming days. I used a reserve chute, but only because it had been tied shut so it would deploy but not open, a trick known as a "Roman candle" in the old days. Once I pulled, I held onto the handle with one hand, making it spin like crazy. It looked quite dangerous.

Afterward, Walt told me that the crowd went wild, yelling and screaming as they saw me free-falling without a working parachute. People shouted, "Open your chute!" Some covered their eyes, a few started to leave, a couple fainted, and even more threw up, expecting that I would hit the ground with a bloody splat. Nobody wants to see someone die, not really—though coming close was pretty exciting.

Above them, I plummeted to the earth, spinning and kicking like a frantic man. I let go of the dummy reserve chute as I fell below 2,000 feet. That's when I faked an unstable fall to make it look like I knew I was going to die. I was close enough to hear the crowd screaming, but I waited until 1,200 feet to pull the real ripcord.

The canopy snapped open, and the crowd went silent. I came in for a decent landing, far from the bed sheet, and walked through the crowd toward the stage. People came up to pat me on the back and shake my hand, showing genuine concern. I wasn't sure who'd had more fun, us tricking the crowd or the crowd being tricked.

Slim jumped after me, and he missed the spot, too. In fact, nobody hit the spot that day, but no one cared.

THE FIRST DUMMY DROP

I took my chute off, put it on the packing table, and made my way through the crowd, where Art was talking to a guy about our age.

"You guys think you're hot stuff," he said, as I walked up behind them. "If I had a chute, I'd go for a jump."

This guy's ranting annoyed me, and Art nodded at me over his shoulder. Art and I thought a lot alike, so I knew immediately what we were going to do. I grabbed the guy and lifted him off the ground, while Art took off his own chute and strapped it on our "volunteer." He kicked and flailed his arms but couldn't get away. We had the announcer give him a rousing hometown welcome, and the crowd must have thought this was all part of the show because they applauded.

Now came the dumb part. We didn't know whether the guy would remember to pull his ripcord in his panic, so we found a piece of clothesline and tied it to the ripcord.

"You guys are crazy," the guy yelled. We didn't even know his name.

"That's what we've been trying to tell you," Art answered with a shit-eating grin.

We dragged the guy, kicking and shouting, and stuffed him into the airplane. I didn't take the time to wonder why some spectator didn't step in. They must have still believed this was part of the act. We tied the end of the clothesline to the strut, and Art took the controls, while I held onto our jumper.

Saginaw Woman Has Her First Parachute Jump

SAGINAW, March 31 (UP) — Mrs. Regina Schneidegger, a 42-year-old beauty parlor operator, nursed a slightly stiff hip today but no other injuries after making her first parachute jump.

Mrs. Schneidegger, who got the idea from her paratrooper son and pre-jump instruction from her living room, made the leap from a plane 2,500 feet over Janes Road Municipal airport in Saginaw while her husband, Charles, a Detroit automobile mechanic watched and chain-smoked cigarets.

Her son, Walter, who is a barber in Royal Oak, and a member of the Michigan parachute team, was the first one to reach her after she jolted to the ground. He is a veteran of the 11th airborne division, and had given his mother instruction in the living room of her home.

"Mom," said Walter. "You made one jump and it was good. No more. Period."

Walt's mom—she jumped only once

"You can't really do this," our unwilling participant pleaded. "You're really going to do this? What am I supposed to do? I've never jumped before. You can't really do this."

74

I gave him as much instruction as I could in a few seconds for someone who had never jumped before. Mostly, I just said, "We have your ripcord taken care of. Don't worry, these chutes always work. Parker knows how to pack them. That's why we never wear reserves ourselves. Just bend your knees when you land."

By the time we reached altitude, he seemed to calm down a bit, as if facing the inevitable. Or, at least, his pleading had stopped. I had a hard time getting him stable as I pushed him out of the aircraft, so he turned upside-down. The clothesline snapped and pulled the ripcord. I reeled in the clothesline and found the pins on the ripcord bent 90 degrees. The chances of a clothesline rope being strong enough to pull the ripcord without breaking were probably 1 in 50,000, but on this sunny day in Caro, it worked, saving us from killing a man and saving him from a gruesome fall.

Looking out the plane's door, I could see that his chute had opened, and he drifted down to a decent landing at the airport. I turned and looked at Art with relief, suddenly realizing what we had done.

"I bet he got a fucking standing ovation," Art said.

"Whoever he is, he's now an honorary member of the Michigan Parachute Club." I silently thanked God for saving us all from ourselves.

Art chuckled. "Yeah, but imagine what he did in his pants on the way down."

And that was the only living person I ever threw out of an airplane—though you could say I was responsible for Walt's mother parachuting. On March 30, 1958, Walt had convinced his forty-something mother, Regina Schneidegger, to become the first woman to jump. I was flying the plane. When she balked, I banked the plane hard, and Walt physically threw her out of the plane. It was her only jump.

THE SECOND DUMMY DROP

We had cheated him again, the Grim Reaper. Seeing the bent pins on the ripcord should have been a wake-up call. But we had one more stunt, which would surely thrill the crowd, and we couldn't stop. The unique thing about this air show, something impossible to replicate in the many other shows we did, was the complete immersion of the hometown crowd. Everybody in town was part of the show, and it was real folksy.

The town doctor volunteered to make a jump. Doc was over sixty, overweight, and absolutely loved by all. He was the only doctor in town, and he had delivered every baby for two generations.

I didn't know this was going to happen because I'd been working when the guys came up with the idea. And then they decided to keep me in the dark. So when Art told me the doctor would make the jump, I said, "Are you guys fucking crazy? We just damn near killed a guy, and now you're going to do it again?"

"It will be okay," Art said. "We told the doctor what to do last week. He's all set."

I just shrugged. When I look back now, I really think we needed better mentors. My parents were old, but I needed someone to sit me down and say, "Listen, you little bastard, the stuff you're doing is crazy." We all needed it—and nobody had that. So the show went on.

The spectators laughed nervously, as the doctor stepped up to don his parachute. Not even the most naïve person could conceive that we would kill off the only doctor in town, even after our last stunt. They assumed he would make a symbolic jump out of the airplane as it sat on the runway. That would be a good stunt, and the crowd would enjoy it and feel relieved at the same time. Everybody would have a good laugh and a pat on the back, and the show would end on a high note.

The crowd gave a collective gasp of surprise as we loaded the doctor into the airplane with Parker, Walt, and Art. They taxied out for takeoff, with the town ambulance in close pursuit. From the ground, I watched with the crowd as the plane rode along the runway and disappeared behind a stand of trees, then took off a half mile away at the end of the field. The ambulance took up position at the center of the airport.

"He's not really going to jump," one spectator said.

"It's probably going to be that guy Walt, with a pillow in his coveralls," another reassured everyone. All necks were craned upward, watching the little airplane circle the final pass for the drop.

A sudden cry from the crowd signaled the moment two jumpers exited the plane. Then people went deathly silent, noticing that something was wrong with one of the jumpers, who was spinning and tumbling down toward the ground. I sensed panic and anger overtake the crowd. They were ready for a lynching should anything happen to their beloved Doc. We might have gone too far.

Art opened his chute at 1,000 feet, but the other jumper continued to plummet downward. It looked like he could not possibly survive. I heard weeping in the crowd as the jumper hit the ground, his parachute never opening. Everyone ran toward the center of the field, where the ambulance was ready. The driver put the body on a stretcher, and they rushed toward the first-aid tent with lights flashing and sirens wailing.

I thought the doctor was dead. All I could do was stand there with my hands on my head, trying to hold it together. The crowd milled around me in a silence so deep, it seemed to echo. When the stretcher was pushed into the first-aid tent, the crowd circled it in apprehensive silence. I couldn't believe it—and then I could. Common sense said that at some point, someone would get hurt. I just never expected it to be a stranger.

A few seconds later, a large man with dirt on his face and a torn shirt walked out of the tent.

"What a horrible landing," Doc said. "Has anybody got a drink?"

The people were stunned; it seemed impossible that he could have survived. I was speechless.

"Gotcha," Art said, punching me in the shoulder. He was laughing his ass off.

After a second, I had to laugh, too. It was funny, and I felt so relieved. We tried to explain the old bait and switch, but nobody would listen. When the airplane and the ambulance had disappeared behind the stand of trees, Doc jumped out of the plane and circled back to the first-aid tent. Art had a dummy already waiting in the plane. People just shook their heads, unable to believe that a miracle hadn't just happened.

After that, we all went up and made a mass jump from the Cessna, and the show was over. The town was happy, and we made $300. We did many other air shows, but none ever measured up to the Great Caro Air Show.

After that last story, most of the guys had either conked out or gone to bed. The sound of a chair scraping the floor interrupted my thoughts. Art had bumped into the chair and now leaned against it to steady himself. He had drunk so much, he was beyond passing out. As a rule, he probably drank enough to kill an ordinary man, but he was no ordinary man, and neither were the other guys.

"That time in Africa—" Art belched, then hiccupped. We both laughed at the shape he was in. "That rusted-out piece of crap C-46 cargo plane left over from the war. We bombed the shit out of them."

Another belch and a chuckle from Art, as he remembered the Biafra war. He'd gotten caught up in it through a deal his boss had made to fly some weapons to someone.

Just to show him I was still paying attention, I said, "That's when I flew cargo for Zantop, I think."

"Fuck it, I gotta take a leak." Art staggered off toward the bathroom.

I knew he'd hit his limit and that was his way of saying, "Good night." We'd pick up the Africa memory another time.

CHAPTER 5

THE FOURTH BILLABOG REUNION

n the spring of 2001, we had our fourth Billabog gathering at Art's cabin. Spirits were high the first night, and the next morning everyone except me woke up with a crashing hangover.

Walt turned to Art. "Are the mosquitoes worse here or in Alaska?"

"Tough question. Both places, the season starts in May. But this here is a swamp."

"How the hell did you guys end up in Alaska?" Mike asked.

Walt said, "It all started when I read a magazine article in '58. Those colored photos of Alaska—"

I choked back laughter. "Don't rewrite history, Walt. You were running from the mob."

He grinned. "Busted. I figured some of you geezers must be senile by now and you forgot."

Never Trust a Sure Thing

By September 1958, just doing jumps—even though we made them more and more dangerous—didn't seem like enough. And though we shared everything, profits and expenses alike, we weren't in it for the money. I saved up enough working at the GM plant, but Walt seemed to be having troubles. Working as a barber would never make him rich; it might not even let him live comfortably.

Before I knew it, Walt had gone to Alaska.

It happened a few days after we made a racetrack jump for the Purple Gang. It was an interesting concept, the racetrack jump. But *interesting concept* is just another way of saying *swindled*.

Four of us planned to bail out of Ward's Cessna at 5,000 feet onto the racetrack—for $100, if we hit inside the track, or $50, if we hit outside. Walt had set up a day to meet his old friends in their office at the track, and we were supposed to wear suits—except for Art, who didn't have one.

They'd tried their best to make this place look like Vegas. It was all part of their mystique, a place where us common folk could rub elbows with the mob. I'm sure that's how they wanted us to see it. The carpet was thick and bouncy, as we walked single file past a covey of stooges or Mafia wannabes. Walt held the door as we went in.

The plush office had velvet drapes and horse pictures everywhere you looked. It belonged to a lady in a tight dress and false eyelashes, too heavy to wink, but she winked anyway. We stood there like a bunch of dopes, not knowing what we were getting into.

Then she said, "You may go in now," and we did.

"Gentlemen, thank you for coming," is how it started.

He said some more jibber-jabber, and then he asked, "Did your friend Walt tell you we're not going to pay you?"

We all looked at one another.

"We only do this once in a while when folks like yourselves have done a good job for us and we want to reward them. We let the ponies pay them."

He had our attention.

"You've heard all races are fixed," he said.

We all mumbled we knew that, so we wouldn't seem stupid. I later learned that the racetrack betting was reportedly run by a Detroit mob called the Purple Gang.

"The horse that's going to win this race is a twenty-to-one shot, and we can either give you your fifty dollars or let it ride on 'winner take all,' which pays twenty-to-one odds."

And all of us said, "Let it ride."

Everyone except Walt. He put Ward's airplane up for collateral, saying it was his, and he threw an extra thousand on "winner take all."

"We've known Wally a long time around here," the boss said. He walked over to Walt, shook hands, and said, "Smart bet, Wally, you're covered."

That's why Walt left town so fast that day in the fall of 1958. Not because of some magazine article, but because he owed the mob money.

Eventually, we all learned that whenever Walt was going somewhere, he was being chased by somebody.

It didn't take him long to pack because he had mostly summer clothes, and thin clothing is of little use in Alaska. He did have a good Hertz car, free of charge, because repositioning a car for car rental companies was common in those days. They still do it today, but I heard they charge around ten bucks a day now. I'm absolutely certain that if Walt had not been in a hurry, he would have saved money on an airplane ticket, as opposed to all of that gas he had to buy for the rental car—unless, of course, Hertz gave him a gas allowance.

Walt stopped by the Lussier house to let all of us know he was heading to Fairbanks. Only Art's brother-in-law Frank was there, and when he heard that, he hustled home and brought back an air force parka. He gave it to Walt—along with three pounds of welfare cheese and whatever money he could scrape up.

Terrors of the Tundra

In the fall of 1958, Walt made the drive to Alaska in ten days. The only exciting event on that trip was a bear looking for food that broke into a house he overnighted in. The landlady threw a loaf of bread out the door, and the bear chased after it.

According to Walt's first letter, he arrived in Fairbanks to 12 below zero temperature and with $7 in his pocket, looking for some guy named Sinclair.

That night it was close to 30 below when Walt surrendered his rental car. He walked back out onto the empty streets of Fairbanks. He needed clothing, food, warmth—he needed everything.

He tried the open door of "The Persian Room" and went in. The tavern was only about 50 degrees, but it shut out the Arctic wind, so it felt warm.

A man named Russ Ferrell was tending bar that night. He had a habit of staring down strangers.

"Pour me a draft," Walt said, "and tell me if you know a man named Brody Herald."

Ferrell brought the draft and stood in front of Walt with both hands on the bar, looking hard.

Walt drank the beer down without a breath and said, "Again."

"That beer just cost you a buck, mister, and another buck for this one."

Walt laid $5 on the bar. Ferrell didn't touch it.

"Well, do you know where I can find Herald?"

"What's Herald to you?"

"Mister, I don't know a soul up here, including Brody Herald. I wrote a letter to Herald before I left Flint because he's president of Midnight Skydivers. I thought maybe he could help me out, that's all. I'll be needing a job and a place to stay."

"You a parachute jumper, are ya?"

Walt nodded.

"Where'd you learn?"

"Fort Campbell, Kentucky, 503rd Infantry, Eleventh Airborne."

Ferrell reached for the five on the bar and pushed it toward Walt. Walt was puzzled.

"I went into Normandy with the 503rd on the D-Day invasion," Ferrell said, looking down. "Lost damn near everybody. We were warned not to make friends, but we did anyway. How do young men not make friends? What genius made that one up? What the hell. Anyway, beer's on the house, Trooper. What did you say yer name was?"

After the bars closed, Ferrell drove Walt over to a boarding house, where Brody Herald got Walt a room.

"What brings you to Fairbanks?" Herald asked.

"A business deal gone bad," Walt said.

"I'd say real bad," Herald added. "You and me, we've never met, have we?"

Walt shook his head. "The Parachute Club of America gave me your name."

"You met Ferrell in the bar?"

"That was a great break," Walt said. "We were both in the 503rd."

"Then you know about jumping," Herald said.

"Some," Walt said. "Skydiving, too."

"Our club, Midnight Skydivers, made a commitment to a Pentacostal orphanage for a Christmas Eve Santa Claus jump, but we have to cancel because it will be too cold."

"You can't cancel that one," Walt said.

"Are you Pentacostal?" Herald asked.

"Catholic," Walt said.

"What is it to you, then?" Herald wanted to know.

"I was an orphan," Walt said. "There's no difference between a Pentacostal orphan and a Catholic orphan. They both need help."

"I agree with you there. That's why we offered to do it, but we've been told our chutes might stick together and not open."

"I'll do it," Walt said.

This was Walt's introduction to Alaska—a man who six hours earlier had rolled into town dead broke and now had offered to make a charity jump for orphans in weather that might be 60 below zero.

By 9 a.m. the next morning, Walt had spent $6 of his $7 on breakfast and saved $1 for beer. By 10 a.m., he had a job at a travel agency that transported workers to the DEW (Distant Early Warning) Line and from there back to Fairbanks.[6] It was a perfect job for a newcomer, with a good wage.

Within two weeks, he'd met half the people in Fairbanks, and those he didn't meet at the agency, he met in the bars. Within a month, Walt knew all the bartenders, the owners, and the chippies. Chippies were girls who worked the bars, having men buy them drinks—ginger ale, mostly. Each drink cost $2 and came with a chip in the glass that the girl fished out, then later redeemed at the bar for $1. Some family-friendly establishments considered the girls nuisance and barred them from plying their trade.

Another nuisance was a gigantic bastard of a man named Warren Brewster. Altercations on the Strip were as common as cold weather, and Brewster, who also owned a bar on the Strip, often brought combatants to a quick end with a size-13 boot to the groin. That's why his bar was failing.

Part of the money to buy the bar—$10,000—had been loaned to Brewster by another big man, Charlie Coulter, who worked for an Arctic Circle DEW Line contractor.

In Coulter's absence, Brewster sold his floundering bar for cash and purchased an airline ticket to the Lower 48 from the agency

---

6   The Distant Early Warning Line, also known as the DEW Line or Early Warning Line, was a system of radar stations in the far northern Arctic region of Canada, with additional stations along the North Coast and the Aleutian Islands of Alaska, in addition to the Faroe Islands, Greenland, and Iceland. Wikipedia, https://en.wikipedia.org/wiki/Distant_Early_Warning_Line. For a map of DEW Line sites, see http://lswilson.dewlineadventures.com/.

Walt worked for. Then he began two days of nonstop drinking and celebrating.

Walt quickly got on the teletype to Point Barrow: "R.E. Coulter. Brewster sold the bar. Stop. He's leaving Alaska with your money. Stop. Come quickly. End. Peca."

Coulter arrived in Fairbanks that evening and confronted Brewster. A large crowd had gathered, most of whom Brewster had swindled at one time or another. Coulter grabbed Brewster by the collar and yelled for his money back. When Brewster went limp, Coulter slammed him against a wall and dug through Brewster's coat pockets, pulling out money and disposing of the man's gun and knife.

Coulter counted out his own $10,000, then threw the rest on the bar. He told Twitch the barkeep to timber the bar (buy a round of drinks), then divide the money among the patrons.

"My work is done here," said Coulter. "I'm going back to the Arctic."

Warren Brewster, that vindictive bastard of a man, slowly woke up from the beating and his two-day drunk. When Brewster was sober, he was as smart as he was tall, and now that he had no money to drink with, he was smart and pissed off.

Soon he struck up an alliance with the chippie girls, promising them protection and guaranteeing them access to all the bars. Brewster also convinced local bar owners to pay him a small fee for protection twenty-four hours a day.

So life was good once again for Warren Brewster—until he paid a visit to that new club owned by Eddie Metcalf.

When Brewster walked into the Caravan, he saw Russ Ferrell tending bar.

Brewster demanded, "Where's Metcalf? We have business."

"You got business with me now," Ferrell said.

Brewster figured the fiery ex-paratrooper would cave in and pay him, as had the others. Ferrell took Brewster's verbal abuse and let Brewster puff himself up and spew threats until he had plenty of witnesses in his favor.

"I've killed better men than you!" Brewster shouted at Ferrell. Then, as he had done a hundred times before, Brewster reached into his coat pocket, but his gun and knife had been removed by Charlie Coulter. As Brewster turned toward Ferrell, it wasn't Ferrell's cold eyes he saw but the muzzle of Ferrell's .38, just as it went off.

Walt heard Brewster's last words as he hit the hard floor: "Get me a priest."

Odd words for a man who'd never committed a good deed in his life.

After Brewster's carcass was hauled away, Eddie Metcalf lamented, "All I ever wanted was to make an honest living by operating a friendly, sociable, family-oriented tavern."

Eddie topped off his customers' drinks and asked that they take their chairs outside and get comfortable. Metcalf then brought a bottle of his own and a chair, and before he took a seat next to his good friends Russ Ferrell and Walt Peca, he set a match to the Caravan.

Eddie, Russ, Walt, and friends sat and drank good whiskey, as they watched Eddie's dream burn level to the Alaskan tundra for the insurance money.

Socks on the Propeller

In the Lower 48 in a barn near Saginaw, Michigan, a 1943 Stinson Reliant was coming alive. Now and then, a letter would arrive from Alaska. We all felt better knowing Walt had a job. He told us about jumping for the orphans in 40 below weather but left out the Warren Brewster story.

I was reaching new horizons on rebuilding the airplane. Remember, I never had one minute of formal training in working on airplanes. What I did have was a good memory. I learned by watching others.

When winter ended and the snow piles had melted, out rolled an airplane fit for any air museum, and she flew as good as she looked.

In March 1959, Art Lussier, Duane "Porky" Polson, and I—seeking adventure, with a change of clothes and a paper sack holding six peanut butter sandwiches—boarded Stinson 79581 and took off from Flint, Michigan, hell bent for Alaska. Our plan? There was no plan at all.

We stopped for customs in Medicine Hat, Canada, on May 8, an Indian settlement with no water or electricity. There were no trees or grass either. This was not the image I wanted to remember the Plains Indian by, descendants of the braves who killed Custer. But this is the image I still have today.

Why is anybody here? I wondered. *In the middle of absolutely nothing? They could have traveled outside this place. If they did, they would never come back.*

We took off for Edmonton, expecting to see Eskimos and Indians and teepees, but instead found people living in high rises and beautiful houses.

After spending one night sleeping under the plane's wing near the Edmonton airport, we were discovered. A pair of socks and two pairs of shorts hanging from the prop got the attention of two men, bottom feeders who wanted to buy our airplane.

A thousand times I've wished I'd told those guys to go back where they came from and I'd walked away from that deal, but I didn't. So we sold a $5,000 airplane for half that price and bought commercial airline tickets to Anchorage.

Splitting up was another mistake, for me. I had planned to go with Art and join Walt in Fairbanks. Anchorage was a city surrounded by the frontier, but Fairbanks *was* the frontier. Except for the drinking without limits, I belonged in Fairbanks, but I stayed in Anchorage with Porky.

Back to the Real World

Porky and I headed home from Anchorage in May 1959, after staying in Alaska only two months. It was time for me to face reality. I had quit my job at the General Motors plant, and the trip had cleaned me out. I would never make a life for myself in a factory, though I respected men like my father who did. Instead, I found a job flying cargo for an outfit called Zantop out of Detroit Metro.

The Wrong Bonfire

On May 15, 1959, Russ Ferrell had left the Persian Room and was tending bar at the Silver Dollar Saloon. Art and Walt were there that night, when one of the barflies wanted to make a parachute jump. It had been brewing for a couple of weeks, ever since he and his pal were in the bar the night Walt and one of the chippie girls jumped into the pasture of Creamer's Dairy. It had turned into a bet between the two barflies, with the loser agreeing to timber the bar. They told Walt they'd pay him $20 to borrow his chute and to furnish them with an airplane and a pilot.

"You're in luck," Walt said. "The world's greatest bush pilot just came into town, and he will be your pilot."

While Walt helped the barfly into his parachute, Art continued to slug down beer after beer. After this, they went to Phillips Field to rustle up an airplane someone had left the keys in.

Meanwhile, other bar patrons would go to the Creamer's Dairy pasture and wait for their friend to land, so they could take him back to the Silver Dollar for the timbering of the bar. They built a bonfire and hung around the fire until all the beer they'd brought was gone, but their buddy never showed up. Then they piled back in their car and returned empty-handed to the Silver Dollar.

The mix-up had happened in the airplane. There had been two fires that night, the bonfire at the dairy and another one. Walt had told the parachutist to jump at the first fire. The man spent the night huddled up in his parachute underneath a bush. When asked why he'd never answered their calls, he said he'd been afraid the bears would get to him before they did.

There's a Downside of Drinking and Flying?

Rays from the setting sun filtered through the trees and flickered on patches of water in the swamp. We sat on the cabin porch at the Billabog, swatting at mosquitoes and drinking beer. Art and Walt could barely get the next story out. They kept laughing and interrupting each other to add more to it. It seems that in Fairbanks, Art found part-time work flying a floatplane for some poor sap. Art's bar tab exceeded his income, but that was incidental to having a good time. Eventually, he did find another job on the DEW Line and was able to stash away a few grand.

When Art had time off work, Walt joined him and brought parachutes (he never told me how he got his hands on those). They resumed our silly free airshows, flying and jumping out of airplanes, until they became household names in every gin joint in Fairbanks. A bar owner who had been in the 101st Airborne made his place home base. The guys were drinking hard and jumping in darkness and sunshine, in storms and fair weather, and probably breaking a ton of FAA rules. They were too hammered to care, and Alaska really was the Wild West, the last frontier of aviation, where the only law was no law.

Pretty soon every drunk in Fairbanks wanted to make a parachute jump. So every night around 11 p.m., Art and Walt gave five minutes of ground school to a drunk and then flew about 1,000 feet above ground and pushed him out of the plane. The gist of their instructions was, "When we say go, you jump out the door and shout, 'Geronimo!' then pull the ripcord." Art always added, "Hold onto that ripcord. They get expensive."

I had to laugh—this was the same command he'd given me after our first few jumps.

The object was to drop people close to the ground so they would be easy to find when they landed, but with a drunk jumper, a drunk pilot, and an even drunker jumpmaster, they seldom hit the target. They relied on all the drunks watching to track down their guy.

It worked every time, except once, Art and Walt claimed. That night the plan started to unravel around ten-thirty, when the volunteer seemed wishy-washy. It was a stretch to call him a volunteer because the night before, his buddy had jumped and said, "Jim's next." Without a whole lot of thought and with a belly full of beer, Jim had said, "Hell, yes!"

Now Art told the newly sober, hesitant Jim that nothing bad would happen.

Walt added that his mom had jumped out of a plane when she was in her forties. He forgot to mention that after we got her into the air, his mom had second thoughts, but Walt gave her an encouraging little push out the door.

"Only two things fall out of the sky, paratroopers and bird shit. Which do you want to be?" Art asked Jim.

"Give me a fucking chance to work up my courage, and I'll do it."

Everyone cheered, and they headed to the bar to get some courage. There were drinks all around. Then another round. Time ticked by, and the drinks still came. Finally, around two in the morning, Jim could barely stand, but he announced that he was ready. Nobody was sober enough to stop him.

A procession of drunks piled into old junk cars and proceeded to the airport. Laughing their asses off, Walt and Art said it took a long time to strap the drunk into a parachute because he kept falling down. Walt, as jumpmaster, wasn't much better.

Art relieved himself on the wheel of the airplane, never mind the ladies in the crowd, in preparation for the flight. He started to have a bad feeling about the jump, but everything was in the works, so he didn't say anything to Walt. Instead, once they loaded up and took off, he decided to fly to 2,500, instead of their usual 1,000 feet. The decision made by a drunk actually saved a drunk because, unbeknownst to Art or Walt, someone had convinced Jim that he had to count to 10 before pulling the ripcord.

When they got to altitude, Jim was clearly as scared as he was sober. "Go!" Walt shouted.

Jim didn't move. "Are you sure it will be all right?"

"Go, get out the door," Walt said, ignoring Jim's question.

Art craned his head back and took action to "resolve the situation," as he described it with a chuckle. He tipped the wing down 60 degrees, and Jim tumbled out. They looked down toward the space where Jim fell, and suddenly they realized what they had just done. They'd flown way beyond the drop zone, hovering over the bush, and Jim was falling without pulling the ripcord.

"Pull, pull!" Walt yelled frantically, but Jim kept spinning and tumbling out of control. Art and Walt looked at each other, silent and sober. A puff of white below let them know that Jim finally opened his chute, but he ended up somewhere in the bush.

When they landed the plane, they joined a motley search party on the ground and tramped through the bush for over two hours, calling for Jim. People in the crowd said they'd heard Jim from down below, counting to ten before he said, "Time to pull."

When they finally found Jim huddled in some brush, he was a mess, both from relieving himself on the way down and from terror.

"Drinking and flying has a downside," Art said to me. "Who knew?"

They had learned a lesson. Art and Walt never quit drinking, but Art flew another 29,000 hours (about 6 million miles), all of them sober.

You Can't Kill a Bear with a Propeller

Making a parachute jump after getting a snoot full of booze at the Silver Dollar Saloon had become a regular thing. Walt and Art estimated that forty or more drunks took the dive, while Walt said he made another forty himself.

That's why I said, thirteen years later, that with Walt having forty night jumps, plus being a para-rescue specialist with the Thunderbirds exhibition team and a military escape and evasion specialist, he was the most qualified person in the world to make the world's most notorious parachute jump.

Yet the boys eventually tired of Alaska. And the FAA had tired of them. Even the bears wished they'd go home. Returning from their last bear hunt, Lussier—with too much to drink and impaired reflexes—had skinned up their borrowed airplane diving at a bear and breaking off a tree limb, which lodged itself through one wing.

Walt, without as much to drink, became the voice of reason, saying, "It's time to take us home, Art, right now."

Art came back on the stick, added power, and lit a cigarette in the blackness.

Then the darkness bit back. High voltage lights and burning sparks flashed, and everything turned black.

"What the fuck was that?"

"It's a good thing we were at full power," Art said quietly.

"Why?" Walt asked.

"I read somewhere you're supposed to apply full power when flying through power lines," Art said.

"We got a small tree growing through our wing and now this," Walt said.

Not another word was said until they were in their car, tearing away from Phillips Field. By daybreak, the FAA was on the case.

"Here's the cause of our power loss," one agent was heard saying. "Look at the burn marks on that prop. Someone is going to pay for this, and I know who that someone is."

The next morning a deal was struck, as Art, Walt, and Bob Sinclair drank beer in the Silver Dollar Saloon.

"How much time is left on your contract with Pacific?" the feds wanted to know.

"Six months," Art told them.

"Six months it is. When you get back from the DEW Line, your license will be in my drawer," one of the feds told Art. "Nothing on yer record."

Art laughed. "I'll be going down under after that. Walt's going tomorrow."

"I wish I was going," Sinclair said.

Leaving Alaska

"When we sobered up for real, we knew we needed a change," Walt said.

They decided to go to California. Before Walt left Alaska in January 1960, he went to see his friend Paul Twitch, the bartender at the Silver Dollar. Walt told Twitch that in two months, he'd send an L.A. address that Twitch could post on the bar for Art, who would join him and Sinclair in California. Twitch agreed to do it.

When Art left Barrow for Fairbanks two months later, after finishing his DEW Line contract, two of their friends were dead: Bob Cooper and Twitch. Bob Cooper had been "flying bush" in a cabin Waco, when it crashed somewhere in the Yukon. Before he died, Cooper had stripped to his socks and shorts. He had survived the crash but perished of the elements in 40 below zero weather.

Twitch had died in a parachuting accident at Creamer's Dairy. His ripcord handle was still in the pocket.

Days before his death, Twitch had received a letter from Walt and taped it to the bar mirror. Art saw it and then found his friends holed up at 447 Hope Street in L.A.

"They Don't Last Long at This Price"

In March 1960, Art was flush with DEW Line money he hadn't had time to spend, but Walt was busted and working in a meat locker. Sinclair spent weekends drinking with Art and living off their crumbs—but life was different in L.A.

Alaska was a tough act to follow. With its tolerance for the untamed, the bizarre, and the lawless, Alaska was a perfect backdrop for their renegade behavior. L.A. had its own urban goofiness, but it wasn't the same.

One day Art told Sinclair, "Me and Walt's going to Hemmet to jump with Sanborn . . . you coming?"[7]

Art dipped into his DEW Line money and purchased a used Cadillac for five hundred dollars.

---

7   Lewis B. Sanborn started jumping in 1948. The most recent record he set was the SOS (Skydivers Over Sixty) World Record 23-way at Skydive Elsinore on October 6, 2001. He was an early developer of the free-fall method of skydiving who, along with Jacques-André Istel, helped popularize sport parachuting in the United States. He is considered by many to be a pioneer and a legend in the sport. See http://www.parachutehistory.com/men/sanbornl.html and https://en.wikipedia.org/wiki/Lew_Sanborn.

"They don't last long at these prices, sonny," the salesman assured him.

He was right. The transmission gave up before the ole Caddy got off the lot.

Next was an "ugly ole Lincoln," Walt said. It carried the same guarantee. Walt told me the salesman repeated, "They don't last long at these prices." But it did get the boys to Hemmet.

Now they had nothing better to do than parachute jump, drink, and hit on George Flinn's attractive girlfriend—especially Art.[8] Far from debonair, he was a bumbler where women were concerned, and he had a severe case of DEW Line fever. Eight months of darkness and never touching a woman, while cooped up in a Quonset hut on the Arctic Circle, will do that to you. Nobody could figure out whether the girlfriend was stringing Art along or trying to make her boyfriend jealous.

After listening to the two of them mollycoddle each other for a week, Flinn concocted a plan. He told them the Hacienda Hotel in Vegas was hiring parachute jumpers for air shows.

Putting Vegas on the Map

In the spring of 1960, Art and Walt took off for Vegas in the old Lincoln. Bob Young, a pilot they'd met at Hemmet, followed them in his own car.

Once again, the words of the cigar-smoking car salesman from L.A. rang true: "They don't last long at these prices, sonny." With the lights of Las Vegas glowing vividly in their sights, ole ugly lurched its last gasp and headed for the ditch.

Art ripped the elbow out of his white shirt peering beneath the car and trying to figure out why the motor was racing.

---

8   George Flinn was a pilot and one of the founding members of the Parachute Club of America. I met him in Hemet, California.

"I could've saved you the trouble," Bob Young piped up. "The drive shaft bounced past me heading south about a mile back. Better put your gear in my car."

Bob could pass for presentable, but Walt and Art entered the Hacienda in tatters. Their early Alaska garments were dirty and torn, and Art had a three-day beard. That didn't stop Art from demanding to see the manager.

Dick Taylor had watched the three enter. Parachutes draped over their shoulders, Walt and Art appeared in need of a good scrubbing.

Just as the guy at the desk was about to escort them out the door, Taylor's curiosity got the better of him.

"What brings you boys to Vegas?"

"We're here to put this place on the map," Art said.

Taylor laughed. "A lot of stuff that goes on here has already put us on the map, but what is it that you do?"

"We draw huge crowds doing parachute jumps. We heard you were hiring."

"Who told you that?"

"George Flinn, down at Hemmet."

"I think Flinn was having some fun with you boys. I never heard of such a thing, and I run this place."

Art kept trying, and after some more back-and-forth discussion the manager relented.

"Okay, boys . . . tell you what. I'm not paying you anything, but I'll give you one room and our famous morning buffet for two weeks. Unless, of course, your act bombs. In that case, I'll give you a day's notice. Without knowing anything about you, that's the best I can do."

Day One of the air show at nearby McCarrell Field drew unexpectedly large crowds. Art's dangerously low bomb-in so close to the desert floor brought applause. But along with that show came a coincidental occurrence: *Ocean's Eleven* was being filmed at the Sands at the same time.

The film's plot centered around a bunch of ex-paratroopers led by Frank Sinatra, pulling a major heist from the vault at the Sands Casino. Dean Martin, Sammy Davis Jr., and the entire Rat Pack were in that movie.

The unaware public might have assumed that somewhere in that movie were parachute jumps, probably during the heist. So Walt and Art must be the stunt men, practicing.

Being fresh back from Alaska, the boys had never heard of the movie, so now the name *Ocean's Eleven* was being bantered around the bars, and they had no idea what it meant.

Some kind of slang talk that became popular while we were in Alaska, Walt thought. Not wanting to appear stupidly out of touch, he and Art went along with it.

At Wilbur Clark's Desert Inn, a gentleman bought them drinks and introduced himself as "Captain Mains," manager of the beloved comedian Jimmy Durante.

And another coincidence: Mains had grown up in Flint, just a short distance from Art Lussier.

"Say," Mains told them, "tomorrow is Jimmy's birthday. I'd like you boys to do a little something for Jimmy when he arrives. Can you help me out?"

Art came up with the idea. "How about if I make a parachute jump and hand him a birthday cake when he gets off the airplane?"

Mains bought the plan.

Due to some sort of delay, the jump was moved to the golf course next to the Desert Inn.

Durante, a humble man, said, "I can't believe that anybody would risk their life to do this for me."

Jimmy's 60th birthday (left to right:
Bob Young, Jimmy Durante, Walt Peca)

The Durante jump and the friendship that ensued between Durante and Art Lussier lent more credence to the rumors. There seemed to be a direct link connecting the boys and Durante's crowd, Wilbur Clark, Taylor, and others that convinced even the skeptics.

"What the hell is this 'oceans eleven'?" Walt remembered asking Art.

"I have no idea," Art said, "but don't fuck it up. They're buying us free drinks."

Problems developed with the act that the casino had no answer for. The act drew a crowd alright, but everyone left the gaming tables to watch the boys when they jumped. Nothing like this had ever happened before, and Dick Taylor had people to answer to.

He told the guys, "This is your last act, boys, so make it a good one. Unless you do something real big to turn this around, I'll have to ask you to leave."

On Day Seven, Walt suggested they try a cut-away. "The appearance of a man falling out of his parachute oughta sober them up at the craps tables," he contended.

But this simple plan soon grew complex. Instead of holding the handle of a reserve chute and falling a few thousand feet before pulling and releasing the handle when he felt a tug, Walt decided to fabricate something with needle and thread.

Its enigmatic design defied my simple logic, but it involved the release of cape wells and other technical devices. No one thought much of Art's dizzying spin, which sent the boys back to the drawing board for their last try.

On Day Eight, their pilot Bob Young guided the Cessna 8,000 feet over the desert for what might be the last time. A smaller than normal crowd had gathered behind the Hacienda to see two forms drop below the Cessna through a gorgeous desert sky.

Down they came, one more stable than the other. They fell an estimated 6,000 feet, and their forms became easy to distinguish . . . one stable, the other not.

"Something's wrong with one guy," an observer commented.

They'd fallen a mile now, when one pulled his ripcord, as the other rocketed past.

At 1,000 feet, still he tumbled . . . 500, 400, and the crowd sensed an impending disaster.

The gaming tables emptied. Guests in high heels, ball gowns, and dinner jackets scurried across the desert floor. A woman fainted.

A siren's dim wail in the distance came closer, and a man's coarse voice roared from the point of impact: "Son of a bitch! It's a dummy named Oscar!" He stared at a sack of sand, wrapped in a pair of white coveralls.

"Did you hear that, ma'am?" a doorman said. "It's only Oscar."

"Only Oscar," the woman said and fainted again.

"I don't know what the exact charge will be," said one deputy, "but somebody is going to jail."

Art Lussier was arrested, along with Bob Young.

Walt Peca, who wasn't in the airplane, observed the gathering storm. He walked to the bar and ordered a drink.

Back at the casino, the mood had turned. No more hostilities . . . it was festive.

"Best goddamn stunt I've ever seen," a man commented. "I think they've gone too far, though."

While the party at the Hacienda roared on without them, Art and Bob Young were charged with dangerous flying. After Walt partied until the wee hours of the morning, he finally went to the sheriff and bailed out his friends.

Walt and Art were out of a job and, except for the remains of Art's DEW Line money, had not a penny between them. Instead of setting aside $500 for meals and plane tickets home, they put every last cent they had on the roulette table and gave it a spin. Art won the first few times and got up to about $20,000.

If I had been there, I could have told them that anybody with any sense knows you can't keep winning at a casino—eventually, the house gets its pot. But I wasn't there, so Art just kept saying, "Let it ride, double or nothing," until he had nothing.

Yet the guys were philosophical. They had arrived in Vegas tired, dirty, and hungry, and they left tired, dirty, hungry, and broke.

They were back in Flint three days later, wearing ripped clothes and nearly starving, after buying bus tickets with borrowed money.

Jimmy Durante remained good friends with the boys until he died.

Zantop eventually based me in Macon, Georgia, so I had to drive up to Flint on weekends to see the guys. Walt went back to barbering, and Art got a job as a mailman. Porky ended up back in a factory, and we kept in touch for a while.

Outside the cabin, Parker started some serious target practice, and Walt joined him. I thought, *It's lucky Art doesn't have neighbors.*

Colonel Parker, our honorary team leader, had driven up to the Billabog from Flint packing a .45. Older than the rest of us, he had started to stoop. He had drooping eyes, and if I put him in a character sketch, it would be a 6'4" Basset hound, toting a gun. Yet I can tell you that despite his size, he wouldn't be much without that gun. He always had one.

They say Parker killed people, but I have no evidence of that. In the Detroit riots of 1965, he and Walt were activated into the Guard. Some black guy decided to taunt Parker, an absolutely insane thing to do.

"Great big soldier with an empty gun!" he shouted from behind one of the steel mailboxes that used to dot Detroit's landscape.

Parker was never a man without bullets, either. In fact, that day he had one in the chamber. When his .30-06 round ripped through the steel plates of the mailbox, it exited in a hole the size of a quarter. It did so much damage, the man's arm couldn't be saved.

I guess Parker could kill someone, if he had a mind to. Ask the man who hid behind that mailbox.

Moonshine and "Good Old Boys"

In September 1960, I almost didn't make it to a party at Parker's where I met my future wife. I was blue-lighted by cops in Forsyth while driving to Atlanta from Macon, Georgia. The cops peered into my backseat and saw four quarts of liquor I'd picked up in Juarez, Mexico.

"We're looking for a car matching the description of this one for running shine," he said.

One cop put me in the patrol car, and the other got into my car and drove off. We pulled up to the sheriff's office in a worn-out storefront facing the courthouse, a Civil War cannon on the front lawn. I got out and started talking with the sheriff, when my car drove up.

"Whooeee!" the cop said. "They said it was nice, but that is exquisite, Carl. You sure that's your car, Carl, not Mama's or Daddy's?"

"It's mine," I said.

"I just had a thought," the old sheriff said, looking as if he'd stepped right out of a *Smoky and the Bandit* movie. "Let's take a walk, Carl. I'd like to show you something."

He called me "Carl," not "boy," as his kind normally would. We stopped at a brick building and entered in total darkness.

"Go ahead, Carl," the cop said. "There's a fella here I want you to meet. Say hello, Carl. . . . We'll see if he answers."

I said, "Hello," fairly loud, and through the darkness came, "Help me."

I turned and saw the old man giggle. "Who is he?" I asked.

"I don't know," the sheriff said, "but he's still alive."

On the way back, the sheriff told me, "He was a vagrant. I caught him hitchin' a ride through town the same night as we had a break-in."

"So you used him to solve that crime," I said.

"Kind of like you, Carl," he said. "You didn't commit no crime. We got you on a technicality we never enforce. Hell, half the folks in Georgia have shine in their cars. I think we can come to equitable terms on this."

When we reached his office, the old sheriff said, "What would your daddy tell you to do about this predicament you got yourself into?"

"Keep myself out of your jailhouse," I told him, and again he giggled.

"It's a smart boy that listens to his daddy," he said, holding the door open for me.

We then dickered over the price to buy back my own car (he won that one), and I wrote out a check from a bank I had no account in (I won that one).

I drove off in haste to Atlanta, where I hid my car. Then I flew from Atlanta to Detroit on a 150-mile-per-hour antique cargo plane and hitchhiked from Detroit to Flint.

I arrived in Flint between 3 and 4 p.m., and Art picked me up that night to go to Parker's party on Carpenter Road. Parker had guns at that party, too. Walt and Joni were there, and Loretta had tagged along with them. They introduced her to me. In those days, men wore suits to parties, and women, party dresses. The tension between me and Parker was instant. Parker told me he was dating Loretta and fully expected she would be with him. Yet she wasn't. Loretta favored me, and Parker could see that.

Loretta accepted my invitation to watch me jump on the weekend. Our group was performing one of our "last to open" competitions, which I won, because my feet nearly touched the ground just after opening. Loretta told her friends I was crazy.

Walt always had a special feeling for orphans. A few years after his jump in Alaska to benefit orphans, he did something similar in the Lower 48. On December 20, 1964—Christmas week—he rented a plane and parachuted down to Our Lady of Providence School in Northville, Michigan, dressed as Santa, and he passed out gifts to the orphans. According to a December article in the *Detroit News*,

Peca injured his left hand slightly when he slipped in the snow as he landed. But it was still better than Alaska. He got tangled in a tree there with the temperature at 40 below.

"It took me quite a while to get down because my fingers were freezing," he said. "The kids kept shouting, 'Please come down, Santa.'"

Art's springtime Billabogs had replaced his mom's parlor as the team's official meeting place. Modifying parachutes and jumping onto racetracks with batwings gave way to drinking beer, shooting guns, and reminding one another of how stupid we were in our youth and how much we got away with.

And it wasn't just parachuting, either. Art and I did foolish things when flying planes, too.

Suicide Mission to Hawaii

I'll start with the worst example, back in 1965—a passenger trip from San Francisco to Hawaii in an airplane without enough fuel capacity, a Model B DC-7. And let's give credit to whoever in corporate offices realized it was somewhat closer to Hilo, Hawaii, from San Francisco than it was from Burbank, which was the original flight plan.

Early on the morning of Zantop's maiden voyage to Hawaii, we assumed we'd thought of everything. The airplane held roughly 100 people, yet we had 102 passengers (bowlers who had chartered the plane), plus 3 flight attendants. We'd brought several cases of wine and beer, so 2 flight attendants would sit on the cases, to give passengers their jump seats. The FAA was supposed to accompany all maiden flights but had not been told about this one. Our head stewardess took the FAA's seat.

Most of the 102 passengers had spent the night on the grass at Burbank Airport and had drunk several cases of beer. When we landed at Burbank, they rushed to the airplane to urinate in one of our two toilets. With all seats filled by people holding beer bottles and two stews perched on beer cases, we set off for San Francisco.

When we were an hour out of Burbank, several passengers beat on the cockpit door with their fists. I told someone to let them in.

"Where's the ocean?" they wanted to know.

Another suspiciously asked, "Where the hell are you going?"

"Frisco," I said.

"What the hell happened to Hawaii?" they said.

"Nobody told you?" I asked.

And then someone said, "It's fuel, isn't it? This is an early DC-7. It doesn't carry enough gas."

That's when the swearing and the threats started.

I continued to fly that airplane, and as soon as I set the brakes at San Francisco, our engineer fueled our airplane to the max. We in the cockpit knew that about half of the overfilled gas would siphon on takeoff.

The three guys we'd talked to earlier then told the other passengers about the fuel situation. I expected a mass exodus of passengers at that point.

The engineer came back into the cockpit, and I asked him how many empty seats he'd seen.

"None," he said. "It's a party back there. One of the new stews was dancing with some guy."

One by one, the engines kicked over, and we taxied for takeoff.

Because we were severely overweight, we used every foot of runway, but that wasn't why the passengers were shouting.

"The gas is all spraying out!" was what they yelled.

Dozens of gallons, perhaps three or four hundred, now blew through the old gas covers, looking like a perfect storm for an explosion.

The siphoning continued until a minute or two after we crossed the Pacific shoreline. Then the screaming stopped, and people's attention turned to another problem: After all of that gas had siphoned out, would there still be enough in those tanks to reach Hawaii?

In close to forty-five minutes, I would have to make the decision whether to keep going forward or turn back for the States while we still could.

Our head stew entered the cockpit. "They're having a party back there," she told us, "and it's about to get a whole lot better."

"Better?" I asked. "How can it get better?"

"That five-gallon bucket sitting in the back toilet is overflowing onto the floor," she said.

Too much piss, not enough gas. Do we go forward or backward? She stood there for a second, waiting for my reply, but all I did was rest my head in my hand.

Then the cockpit door opened again, and another stew stuck her head inside. "The front toilet is overflowing onto the floor."

There really was no one to blame. Partiers had consumed gallons of booze that night, and they had no convenient place to relieve themselves. Plus, a last-minute change of route had added five more hours of drinking on the way to San Francisco. Then, of course, seven more hours of drinking on the way to Hawaii had been more than two 5-gallon buckets sitting under a toilet seat could take.

The engineer said, "Captain Laurin, we must turn back. This much urine contacting our electrical wiring will surely short something out."

Yet he hadn't considered that we had just as many miles to travel if we went forward versus turning back.

In the next ten minutes, I would have to make a life-or-death decision for 109 people: whether to go ahead or turn back.

My decision to continue on to Hilo surprised no one.

The second the stairs lodged against the airplane and the door opened, all passengers who had not yet wet themselves started a rush for survival. They ran down the stairs and toward the miniature terminal like a herd of stampeding zebras, only to find a tiny one-hole toilet with people already lined up.

Then someone started to urinate on the lawn, and every passenger followed, all 102 of them—the ultimate bladder relief.

To find a pilot for that risky flight to Hawaii, the company had done something unheard of in the annals of airline history. They took a secret vote among the engineers, roughly a hundred men, asking which pilot or pilots would absolutely be the most likely to push on to Hawaii, as the plane approached that spot where, if you passed it, you wouldn't have enough fuel to get back to L.A. By the way, they also mentioned that the flight was oversold, and some passengers and crew would have to sit on beer crates.

My name had been written on every ballot the engineers submitted—not one other name on a hundred or so ballots.

I'm still alive today, so we made it.

Why me? I don't know. What I do know is that the answer to why I spent years rooting out D.B. Cooper lies somewhere in these stories.

Back in 1965, the pilot turnover was ridiculous, especially with young guys our age jumping to large carriers for big pay. And during that period of time, there were more assassinations, airplane hijackings, mercenary wars, and drugs than America had ever experienced. More than a few people, especially in Miami, became millionaires overnight. Some of them were people I knew pretty well, right from that little airline, but the results were mixed. Although it's been more than sixty years, the thing I remember most clearly is that for every millionaire who came out of that "get rich quick" era, it left eight or nine dead and just as many more with empty pockets and a good story to tell.

Earlier, I mentioned a book authored by Michael Abrams, and at the end of Chapter 16, he quotes E. Hamilton Lee, one of the first U.S. airmail pilots. Lee said, "There are old pilots and bold pilots, but no old bold pilots."

How Walt Peca, Art Lussier, and I, along with the rest of the Michigan Parachute Team, escaped such a prophecy remains a mystery.

As E. Hamilton Lee said, "All men are not immortal, just a few of us are."

CHAPTER 6

THE BREWING STORM

After Walt got back from Alaska, California, and Las Vegas, he was still very much a part of our Michigan Parachute Team.

Walt and Joni got married on November 3, 1960. During the first years of their marriage, they lived in a rented house at 29142 Cherry Hill, Garden City, Michigan—seventeen miles from Detroit.

The following year, on September 5, 1961, Loretta and I were married.

A Return to Military Life

On September 22, 1961, Walt enlisted in the U.S. Air Force Reserve as a member of the Para Rescue 305th Air Rescue squad at Selfridge AFB. He became a Rescue and Survival Specialist, AFSC B92130A. He was picked to travel with the USAF aerobatic team, the Blue Angels. From October 25, 1961, through the end of November, he was assigned to active duty.

From November 9, 1961, through December 9, 1961, he took part in Operation Long Legs II, a goodwill mission to South America with the USAF Thunderbird Team. His unit also received a presidential citation for participating in the 1961 Berlin Air Lift. He held the rank of Airman First Class.

The military taught Walt the love of jumping, but he never enjoyed the crazy stunts the rest of us guys performed. Walt jumped for a reason; the rest of us jumped for fun.

Walt and Joni get married

A Fateful Meeting

Walt got a desk job at Zantop Air Transport, coordinating communications between the main office at Willow Run Airport and pilots, crewmembers, maintenance people, and airports where Zantop flights went. He worked there until 1963. Art and I were pilots at Zantop; I left the company on Thanksgiving 1969. Sometime in 1962, using the privileges that came with his job, Walt took a trip to Elsinore, California, to visit the drop zone there. He had heard that the CIA was hiring parachutists in Elsinore. Walt met a man named Phillip (Phil) Q, a CIA operative, there, and I believe he encouraged Walt to apply to the CIA. Phil and Walt remained friends for many years.

Gun-Running for the Teamsters

When he returned to Detroit, Walt got work with the Teamsters. He didn't talk too much about the jobs he did, knowing what the union was capable of. We used to joke and call them the Hamsters.

The Teamsters union was different from government work. The government didn't want anybody to know what it was up to. Yet Walt said the government did the same type of thing as the unions and mobsters, trying to get money and power, but kept it under the rug. When people did something the union didn't want them to do, the union sent a thug to bust their kneecaps or burn their houses down. The union wanted everyone to know they did it. That way, people knew that if they revolted against the union, there was a very real certainty something bad would happen. The union ruled by intimidation, and Walt followed them the way he followed anyone in power.

He didn't really make a lot of money, but one day in an audiotaped phone call, I asked him why he did it. He said, "I was hoping for a better position. I always tried to work my way up. You didn't just get in there for doing nothing. You had to do something. In other words, I was proving myself."

"But eventually you made some money, right?"

"At one point, about the same as I would make working on the docks. But they gave me different jobs. There was Dolly Madison, that cake company, and they wanted to beat Hostess. And they opened up an office. I got called up and was told I could take a day off work to go there to apply for a job. I went in and filled out the application, and I wrote down everybody's license plate that was there. I took it back to the union hall, and they gave me $100 and a turkey."

Walt never drew a paycheck from the Teamsters; his pay came through Teamster affiliates: Hostess, Taystee, and Sunshine Biscuit, the company that makes animal crackers. In turn, those companies contributing to the Teamster cause were exempt from strikes and the union's strong-arm tactics. Our government works the same way.

And yet Walt wanted more.

One day, after I started writing this book, I asked him what he did for a living in Detroit back then.

"I was, more or less, in the gun business," Walt said.

"You mean, for the Hamsters?"

"Yeah, well, if you put it that way. I would get machine guns and all that, from Earl's gun shop, and then I would sell them to different locals."

"Oh, okay," I said.

"We had Marcus right there and offloaded guns into the car. Marcus Hamburgers—they used to have loose fried hamburger. And they would put chili over it. They were famous all over Detroit."

". . . And were you still getting money from the cookie company then?" I asked.

"Yeah," Walt said.

Walt was once a Teamsters' employee

Walt bought and sold guns mostly to people who needed a gun but couldn't legally buy one—people in the covert world who for a moment needed a throwaway unregistered gun that couldn't be traced back to them. He often sold to known gangsters but to cops as well. He never made a lot of money. Thinking he had protection, he did his own version of Bonnie and Clyde, and when he got caught, due to his own sloppiness, he always walked. His was a now-and-then cottage industry, mostly meant to elevate his status with the Hoffa union and Murder Inc., a business mainly run by a woman. Walt got to know them all. He was a reliable source, and he kept quiet. Soon he was working for them and with them.

"You can't make a whole lot of money selling guns," I said.

"The kind I was sellin', you could. I was sellin' Sten guns."

"What the hell was that?" I asked.

"The British submachine gun in World War II."

The Sten gun, a lightweight submachine gun made by the British in World War II, started to appear in the States in the mid-1950s. Sten guns were poorly constructed from scrap metal parts. Walt had learned about Sten guns during his stint in Germany as a paratrooper. The Sten itself was hard to get, but if you bought the parts from the UK, it was simple to assemble. It was legal, and in fifteen minutes you had a working gun.

This was Walt's introduction into the underworld. He also used the Sten gun himself. As an instrument of intimidation, it was unparalleled. You didn't have to kill anyone to get results, just fire off a burst of five, then hand the person whatever your boss wanted him to sign.

Walt never fished or hunted. He just liked guns, which he often used. He told me he never killed anybody any other way except with a gun.

Sten guns—Walt sold them

On one occasion in the early 1960s, Walt was caught smuggling a German submachine gun into the country, but before he went to court, the U.S. federal government melted that gun down, and again the case was dismissed for lack of evidence. This happened not once or twice but dozens of times. Walt knew he couldn't be prosecuted.

"You can tell someone somewhere, someplace, likes me," he said. In a note to me, he wrote that some cops had told him, "We're going to see you locked up." Walt, knowing he had friends in high places, told the cops, "You're not gonna do a fucking thing," and he was right. Walt walked, and the cops were transferred.

Another time the cops wanted Walt's books and records, so he showed up with a Bible and a Beatles album. He taunted them and made fun of them and walked away every time.

CIA Application

A year after meeting the CIA operative Phillip Q, Walt made a big decision: he would apply to the CIA, which seemed like an ideal job for him. As a first step, on February 12, 1963, he took a literacy test at army headquarters in Detroit, Michigan. He passed for Russian and Polish.

Soon after the test, Walt sent in his application to the CIA. In the spring of 1963, he was elevated to an enforcer in the Teamsters.

On June 21, 1963, Walt was charged with misdemeanor assault or assault and battery and found guilty.

On September 18, 1963, Walt received a disappointing letter from the CIA in Washington, D.C., informing him that "Operating Officials of the Agency have made a careful analysis of your background and experiences"; however, "we cannot at this time utilize the qualifications which you have made available to us."

Walt's friend Phil (Phillip) Q and his wife, Mary, became Walt's mentors. He told me they did a lot for him. Walt didn't know whether Mary was an agent, but she worked with Phil. Although Walt's application to the CIA had been turned down, in 1964 with Phil's help Walt became an operative for the intelligence community and from then on received his project numbers from Phil. This was not steady work, by any means. Walt continued to work at various jobs.

Hard Times

During another audiotaped phone call with Walt, I questioned him further about his financial problems.

"Going back, you must have done some work . . . for the Hamsters . . ."

"Yeah. . . . Working my way up, in charge of picket lines. We picketed here, picketed there for different problems, like different locals we had. . . . Going in and talkin' to people, when our girls told them, 'You're not doing right by your employees,' or whatever."

"You seem like you should have been making enough money . . ."

"I was," Walt said, "but I thought I could make more at other things, and I think I fought for that. Oh, that made a whole bunch of dope come down on me."

"For the Teamsters," I said.

"Yeah. My pension with them was gone!" Walt laughed. ". . . And then, when everybody was getting on my ass . . . the Ironworkers . . . I went and filed charges against them. Then they threatened me, and I called the FBI. I was protected under the Hobbs Act. I was a federal witness."

"Uh-huh."

"And they went down to the union hall. So I said, 'But that don't mean they still couldn't kill me.'"

"Right," I said.

"And then after a while I said, 'Fuck it, though.' I might as well head out right there, and that's when I left. And went down to see Art in Lauderdale."

"Right, but this would be about '65—"

Walt interrupted me: "'68 or '69."

"Now somewhere between '65 and '68 to '69 then, you fell on hard times."

"Yeah," Walt said. "Real hard times."

"What was the reason for that, do you think?"

"I was workin' iron, but I wasn't a union member. I was working on core bit. You're the last one out of the hall and the first one to be laid off."

"Okay," I said, "but you were collecting money from the biscuit company, right? Or did that stop for some reason?"

"Oh, that stopped," Walt said, "after Big Boy's."

"Okay. So basically, hadn't you been working with the Hamsters during this time and collecting somethin'?"

"Yeah," Walt said.

"How come you worked for them, if you weren't making hardly any money?"

"I was hoping for a better position," Walt said.

"Did you ever prove yourself and get to where you at least made a decent wage? 'Cause Loretta knew this one guy who always made good money with 'em."

"I don't know what's considered good money," Walt said. "What was he doing? What was his job?"

"He was pretty much a goon," I said. "Joni used to run around with Loretta and this girl named Judy. So Judy never knew what her dad did, and Loretta didn't know either. But one time she was over at her Uncle Eddie's—he was a Hamster—and Loretta brought it up: 'Well, my girlfriend Judy, her dad works with Jimmy Hoffa, but none of us know what he does.' Eddie laughed. He was a funny guy, big beer drinker, and he said, 'Johnny? He's a goon. He breaks people's legs.' And he laughed when he said it. That's the first time Loretta found out what he did. She never did tell Judy."

"Okay, here's what happened," Walt said. "I told you about Tom here, that he was a shooter for the Hamsters."

"Tom who?"

"I don't have to say no names."

"No," I said. "Okay."

"And he worked for Hoffa. And then you're talking about this Johnny guy. One day, Hoffa called Tom into the office and told him, 'We don't need you no more or any type of work that you do.' And that was it. Tom was living—" Walt broke off. "He had a horse farm, you know. He lost everything."

"I wonder what happened to him," I said.

"He was an errand boy. He was around too long. They don't keep people around too long that know too much."

In early 1964, while hanging out with a friend and drinking heavily, Walt and a friend talked about robbing a bank. One night he told Joni that he was going out for milk and a loaf of bread. There is no record of a robbery that night, but Walt never came home.

The Big Boy Robbery: June 22, 1965

Walt's day job was union organizer for James R. Hoffa's Local 51 Teamsters in Detroit. At night he did other things. At 4 a.m. on the morning of June 22, 1965, he committed armed robbery of the Big Boy at 1621 East Eight Mile Road in Detroit.

It seems the robbery was his partner's idea, and they were supposed to go into the Big Boy together. But then the partner wimped out, so Walt said he'd do it and proceeded to go in alone.

Big Boy

Both men were obviously drunk, and the robbery seemed like a good idea at the time. Walt told me he'd used a submachine gun that night but wasn't sure which make and model.

During the robbery, Walt said to the customers, "Don't get up, finish your meals, then leave when you're done."

The manager was a pretty blonde woman, probably in her twenties. Walt had her walk him to the basement of the building where they kept the safe. She dialed the combination and opened the door. Walt grabbed the money from the safe.

He told me that some people even applauded when he and the manager came up from the basement. Amazingly, most of the customers had stayed in their seats, finishing their meals, during the robbery. Some even paid their bills.

Walt started handing out money to the employees. The manager followed him toward the door.

"You've been nice to me, young lady," he said, "and I didn't have a chance to give you a tip." He gave her some $20 bills. She stuffed them down her bra.

He thanked people for their cooperation and walked out the door.

The getaway should have been smooth sailing, but as Walt headed toward his partner's car, he saw a police officer beside it, leaning into the window. Walt ditched the gun in some shrubs and walked toward the car.

The officer was writing Walt's partner a ticket for parking the wrong way on a one-way street. Another officer in a patrol car had blocked their vehicle.

The other officer signaled to the first one that an APB was coming in, and he went over to investigate. Walt and his partner couldn't get the car out of that spot, so they waited like sitting ducks. The officer came back and told them the Big Boy had just called in a robbery, and Walt fit the description.

The next day our friend Art called and told me, "Go see Peca. He's in jail in Hazel Park for robbery of a Big Boy."

When Loretta and I arrived, Walt asked whether we'd seen a nice-looking blonde lady leaving. We said no. That would have been the restaurant manager, visiting him. She'd told him, "Too bad we couldn't have met under different circumstances." (Note: Despite news reports of a love affair between Walt and the blonde Big Boy manager, this was not true. The only evidence of any chemistry between them was the manager's comment at the jail cell.)

Walt told us the whole story about how he'd ended up in jail. He said he didn't even know where his partner was.

Loretta and I walked out of the police station in disbelief. We couldn't do anything to help Walt at this point, and we had to get back to our own lives.

The next day the Teamsters bailed him out but told him they were finished with him. Hoffa himself fired Walt, saying, "It's people like you that give my union a bad name."

The next thing I knew, Art told me that Walt had jumped bail. Walt had called Willard the next day, saying he would be on the lam. He asked Art to call Joni in a couple of days to tell her he was sorry things hadn't worked out between them. Joni and the kids left the house they'd been living in at 12751 Joyce in Warren, Michigan, and moved in with her parents.

The day Walt robbed the Big Boy changed his life forever and also marked a change in the whole group. The Michigan Parachute Team seemed to unravel. Living our everyday lives took over. I moved from piloting to owning my own construction business, to running a pizza parlor, before Loretta and I left Michigan to retire on our farm in Florida.

With the Big Boy Robbery, Walt's life took a turn for the worse. From this point on, until the hijacking, Walt was truly down and out, mostly due to his own behavior. It was why, six years later, he figured that if he died during the hijacking, it wouldn't be much worse than the life he was living. He was in a bad relationship, with kids he couldn't support; he'd become a fugitive from the law; he had no money and a crappy job; and he lived in a tiny postage stamp–size town literally in the middle of nowhere. In his mind, he had screwed up his life—a life of promise, beginning with the army, becoming a skydiver, being written up in a major newspaper as the Santa Claus who jumped out of a plane, seeking adventure in Alaska and Las Vegas, becoming a USAF Rescue and Survival Specialist and a member of the Blue Angels aerobatics team, and working for the Teamsters. He had a loving wife with two kids and drove a nice car. And it all spiraled downward because of the Big Boy robbery. That's why he mentioned the robbery so many times in our phone calls.

So he rolled the dice and did the hijacking—and he actually won because his life was better after that. You can see why the D.B. Cooper hijacking had to happen. Walt could see no other way out. He needed money, lots of it, to turn his life around. And the $200,000 (more than $1 million, at today's currency value) *did* turn his life around.

A Comedy of Errors

During one of my daily audiotaped phone calls with Walt, I brought up the Teamsters again, trying to learn more about how he and the organization had parted ways.

"Let's see, so '65, when you did the great jewel—"

"The Hiccup," Walt said.

We both laughed.

"The Maxwell Smart guy," Walt said sarcastically.

(Walt, acting alone, had made an unsuccessful attempt to rob a jewelry show at the Birmingham House Motel at 12:11 a.m. on June 7, 1965, by spraying bullets into the ceiling above the vendors. But he'd made a mistake—it was the wrong week for the show. On December 14, 1967, Walt was interrogated by Detective Richard Chambers from the City of Birmingham regarding the attempted robbery. Walt told Chambers that he'd been working at Sunshine Biscuit at the time of the robbery. The detective called the personnel manager at Sunshine, who informed him that Walt didn't begin work with them until the day *after* the robbery. Walt wasn't arrested, though, because an eyewitness claimed that the man had tattoos on his arms, and Walt did not. No further action was taken, and Walt was later granted an end to his probation.)

"So," I said. "You were just doing a little side job to—"

"Which I shouldn't have been doing because they drop you then."

"If they catch you doing that," I said. "Did they ever know it was you or associate you with that? I mean, the Hamsters?"

"No," Walt said, "not till afterwards when it was all over. But it was all over for me with them with the Big Boy. They stopped everything right there."

"Oh, wow."

"You can't trust anybody with a felony conviction."

"Yeah," I said, "because somebody with a felony, the cops can pull 'em in and make 'em talk. Easier than somebody without."

"They don't make them talk," Walt said. "They run down and make a deal with the prosecuting attorney. 'Cause they don't get so much time. Nobody has to make you talk. Good people with a felony conviction do it themselves."

"Well, yeah. That's what I meant."

"I want a great deal," Walt said. "I don't want twenty years. Give me five to ten and let me out in three. . . . And here's what was goin' on. 'Cause when you got a felony conviction, you're not even in charge of a picket line."

"Yeah," I said. "What year did you rob Big Boy?"

"It must have been '65. . . . It was [around] Father's Day in '65."

"Okay, so basically, then, after Father's Day of '65 you were pretty well out of the Hamsters?"

"Oh, yeah," said Walt.

"And you were just cut loose?"

"Yeah."

"Then this is basically when you fell on hard times."

"Yeah," Walt said.

"So that's pretty much when everything stopped, but the Ironworkers were still after you?"

"Not then," Walt said. "I wasn't even in Ironworkers then."

"In '65?"

"No. That's when I went to look for Don."

On the Lam, in Search of Don

Right after he jumped bail from the Big Boy robbery, Walt boarded a flight to Los Angeles. All he had was $50 that Art had given him and Art's optimistic attitude on his side. He thought he'd try to find Sinclair again or Don Brennan, a smoke jumper friend from Alaska. Whenever Walt was on the run or needed something, he turned to Don, who was a somewhat shady character. After Walt searched in Huntington Beach, the last place Don was living, he learned that Don had taken a job out of town.

As Walt told me about this time in his life, we both agreed: what happened next defied even the most extreme definition of dumb luck. Two ladies walking out the door of the bus station were conversing, and Walt heard one say "Don" and "smoke jumping."

He followed them. "Excuse me, ma'am, did you mean Don Brennan, by any chance?"

"Yes, I did. Why do you ask?"

"I'm looking for a friend of mine named Don Brennan, who was a smoke jumper in Alaska about four years ago. Do you know him?"

"Yes, he's my son."

Walt asked her for Don's phone number, but Don didn't have a phone, though she said he was in Wenatchee. Walt then took a thirty-hour bus ride to Wenatchee, Washington, and walked to the address Don's mother had given him. He found that Don had left that house the previous week to start a new job.

Being broke, Walt offered to do chores for the landlady, and she gave him room and board. He wrote a letter to Don, telling him to call at his old place and hoping that Don had requested his mail to be forwarded. After five days, Don called. They made arrangements to meet at his new place in Bellingham, Washington.

Walt hitchhiked as close as he could to Bellingham and then stopped at a diner to call Don. As they were talking, Walt saw cops outside.

He whispered to Don, "Get here as fast as you can."

Walt learned quickly about being on the run from the law. He told me that sometimes he felt like there was a cop behind every bush. Every person seemed suspicious, and no question was harmless. Yet somehow he figured out that with thousands of warrants out there, an officer can only remember a few of the faces on the posters. What gives people away is their actions. When people try to hide their faces, keep out of sight, or avoid walking by, a cop gets suspicious. Walt knew better, so he kept smiling and talking casually to the waitress, while sipping his coffee.

When he got into the car, Don asked what kind of trouble he was in.

"Armed robbery. I'm on the run. I skipped bail."

"What the hell were you thinking?"

"I wasn't thinking. I was drunk."

"Well, for Christ's sake," Don said. "I get drunk every night, but I don't go out and hold somebody up."

Don just happened to have an extra Social Security card and number from a deceased coworker with the name James Allen O'Keefe. He gave it to Walt.[9]

"Who is James Allen O'Keefe?" Walt asked.

"From now on, you are," Don said and instructed him on how to create a new identity.

Walt as an Ironworker

The next morning Walt went to the library and took out *For Whom the Bell Tolls* by Hemingway to get his library card. From there, it was a cinch to get his Washington driver's license. Using the good old boys network, Don then got Walt an ironworker's card and a job.

"The bad news is, it's filthy work that nobody else will do," Don said.

The ironworker's job was perfect for a man on the run. More than half the guys there were hiding from something or other: busted marriages, bad loans, money collectors, bail bondsmen. The jobs didn't last long because dams and skyscrapers were eventually built, meaning ironworkers moved around like gypsies.

Nearly every evening after their shifts, they all met at a local bar to get rid of their paychecks. Walt was careful to keep his drinking under control and to save some money, just in case.

One day, as Walt walked back to Don's apartment, he stopped at a pay phone to call Sinclair in California. The next morning, he quit his job, got his pay packet, and packed up his belongings.

On the flight to L.A., Walt knew he was better off than he had been a month ago, but he was still a man on the run, who could be turned in, arrested, and shipped to prison at any moment.

Sinclair was there to pick Walt up from the airport early in the morning.

---

9   James Allen O'Keefe is a pseudonym for the actual name on the card.

"What the hell kind of trouble are you in now?" Sinclair said, as Walt settled into the passenger seat.

They stopped at a diner, and Walt told his story again, but with the addition of his new identity and that he was working steel now.

The next day Walt went to the ironworkers' hall and immediately got signed up for a job near Tahachapi State Prison in California. While drinking at a nearby bar after work, Walt met an attractive dusty blonde who told him her name was Carla M__ (but her real name was Florence E__).[10] She worked as a guard at the prison.

Walt told me he was attracted to Carla the minute he saw her—though if he'd known how it was going to turn out, he probably would have run the other way.

He told her his name was James, and they had a good time that evening.

Carla invited Walt back to her place. She had a son, who was sleeping in his room when Walt got there. For the next few hours, Walt felt as comfortable as he'd ever been. Carla wasn't the best lover he'd ever had, but Walt believed there was no such thing as bad sex. Of course, when he told me about this years later, he had to admit that with Carla, he learned that he was mistaken about a lot of things.

By September 1965, Walt was living with Carla. In July 1966, he decided to move to Washington for better work. Carla told Walt she was pregnant and that she was going with him.

Walt and Carla in Washington

On their first day in Washington, in the fall of 1966, Walt went to work and left Carla with her son to look for a job and a place for them to live. She found an apartment, but it took her a few days to get a job as a waitress. While Walt rode to work with Don and

---

10 Names withheld.

Stan each morning, Carla was left to walk a couple of miles to the restaurant. The fact that they needed a car soon became her only topic of conversation. She wasn't making enough for a car, though, because she had to pay a neighbor to watch her son.

Then it started to rain every day. After a week of slogging through the rain, Carla took matters into her own hands and went to the closest car dealership. For $400, she didn't get any better deal than Art and Walt had on their trip to Vegas, and the car broke down after two days.

Before long, Carla got suspicious because Don kept slipping up and using Walt's real name, instead of "James." (It's hilarious that she was upset at him for using an alias, when she was also using an alias at that time. In many ways, they were a good match for each other.) She called the local police, who discovered Walt's actual identity.

That day when he arrived home after work, two men were waiting outside for him. One of them cuffed Walt.

He was extradited to Michigan to stand trial. Again, he walked.

When Walt got back to Michigan, he didn't call me immediately. He was probably afraid I would tell Loretta, and she would tell Joni. But Loretta and Joni had drifted apart, so Loretta didn't know any details about her old friend. At that point, Walt was five years behind in child support, and other than making infrequent calls to his mother, he'd had no news of his wife and kids.

By the time Walt returned home years later, hoping to become the father he never had been, it was too late to help his children. They had made several unfortunate life choices and continued to do so, making it impossible for Walt to be the provider he'd always wanted to be.

I did see Walt again around 1967, when Loretta and I lived at our Portage Lake, Michigan, house. One day a pilot friend from California came to visit with his young son. The pilot and I decided to tie the kid into a parachute harness and hook him to the back of a boat. I gunned the engine but couldn't get him up into the air. A few days later, Walt stopped by to borrow that same parachute, which was now unpacked and loose. But repacking it would be no problem for Walt because he had learned how to do this from Parker. The fact that Walt borrowed a parachute from me indicated that he was still actively jumping at that time.

CHAPTER 7

WALT'S "DARK YEARS"

lost track of Walt from 1967 to 1998 and didn't have any direct contact with him, except for one time when Loretta and I visited him and Joni at her apartment in Westland, in August 1975. During what I call Walt's "dark years," he lost touch with his family and most friends, except for Art and Willard. Even his sister didn't know where he was.

At his trial for the Big Boy robbery, Walt was given probation, with the stipulation that he not leave Michigan. Art offered to let Walt stay in his apartment and picked him up at the courthouse. Waiting back at Art's apartment in Flint were Carla and the new baby boy, born on February 14, 1967.

Looking to get extra money, Walt began selling military guns, automatic machine guns (Schmeisser) on the black market.

Flint, Michigan, where I grew up, was home to big unions and bad water. Walt's problems with the ironworkers escalated after he was extradited from out West. They tried to put Walt in jail for skipping bail, but, surprisingly, the judge rejected the union's request.

The unions in Flint were a mix of good and bad, as were the factories. They got their start in Russia in 1928, with an agreement between Henry Ford and Joseph Stalin to build a Model-T Ford plant in Gorky, Russia. By consent, Henry Ford sent several thousand workers, including Walter Reuther and his brother, to Gorky, and that's where they learned about unions. When they returned to

Michigan, they started the United Auto Workers (UAW), which did a lot of good for the workers at first. Other unions used the UAW as a model.

Early on the morning after the Big Boy trial, Walt parked in the ironworkers' union hall lot, looking for work. Halfway to the front door, he was confronted by three very large men, who asked, "Hey, Buddy, you got a book?" Walt didn't. Moving to full mastery and a union book would mean he could get the good jobs. He hoped that was coming soon.

Walt told them no, and they told him to get the fuck out of there.

Walt turned in silence and walked back to the car. He drove out of the near-empty lot and parked across the street. He walked back into the hall without further interference. In fact, the three stooges ignored him completely. As he approached the agent, Walt struggled to stay calm. He told me later that it took everything he had not to burn the whole place down.

He introduced himself to the agent as Walt Reca and extended his hand. The agent shook hands suspiciously, but his attitude, if not friendly, was at least civil. Walt presented his new card with the name Walt Reca on it and a review of his work experience.

The agent set Walt up with some work "in the air," which a lot of the men didn't do. Walt clearly saw that the ironworkers' union took care of its own. If the good ol' boy network was alive and well, there would be five or six guys sitting in the foreman's shack playing cards, and not one of them would ever get two feet off the ground. Walt didn't like their featherbedding, but it did mean he got a job.

Jobs from the hall came and went, but Walt was always the last one hired and the first laid off. He still managed to make a living, so he and Carla got a modest apartment and a dependable car. He had hopes that his baby would have a decent life.

The main bright spot in Walt's life in Flint, though, had been Art. Art had started his own cargo business out of the same airport where we'd all met. The other guys had gone off in different directions, but Art stuck around for a while. Then one day he came home from work and told Patty to sell the business, they were moving to Ft. Lauderdale. He'd gotten tired of freezing his ass off and fighting the snow.

The next day, Walt went to the agent and demanded his book. The agent told him to get the hell out of there and that he'd never get a book from that hall. I believe that the agent would not let him be admitted into the apprentice program unless Walt gave him a bribe.

Frustration and anger built up, and Walt found himself on a mission—once again breaking the rules he had set for himself. Once again with consequences. He knew about union corruption; everybody did. He explained it to me like this:

New people in the ironworkers' union were trying to become journeymen, which allowed them to work in a variety of positions at premium pay scale. Once accepted into the journeyman's program, they got a *member number* or a *card* or a *book*. All three terms were used interchangeably.

All work was assigned first by seniority, then to any journeyman, then to certified members from the local, and then to individuals from another local. This, of course, placed Walt near the bottom of the rung for being dispatched to a job.

The journeyman's program was a four-year course, and welding was taught in the second year. During this second year of the program, someone could be certified in welding, provided that he pass a proficiency exam and a written test.

Another variable concerned workload. If Walt were a welder, he might have one day on a job to complete a required weld, then be off for a few days because the cranes would have to bring in the tubes to be positioned or because the tubes did not arrive at the job site on time, and so forth.

He didn't belong to Local 29 but to the local in Detroit; he was not a journeyman, so he was at the bottom of the pay scale and had only a few jobs that he was qualified to do.

Walt Takes on the Ironworkers

All Walt wanted was to get what he deserved, what he should have gotten without even asking. He was determined to find a way. Having no experience with labor law, he went to the library and learned all he could. Then he started a letter-writing campaign to any politician he could think of.

One after another, the replies came: "I'd really like to help you, but . . ." The reasons were slightly different, but reading between the lines, Walt knew nobody was prepared to take on the unions.

What happened next made Walt suspect that the ironworkers' union had found out about his letter-writing campaign.

One day the union agent called Walt and said they had a job for him. They sent him to a remote area out of town to measure up a building. Walt knew something was off—there was no way the union that built the building wouldn't have the dimensions and the blueprints for every single job.

When he arrived at the spot, new snow had fallen. Walt observed footprints leading in but not out of the building, indicating that whoever those footprints belonged to was inside waiting for him.

Only the union knew he was coming. No car tracks were in the driveway, so Walt surmised they had driven past the building, parked the car, and then walked back, so the building would appear vacant. But those footprints told a different story.

Continuing on, Walt spied their empty sedan. He got out of his car and checked the hood of the expensive sedan. The hood was warm.

He had been set up for a hit.

He let the air out of their tires and then drove home, wary about what the union would try next.

The next day, he went to the union hall and told the agent his car wasn't working, so he never made it to the building. The agent clearly knew better, but he gave Walt another job. Walt had to take it, yet he was careful when working out on the iron to keep his distance from his coworkers.

Walt moved his family to a trailer park at 30030 W. Eight Mile Road in Farmington, Michigan, under an assumed name. That worked for a while.

He kept sending letters to politicians; then, on a whim, he decided to go to the top. The response from the National Labor Relations Board came more quickly than he expected.

> Your letter to President Lyndon B. Johnson of July 31, 1968, was referred to this agency.

During autumn of 1968, Walt sent letters about his case to the following individuals and received replies: Francis E. Dowd, Assistant General Counsel, National Labor Relations Board; Michigan governor George Romney; Senator Robert P. Griffin; and Senator Philip A. Hart. (Senator Hart requested that Walt attend the January 6, 1969, hearing in front of the NLRB.) On December 13, 1968, Walt sent a letter to the Wage & Hour Division of the Department of Labor. In January 1969, Walt received a letter from W. A. Kolar, Director, Intelligence Division, Internal Revenue Service, U.S. Treasury. All of these letters were sent to and from Walt's address at the trailer park on Eight Mile Road.

Walt's simple goal of acquiring a workbook and getting the unions to pay the little guy started a shit storm of Olympic proportions, as the government began its investigation. Before it was all over, the National Labor Relations Board, the FBI, the IRS, and a swarm of lawyers and agencies had taken up Walt's case. Even President Lyndon B. Johnson sent a letter dated September 9, 1968, to the National Labor Relations Board. The NLRB absolutely pounded the union.

The basis of the lawsuit #7CB 1794 against Ironworkers Local Union 25, AFL-CIO, as stated in a letter dated October 24, 1968, says that money was collected from union members (card holders) for which no corresponding benefit was derived. In other words, the union collected money for benefits they (card holders) did not receive, such as health care and retirement benefits.

The suit started in Flint, Michigan, a city where the United Auto Workers under Walter Reuther ran everything. Walt grew up in Detroit, a city much like Flint, so he knew how the power structure went. If you fought the union, as he did, even if you win, you lose. You are one, and they are many. The union fought back in the way that years of practice had perfected for them. First, they got to Walt's probation officer and tried to put pressure on him, making him say Walt would go to prison if he didn't drop his case. The union also tried to kill Walt a number of times.

Despite this, Walt took them on and prevailed, costing the union millions. That was the day he became the union's worst enemy. That was the day he became a fugitive.

Although Walt did eventually win his case against the Ironworkers, it was a class action suit, and he didn't get much money out of it—maybe $200.

Walt felt that surely the federal government would protect him, but he was wrong. The government was just another big guy, cashing in on the little guy. Just like the lawyer who said he would get money for Walt's mother after his father died, the government did what it wanted and left Walt to dangle in the wind. If anyone would benefit from all of Walt's sacrifice, it would be somebody else.

Then one day Walt and Carla went out and left their oldest son locked in the trailer.

Walt said, "Carla and I went out to the Teamsters Hall, and they took us out to dinner at Carl's Chop House. . . . It was Farmington. Grand River, Eight Mile. Confusing place."

When they got home, they couldn't find their oldest child and called the police. After a quick check, the police found a vacant trailer with footprints by the door. They busted a window and smelled gas.

"All the gas was turned on in the trailer," Walt told me in a taped phone call years later.

The child was unhurt, but Walt again decided they had to go on the run. Which meant he would violate the terms of his probation.

He made a quick call to Willard, saying he'd miss him and always value his friendship. Willard, now a responsible family man, understood the trouble Walt was in and wished him the best.

On the Run Again

Walt told me, "We went to Louisiana after that to get away, first between Port Allen and Baton Rouge. I worked on a bridge."

In Louisiana, Walt visited the dog pound, asking for a dog that would bite and protect his family. He named the dog Hitler to scare people—especially the Ironworkers who were chasing him. Two weeks later, it wasn't the union men who were bitten but the postman. A lawsuit was filed against him and his dog Hitler. Again, the Peca family went on the run, this time to Florida, hoping to meet up with our old friend Art, the mercenary. He had been in Nigeria, fighting a war he knew couldn't be won.

Walt—The "dark years"

On Highway 10, on the way to Fort Lauderdale, the Peca family took a break. They saw a beautiful beach and pulled over. The kids played in the sand, walked in the water, and for a few minutes anyway, life was as normal as with any family.

Then Carla said, "I can't take this anymore."

No reply from Walt.

Carla said, "How do we even know Art will be home? When did we see him last?"

Walt was uncertain. "Just before we moved to Eight Mile, I think. We stopped at Art's mom's house, and she told us he was in Nigeria."

"Some friend of yours had just been killed," Carla said.

"Don Merryman," Walt said. "Nicest guy you'd ever meet."

"So now he's dead," Carol said. "His troubles are over."

At ten past eight, Walt and his family pulled into Art's driveway. The door opened.

"What the hell are you doing here?" Art said.

"I'm on the run, Art. What's yer problem?" Walt asked.

"They're trying to take my citizenship," Art said.

"They're trying to take your *citizenship*? They're trying to *kill* us, Art. Can we come in?"

Once the drinking started, which was immediately, it carried on for three nights and days. Art and Walt talked about their close calls, and Patty and Carla about how miserable they were.

"I'm going to the airport in the morning," Art said. "I need some work."

"We'll be leaving as well, heading north, I suppose."

"Ya can't keep this up much longer, you know," Art said.

"Russian missiles exploding just below your plane," Walt told Art. "Another five hundred feet and you'd have been dead last week. You can't keep this up either."

In the morning, after coffee, Art drove to his old employer, Carolina Leasing, looking for work. Tom Boy, the owner and manager, greeted Art and told him to wait downstairs.

"Tell the girl to get you some coffee," Tom said. "By lunch, I think I'll have something for you."

Tom Boy had something all right: the second of three attempts to overthrow Cuba. After Art and the crew that hired him loaded the C-4 explosives, the ATF arrested everyone on the scene.

"I was the only one without a gun," Lussier said.

A Short Stop at Briny Breezes

Walt and family drove north on I-95, checking in with local ironworkers' unions as they went. Just north of Lauderdale, the local sounded promising, so they stayed in a motel near a community of about five hundred small, old trailer homes called Briny Breezes.

"I know a guy close to here," Walt said to Carla. "After we get the kids settled, remind me to give him a call."

Meanwhile, in the motel office, the manager was renting the room right below Walt's second-story room to an upstart rock band. A short while later, as Walt's children tried to nap, the noise—music, to some—became unbearable.

Walt went downstairs. In a minute, he was back.

"They didn't stop," Carla said.

Walt went to his suitcase and reached into a side pocket. "They'll stop now."

Years later, Walt chuckled as he related this story. "Hippies were running every which way," he said. "I made sure I put a bullet in every instrument."

"So, how did you get away?" I asked him.

"I ran up the beach to Jerry Grady's house, the guy I called just before the hippies got there. He took me to the local the next day and

Grand Coulee Dam

got me work. The motel didn't press charges, didn't want any kind of publicity."

Nobody had even called the police. Still, it wasn't long before moving seemed like a good idea to Walt. They cleared out of Florida in 1968 and headed north, with Walt working his way across the country through Atlanta.

The car died in Atlanta, he told me years later. Then he laughed. "Damn cars, sometimes I think every bit of trouble I've gotten into is because some fucking car broke down."

Walt and his family eventually returned to Washington State.

In 1970, Walt was reunited with Phillip Q, the CIA operative. On January 1, 1971, according to Walt, Phil got him a job with Vinnell Corporation, a spook outfit that worked with the CIA. (For more on the Vinnell Corporation, see Appendix A.) Walt was free to work where he pleased, but at this time he chose to be a welder on the Grand Coulee Dam in Washington State.

By his own admission, Walt was nothing more than a worker on the dam who, like many workers, left for other jobs but then returned once those jobs were over. He said the dam always let him come back because they had problems getting workers, due to the horrible conditions of the job.

CHAPTER 8

THE HIJACKING

November 24, 1971

Walt felt slightly nervous boarding the plane. He'd wanted to look like any other businessman going on a trip, in his dark suit with the thin black tie and loafers. His briefcase looked like every other briefcase carried by every other executive climbing up the stairs for Northwest Orient Airlines Flight 305. November 24 was cold and rainy, but he took off his raincoat and slung it over the arm holding the briefcase.

He had been living in a town called Hartline, seventy-five miles west of Spokane on Highway 2. It was on the eastern side of the Cascade Mountains, and as you came out of the mountains, you ended up on a flat plain, a farming area. Back when it was a mining town, about 250 to 300 people lived there. But the mines played out, and everybody moved away. There were towns like that all over the West, especially from silver mining.

From the time Walt concocted the plan to the time he sent his family away for Thanksgiving, he had repeated the same thing, "I don't really have to do this. At any point, I can turn around and hitch a ride home."

But, he thought, *I love them two kids. The babies. I don't have much money, and they're ready to start school. I have no future. Prior to this, I thought if I fell off the iron and got killed, at least workman's compensation would give 'em enough money right there so they could buy a home.*[11]

---

11   Audiotape transcript of Walt Peca's phone call with Carl Laurin (00:49:57, 2008).

So he went to a local stationers shop outside of Hartline and rented a typewriter. Typing wasn't one of his skills, but he pecked his way through the note. He also hand-wrote a similar note. He sat down with the briefcase and used road flares and wires to make what would pass for a bomb. It required a light touch.

The Unplanned Plan

A few days prior, Walt had called a close friend, Don Brennan, to get together for a drink. They'd met in a tavern on Highway 2 just east of Seattle. It was just the kind of nameless, nondescript place that he liked, and they settled in for a night of hard drinking. Walt told Don that he was going to hijack a plane. Don never responded and later said he was too drunk to remember anything.

Walt had formulated his plan earlier while watching a TV show where the hijackers asked for a bus and then a plane for their getaway. It occurred to Walt, *Why not eliminate all that by just getting a plane?* He could use a parachute to exit the airplane with the ransom money. He would only need his pocketknife, several packs of his usual brand of cigarettes, some glue, and a disguise. He was naturally blond, but during his years on the run, he had been dying his hair dark brown. His normally light skin was deeply tanned from months of outdoor work. He decided to pass himself off as a businessman with a suit and his briefcase.

Somehow both Walt and Don left the bar and made it to their respective homes.

Let the Adventure Begin

The morning he left home, November 23, 1971, had dawned bright and sunny. He put on insulated underwear bottoms and the items he'd purchased for $10 in a thrift store: a dark suit, a white shirt and a tie, a raincoat, and loafers. He took no change of clothes, nothing to eat, and about eight packs of cigarettes, stuffed in his pockets. Then he hopped into his car and drove the eighty miles east to Spokane. All the way there, Walt kept thinking, *This is a fucking stupid idea, and I don't have to go through with it. I'll just go through the motions right there and see how I feel.*

In Spokane, he left his car in the bus station parking lot. From Spokane, he took a bus southwest to Portland. He kept his briefcase between his ankles on the floor.

A woman with a baby sat next to him. She tried to keep the baby busy, but he would not stop crying. Even though the woman wasn't attractive, Walt felt a little sorry for her and tried to make the baby smile. When that didn't work, he held the bottle for her for a few seconds while she burped the baby. He felt relieved when they got off early and didn't go all the way to Portland.

When he arrived in Portland, he took a taxi to a motel he was familiar with. He realized that if he went through with this, he could die. So he repeated his "out": he could still just go home. Even as he checked in, he thought about giving up on the whole thing, but he was propelled forward. Even as he told himself he didn't have to do it, he somehow knew he would.

In the motel room, he decided that a drink would be good right about then.

The motel had a businessmen's bar in the basement, and for dinner they had good-looking waitresses in short skirts. Walt talked to the barmaid. He remembered her name was Cindy.[12]

Then he went back to his room. He wiped his fingertips with rubbing alcohol he'd brought in a little bottle. This would get rid of his fingers' natural coating of oil. Then he covered each finger with

---

12   Audiotape transcript of Walt Peca phone call with Carl Laurin (01:10:58, 2008).

quick-drying glue, so he wouldn't leave any fingerprints. He'd tested this earlier, by tapping his fingers on an inkpad, then on paper, and all they left were blurry circles.

He had a hard time falling asleep, but eventually he did because he told himself, *I don't have to do this*.[13]

The next morning hazy light filtered in through the window, waking him so he could get ready. The insulated underwear bottoms would be important because it was very cold at an altitude of 10,000 feet. He put on the suit and the clip-on tie, then slicked back his hair.

His stomach felt too crazy to eat, so he just gulped one cup of black coffee before taking a cab to the Portland airport.

The airport was almost empty on the morning before the holiday, November 24, 1971. Most Americans had already settled in with their families. And the storm had scared some people off. It was not a great day to fly.

Walt had not chosen a flight in advance. He stood at the check-in counter and filled out the forms, purchasing a one-way ticket to Seattle on Northwest Orient Airlines Flight 305.

The airline clerk told him that his ticket said Dan Cooper, but his luggage tag said Dan Copper. The clerk, Hal Williams, asked which was correct.

Walt said it was Cooper, and he erased the first P and wrote in an O.

"I was the Northwest Airlines gate agent who worked on Flight 305," said Hal Williams. "I personally saw Dan Cooper and was probably one of the few people who ever [sic] saw him without sunglasses. . . . It was a raging, rainy, stormy day. A nasty day. . . . he was conspicuous. This was 1971, when we wore polyester and plaid and funny shoes and gaudy shirts. The boarding area had lots

---

13   Audiotape transcript of Walt Peca phone call with Carl Laurin (01:11:26, 2008).

of businessmen dressed just like that. All except this one man, Dan Cooper, who was dressed all in black. It was unusual: black pants, shoes, black raincoat. It was like he was trying to hide, in black. But when you try to look inconspicuous, sometimes you make yourself even more conspicuous.[14]

"He stood right smack in front of me while I was doing the things you do when checking people in at a ticket counter and boarding area," Hal said.[15]

"It was about three in the afternoon, and the other 20 or 30 people waiting for the flight to Seattle were milling around—laughing and back-slapping. But he stood off to himself . . . very calm and quiet . . . and looking out the window most of the time.

"No, I didn't suspect anything bad while observing him. He looked like a sharp looking businessman to me. But I noticed him quite a bit because his behavior was different from the others, and he was all in black during the day of polyesters and plaids."[16]

Walt left the check-in counter for the bathroom, where he put another coat of quick-drying glue over his fingertips. He threw the glue in the trash and bought a newspaper at the stand.

Hunched in a corner and waiting for his flight to be called, he thought people were staring at him. He held the newspaper in front

---

14 "Woman Searches for Clues as Elusive as D.B. Cooper," by Margie Boulé, columnist, *The Oregonian*, August 13, 2000. Interview with airline ticket clerk Hal Williams: "I looked at hundreds of pictures over the years," he said. "You can't believe how many pictures, over and over and over. The FBI came to my house frequently. I suppose it was exciting at the beginning but then it got to be a real pain. I wished that I'd never been there. It just never seemed to end." Later, Hal was one of the witnesses who helped the FBI create composite drawings of Cooper. "But I never did think they were very good. They didn't look like him at all. But I was just one of many who helped put them together."

15 Ibid.

16 "Ticket Agent Won't Forget Man in Black," by John Guernsey, staff, *The Oregonian* [date unknown], http://www.dropzone.com/cgi-bin/forum/gforum.cgi?do=post_attachment;postatt_id=112448;guest=247133683.

Walt took seat 18-E

of him but didn't read it. His mind raced a hundred miles an hour. The thought went through his head, *I should just forget all this shit and go home.*

Ready for Takeoff

When the call came, passengers boarded on the aft stairway of the 727. Walt took a seat, 18-E, in the middle of the last row on the plane—which happened to be empty. There were no seat assignments. He realized that at this point, he was beyond changing his mind.

He kept his wraparound sunglasses on, as he would during most of the flight. He flagged down a stewardess named Flo Schaffner and asked for a drink, choosing bourbon and 7-Up, instead of his usual beer. He nursed the drink and lit a Raleigh.

The stewardess told him the pilot had put on the "Fasten Seat Belt" signs, which meant no smoking during takeoff, so he put out the cigarette.

A Note and a Bomb

Flo sat in the stewardess seat behind the passenger. After she had been seated about 30 seconds, as the plane taxied toward the runway, he turned around and handed her a note.

She didn't read it immediately. At first, she thought he was making a pass at her, but he repeatedly turned around to look at her, as if asking her to read it, so she did.

The handwritten note said, "Miss—I have a bomb here and I would like you to sit by me." *MISS* was printed, and the rest of the note was legibly handwritten.

Flo read the note twice, then looked directly at him and asked if he was kidding.

He replied in a serious, calm voice, "No, Miss, this is for real." At that moment, he wondered, *If I get killed, am I going to hell?*

Another stewardess named Tina Mucklow then came to the rear of the plane. As Tina faced the barrier strip, she saw Flo drop the note, stand up, and then sit beside the man in 18-E. Flo appeared emotional and tried to speak, but only the word "Tina" came out. Tina picked up the note lying at her feet and read it.

Flo again asked the passenger if he was kidding, and he said, "No, Miss."

Walt built a realistic-looking bomb

He opened the briefcase and showed her six or eight reddish sticks, each 6 to 8 inches long, which appeared to be taped together. The briefcase also contained a 6" X 8" X 2" dry-cell type battery. A small wire with red plastic coating ran from the bundle of sticks toward the battery. The last inch of the wire was bare, and the passenger held it between his fingers, as if to indicate that he could detonate the bomb by touching the wire to a contact.

Tina went to the rear of the plane to call the pilot on the phone. "We're being hijacked," she told him. "He's got a bomb, and this is no joke."

Flo asked the hijacker what she should do, and he said, "Take this down."

Tina leaned over the aisle and saw Flo writing down the hijacker's demands, using her own notepad and pen.

> "I want $200,000 by 5 p.m. in cash. Put it in a knapsack. I want two back parachutes and two front parachutes. When we land, I want a fuel truck ready to refuel. No funny stuff, or I'll do the job."

Then he said, "No fuss."

"Okay," Flo said.

The hijacker told her, "After this, we'll take a little trip."

Flo got up and went to the rear of the plane to get the note from Tina that the hijacker had initially given her, then took both notes up to the cockpit and gave them to the captain. First Officer Bill Rataczak told her to stay in the cockpit and sit behind the captain, Bill Scott. Rataczak gave her a headset and showed her the clock and told her to take notes whenever they communicated with traffic control or the company on a select frequency, and also to record conversations between him and Captain Scott.[17]

---

17   Videotape of a speech given to Northwest employees by First Officer Bill Rataczak at the Northwest Airlines Museum in Minneapolis in 2012.

Then Tina sat in the aisle seat beside the hijacker.

He showed her the contents of the briefcase and said that it was an electronic device. He suggested that the crew use the radio as little as possible. He didn't think the transmissions would set it off but wanted to warn the crew anyway.

Conversations with Cooper

All of the nearby passengers were moved up three rows ahead of where the hijacker was seated. During the flight, Tina assured him that he would have the full cooperation of the crew. She questioned him about his destination, and he said not to worry, the flight wasn't going to Havana but to a "pleasant place." He asked where she was from and she said Pennsylvania, but she was living in Minneapolis. He said that was a very nice part of the country. She asked him where he was from, but he adamantly refused to say. She asked him why he'd decided to hijack Northwest Airlines: did he have a grudge against them?

He laughed. "It's not because I have a grudge against your airline, it's just because I have a grudge."[18]

They talked about personal habits and smoking. She used to smoke but quit. However, when he offered her a cigarette, she took it. She offered him food or drink, but he said no.

At one point a male passenger came wandering down the aisle, looking for a sports magazine, but Tina managed to redirect him and gave him a *New Yorker* instead. After this incident, the hijacker said, "If that is a sky marshal, I don't want any more of that."

Tina assured him that no sky marshals were on board.

Shortly after that, the pilot called back and asked if the hijacker wanted the passengers to be informed. The hijacker said no, and the

---

18   FBI report of interview with stewardess Tina Mucklow dated December 3, 1971. Report by SA Patrick Joseph Kelly and SA John William Culpepper, File Philadelphia 164-133.

pilot said he'd make up an excuse to tell the passengers about why the flight was being extended.

"Miss Mucklow recalled that it was at this time that the hijacker requested that all notes, including the one he had furnished to Miss Schnaffer [sic] and those written by Miss Mucklow to be returned to him."[19]

Tina called the cockpit, and Flo brought the notes back.[20]

When Tina lit a cigarette for him, she attempted to discard the matchbook cover, but he insisted on keeping it.[21] He repeated his previous instructions, saying that all of the items he requested had to be in place on the ground before he would permit the plane to land.

First Officer Rataczak had "the impression that the . . . hijacking had been carefully thought out in advance in that the hijacker specified that the money was to be furnished in a knapsack and even insisted that a discarded match cover be returned to him. He also insisted on the return of the original note and the envelope and appeared especially careful to see that nothing of his was left behind."[22]

Right now, Walt imagined, *the pilot is radioing instructions for the parachutes, and some bigwig is getting the money from the bank or a safe full of cash.*

His thinking wasn't far off. From 1968 to 1972, there were a total of 133 hijackings in the United States, so airlines had a protocol in

---

19 FBI report of interview with stewardess Tina Mucklow dated November 30, 1971. Report dictated on November 26, 1971, by SA H.E. Hinderliter Jr. and SAC Harold El. Campbell Jr., File LV 164-60-139.

20 FBI report of interview with stewardess Florence Schaffner in Seattle, Washington, dated November 26, 1971. Report by SA Daniel S. Jacobs, File SE 164-81.

21 FBI report of interview with stewardess Tina Mucklow dated December 3, 1971. Report by SA Patrick Joseph Kelly and SA John William Culpepper, File Philadelphia 164-133.

22 From FBI eyewitness report of First Officer William John (Bill) Rataczak on December 1, 1971, by SAC Harold El. Campbell Jr. and SA H.E. Hinderliter Jr., File LV 164-60-158.

place. Banks had prepared packets of money to ensure that hijackers received their demands quickly. The news reports were always full of hijackings; mostly, they seemed to be people hijacking planes to get to Cuba. There had even been some talk about putting in regular airport security, like metal detectors and searches, across the nation. But the FBI and the Federal Aviation Administration (FAA) were still battling over who had jurisdiction. Of course, Hoover thought it should be the FBI. Luckily for Walt, they hadn't figured it out yet—though the new laws making plane hijackings a federal crime meant that he was taking a real risk.

First Stop: Seattle

As the plane neared the airport for landing, the pilot announced that because of mechanical difficulties, landing would be delayed. According to First Officer Bill Rataczak, initially the airport wanted the plane to go into a holding pattern five miles out, over a residential area near Sea-Tac (Seattle-Tacoma International Airport). Instead, they circled over Puget Sound for more than an hour, arousing the suspicions of some passengers.[23] Tina made numerous phone calls from the rear of the plane.

Walt figured that waiting on the runway would be the tricky part—that was when they might try to get him.

First Officer Rataczak noted that all of the hijacker's demands "were forwarded to the cockpit through hostess Mucklow and at no time did he have occasion to personally observe or have any direct contact with him."[24] Rataczak also stated, "It was further established that hostess Mucklow was to act as intermediary between the hijacker

---

23 Videotape of a speech given to Northwest employees by First Officer Bill Rataczak at the Northwest Airlines Museum in Minneapolis in 2012.
24 From FBI eyewitness report of First Officer William John (Bill) Rataczak on December 1, 1971, by SAC Harold El. Campbell Jr. and SA H.E. Hinderliter Jr., File LV 164-60-158.

and the individuals meeting the plane to supply his demands. The chief pilot for Northwest Airlines and one other individual were to be in the first vehicle with the money. The second vehicle was to carry the stairs so that the hostess could exit from the front of the plane with only one driver designated for that vehicle, with a third vehicle being a fuel truck containing a driver only which was to remain in a 10 or 11 o'clock position from the plane in order that all would be in full view of the hijacker at all times."[25]

After the plane landed in Seattle, Tina got up and went to the front of the plane. An announcement from the cockpit instructed passengers to remain seated, due to mechanical problems. The hijacker's 5 p.m. deadline passed, and Tina called the cockpit, saying the hijacker wanted to know what was going on. He'd asked, "Where's the money? Where's the parachute?" Rataczak said that the chutes had to come from McChord Air Force Base. The hijacker said, "That's only twenty miles away." Rataczak turned to Florence, sitting in the cockpit, and said, "Florence, jot that down. That's an important fact. This guy [knows] something about the Pacific Northwest." Rataczak sent this information to the airport, along with the hijacker's knowledge of flap settings on a 727, so they could start vetting the thirty-five passengers.[26]

Eventually, Tina left the plane via the front stairway and returned carrying an off-white canvas drawstring bank bag with the money and gave it to the hijacker.[27] She said he complained that the money had been given to him in a bank bag, instead of the knapsack he'd asked for, and he told her that he would "be forced to use one of the parachutes to rewrap the money since he had not been furnished a

25 Ibid.
26 Videotape of a speech given by First Officer Bill Rataczak at the Northwest Airlines Museum in Minneapolis in 2012, to Northwest employees.
27 Ibid. Although several passengers, an airline official, and FBI agent Larry Carr described the bag's dimensions, only First Officer Rataczak mentioned it being a drawstring bag.

knapsack container."[28] Years later, in a 2012 speech, Rataczak said the hijacker got upset because the money wasn't in a knapsack and threatened to blow the plane up.[29]

The hijacker opened and inspected the bank bag, then declared that everything seemed okay and that the passengers could leave the plane. He lifted the bag of money, commenting on how heavy it was.[30]

As the passengers were leaving, Tina jokingly asked if she could have some of the money, and the hijacker took out one bundle of bills and handed it to her.

"You've all been nice to me," he said. "I never had a chance to thank you."

Tina noted that "the money was packed in small packages with bank-type bands around each package."[31] She returned the money to the hijacker, saying that she wasn't allowed to accept gratuities.

After all of the passengers had exited, Flo, Tina, Alice, and the other stewardesses conversed with the hijacker. He asked Tina to get the parachutes. After she brought back the first large chute, he asked her to lower the shades in his section of the aircraft. He assumed a sniper was out there. Tina made several trips outside to carry back all of the parachutes.

It later occurred to William John Rataczak, the first officer on duty, that during this period after the passengers had disembarked

28 From FBI eyewitness report of stewardess Tina Mucklow on November 24, 1971, in Reno, Nevada. Report by SA H.E. Hinderliter Jr. and SAC Harold El. Campbell Jr., LV 164-60-139.
29 See the videotape of a speech given to Northwest employees by First Officer Bill Rataczak at the Northwest Airlines Museum in Minneapolis in 2012.
30 First Officer Bill Rataczak said the $200,000 weighed about 22 pounds. (Videotape of a speech Rataczak gave to Northwest employees at the Northwest Airlines Museum in Minneapolis in 2012.)
31 From FBI eyewitness report of stewardess Tina Mucklow on November 24, 1971, in Reno, Nevada. Report by SA H.E. Hinderliter Jr. and SAC Harold El. Campbell Jr., LV 164-60-139.

and Tina was off the plane gathering the parachutes, the rest of the crew could have left the plane, leaving the hijacker alone on board.

According to First Officer Rataczak, the hijacker hadn't realized this either—that when Tina was out of the plane, making four trips to carry the parachutes, the other stewardesses could also have gotten off the plane, and the cockpit crew could have easily left through the curtained first-class section without the hijacker seeing them. Rataczak later said, ". . . and in the meantime I had told Andy to tell the other two [Flo and Alice] to leave the airplane, stay out of the airplane, we could pack up, go outside, and say, 'Hey, check the cockpit. If you [unintelligible] you can fly it. It's all yours. We're gonna stay down here.' . . . But, of course, they didn't cooperate. . . . That was his [the hijacker's] tactical error because Tina had to make trips out of the airplane . . . If those other two had gone out when we told them to go out, they all would have been out. . . . He would have been in back alone and we could have packed our bags and our peanut butter sandwich and gone out . . . but they chose not to."

Rataczak also later said, "Tina had made her last trip out of the airplane but is now seated back next to the guy. They decided then it was time to go. And we talked about it in the cockpit, 'Should we bail out?' We've got escape ropes in the overhead and they're resin-impregnated . . . that . . . you . . . put out the window and you slide out that way. Well, with that curtain drawn, he wouldn't have seen us anyway. We could have packed our bag and . . . gone out the main door. . . . Scotty said, 'Whaddya think, you guys? Should we leave Tina back there with him and get out and then they can't go anywhere cause they don't have a crew to fly it?' And I said, 'Well, Scotty, if you give me a direct order to go out of the airplane, I'm gonna say, "No, I'm not. I'll tell everybody you gave a direct order to your irascible copilot, but he decided to stay there." I said, 'I can't in good conscience leave Tina alone back there with that guy.' So we all agreed that was the way to go. So we stayed there."[32]

Altered Plans

At first, Flo thought the hijacker seemed unsure of his destination because he mentioned going to Mexico, Phoenix, or San Francisco.

But then Tina Mucklow used one of her pay sheets to write down his further instructions:

> "Going to Mexico City—or anyplace in Mexico— nonstop—gear down—flaps down—do not go over 10,000 feet altitude—all cabin lights out—do not again land in the States for fuel or any other reason—no one behind the first class section."[33]

Flo asked whether the stewardesses could leave, and in a calm, disinterested voice the hijacker said, "Sure, go ahead."

Walt had noticed a sign in red letters over the side door that said, "Open here." He had planned to jump from the side door.

But then Tina mentioned, "There's that tail door there," and he said, "Well, that's fuckin' good."[34]

The rear door had a staircase built in. When Boeing designed it, they had to consider all possible uses, one of which could have been

---

32 From FBI eyewitness report of First Officer William John (Bill) Rataczak on December 1, 1971, by SAC Harold El. Campbell Jr. and SA H.E. Hinderliter Jr., File LV 164-60-158. See also the videotape of a speech given to Northwest employees by First Officer Bill Rataczak at the Northwest Airlines Museum in Minneapolis in 2012.

33 FBI report of interview with stewardess Tina Mucklow dated November 24, 1971. Report by SA H.E. Hinderliter, Jr., and SAC Harold E. Campbell, File LV 164-60-139.

34 Audiotape transcript of Walt Peca phone call with Carl Laurin (01:14:07, 2008).

The 727's back tail door after it was altered
to include the "Cooper Vane" to prevent it
from opening during flight.

Lowered tail door stairs

a clandestine air operation for the U.S. military, which led to the rear door being built to open in the air.[35]

He also stated that he wanted the plane to take off with the rear door open and the stairs extended.

The crew informed him, through Tina, that taking off with the door open and stairs extended would be impossible. They finally agreed to take off with the door closed, the stairs retracted, and Tina would remain on board to lower the door after the plane was airborne. After she had done this, she could go to the pilot's compartment.

---

35 In 1972, following the D.B. Cooper hijacking, the FAA required all operators of the Boeing 727 to install a spring-loaded, hinged vane device to prevent the aft air stairs from being lowered in flight, thus eliminating the possibility of "copy cat" parachuting skyjackers. The simple device allows the stairs to be deployed on the ramp, but when the aircraft takes off, the airflow pushes the paddle parallel to the fuselage, and the plate is moved underneath, preventing the stairs from being lowered. Douglas DC 9 aircraft with aft ventral air stairs were also equipped with Cooper vanes. See https://aviationglossary.com/d-b-cooper-vane/.

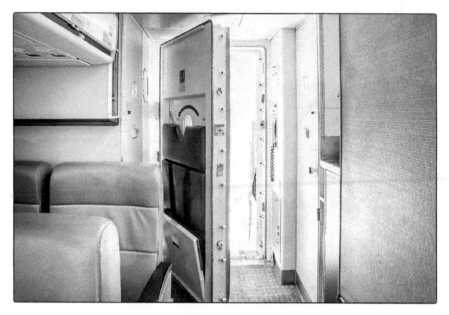

The back tail door opened

About one hour had passed since landing, and the hijacker became annoyed with how long refueling took, displaying extensive knowledge of the aircraft and refueling procedures.

Tina offered to get him something to eat or drink, but he refused.

Just before takeoff, the crew called on the intercom and said they didn't have enough fuel to make it to Mexico City or anywhere in Mexico. They recommended San Francisco as a refueling stop. The hijacker disagreed and suggested Phoenix. The crew said the distance was too far; they could make it either to Yuma, Arizona, or Reno, Nevada. The hijacker preferred Reno, so they settled on that.[36]

---

36 From FBI eyewitness report of stewardess Tina Mucklow on November 24, 1971, in Reno, Nevada. Report by SA H.E. Hinderliter Jr. and SAC Harold El. Campbell Jr., LV 164-60-139. See also FBI eyewitness report of First Officer William John (Bill) Rataczak on December 1, 1971, by SAC Harold El. Campbell Jr. and SA H.E. Hinderliter Jr., File LV 164-60-158.

Cooper Vane: Named after D.B. Cooper

Alice Hancock, another stewardess, then went to the back of the plane and asked if the stewardesses could go. The hijacker said, "Whatever you girls would like."

Flo and Alice left the plane, while Tina remained in the rear, talking on the phone.

The Great Escape

The plane took off from Seattle at 7:36 p.m. Tina observed that the hijacker was occupied with opening one of the parachute packs (which was a bright pink-orange color) and "attempting to in some way pack the money in a parachute container in order that he could in some way attach it to his body along with the regular parachute straps."[37]

---

37   From FBI eyewitness report of stewardess Tina Mucklow on November 24, 1971, in Reno, Nevada. Report by SA H.E. Hinderliter Jr. and SAC Harold El. Campbell Jr., LV 164-60-139.

She "clearly remembered him removing a small jack knife from his pocket and cutting some portion of either the outside container or the parachute in order to secure the money in this rather than the white bank-type bag which he had been furnished."[38] She "did not see him tampering with the two large parachute containers other than to cursorily inspect them when she had brought them aboard."[39]

" . . . she saw that he had one chute cut open and nylon cords out and he was cutting them with his pocket knife. He took the nylon cord and wrapped it around the neck of the money bag numerous times and then he wrapped it a few times from top to bottom and with the same piece made a loop like a handle at the top. This nylon cord was pinkish in color. He appeared irritated because they didn't give him a knapsack for the money which he had initially requested, and after trying to put the money in an unfolded parachute, he decided to leave it in the canvas bag."[40]

Possibly, the FBI figured that he'd asked for the extra parachutes for a hostage. Yet Walt had cared only about his own survival when he'd asked for four parachutes. He just wanted a backup in case someone had booby-trapped the chutes by tying off the bottom part so that they wouldn't open. After opening one of the main chutes, he'd checked it out. It hadn't been rigged. He then used the second main chute for himself. However, he discovered that one of the reserve chutes was a dummy chute.

At some point, Walt took off his clip-on tie and tossed it onto a seat, not bothering to remove the tie pin. He cut up one of the parachute's cords and used it to tie the money to his neck, waist, and crotch. He

---

38 Ibid.

39 Ibid.

40 FBI report of interview with stewardess Tina Mucklow dated December 3, 1971. Report by SA Patrick Joseph Kelly and SA John William Culpepper, File Philadelphia 164-133.

then put on his overcoat and used his belt to secure everything. He took a rubber band from his pocket and used it to hold his glasses to his head. Finally, he put on his parachute.

Tina asked if they could use some nylon cord from the parachute to tether her to a seat so that she wouldn't be sucked outward when she opened the door. But instead, he asked her to demonstrate how to open the rear door and extend the stairway. He said he would do it himself. She told him oxygen was available, if he needed it, and he said, "Yes, I know where it is. If I need it, I will get it."

Less than five minutes after takeoff, he was ready. He told Tina that he would take it from there, just to close the curtains to first class and go into the cockpit with the others. Before she left, she pleaded with him to take the bomb with him, and he agreed to or would disarm it.

Walt opened the rear door, following the directions on the placard. About ten minutes after Tina had left him and entered the cockpit, he called one of the officers in the cockpit on the interphone, saying he couldn't get the rear stairs down. The pilot said he would level the plane and reduce the air speed, and shortly after that, Tina observed a red indicator light come on in the second officer's panel showing that the stairs were down.

Walt stood on the precipice between light and darkness, between capture and freedom. There was a chance he could die, but deep down he knew that he could make this jump.

The plane's roaring and creaking, with its open door, beat against his ears. He had always felt like two personalities, Dr. Jekyll and Mr. Hyde. *And right now*, he thought, *Mr. Hyde isn't scared of shit.*[41]

He tossed the briefcase out of the plane, along with the dummy chute. He didn't wear a reserve because neither of the main chutes

---

41   Audiotape transcript of Walt Peca phone call with Carl Laurin (01:31:54, 2008).

A look down the rear stairs

were fitted with D-rings, which are required to attach them to the front (reserve) chute. He also knew he probably wouldn't have time to deploy a reserve at what might be a very low altitude. And finally, the reserve chute would have been too bulky with the backpack and the money under his raincoat.

He said what he called his "contritions."

He hadn't planned for this to be a night flight. The wind, the whirling darkness, the cold and the storm. It would be insane to step off into that. There was a moment when he knew it. But that moment passed. He had jumped in worse conditions back in Michigan and Alaska, and he felt confident now. He looked at his watch and stepped into the turbulent sky.

CHAPTER 9

CRANKING UP THE WAYBACK MACHINE

The 1960s and '70s were among the most volatile in American history. Reflecting the times, the FBI was an agency out of control. The controversial director J. Edgar Hoover had a nearly fifty-year stranglehold on the nation's most powerful law enforcement agency. No wonder the FBI had bungled so many high-profile cases—including the D.B. Cooper hijacking.

Hoover was appointed the director of the Bureau of Investigation on May 10, 1924; was promoted to director of the Federal Bureau of Investigation on May 22, 1935; and continued in that position until his death in May 1972. Hoover transformed the Bureau into his own personal police agency, which kept politicians and even presidents at bay. President Truman was quoted as saying that Hoover was, "dabbling in sex-life scandals and plain blackmail."

Illustrating the Cold War intrigue of the era, the FBI recently released more than 2,800 once-secret documents, including a July 4, 1964, memo marked "SECRET" that detailed the haggling between Cuban exiles and businessmen with ties to organized crime over the cost to kill Fidel Castro and Che Guevera.[42] The FBI claimed

---

42   Ernesto *"Che" Guevara* was an Argentine Marxist revolutionary, physician, author, guerrilla leader, diplomat, and military theorist. He played a major role in the Cuban Revolution. (Wikipedia, https://en.wikipedia.org/wiki/Che_Guevara, accessed February 11, 2018).

the $100,000 plot to kill Castro was not a "government effort."[43] However, intelligence agencies commonly used assassinations and clandestine endeavors to carry out their tasks. U.S.-Soviet relations fluctuated from tense to incendiary during the Bay of Pigs fiasco and the Cuban Missile Crisis. In addition, covert agencies' spy-versus-spy tactics cast a shadow of suspicion over JFK's killing that fuels conspiracy theorists to this day. The CIA's fixation on Fidel Castro wasn't helped by the fact that Lee Harvey Oswald, JFK's alleged killer, traveled to Mexico City and contacted the Cuban Consulate there, resulting in the Agency wiretapping that consulate.

In a deposition of Richard Helms, former director of the CIA, given before the presidential Commission on CIA Activities in 1975, attorney David Belin asked him whether the CIA was involved in Kennedy's killing. Just as Belin asks, "Is there any information involved with the assassination of President Kennedy which in any way shows that Lee Harvey Oswald was in some way a CIA agent or agent . . ." the document suddenly cuts off.[44]

One recently released FBI memo detailed antagonism between the CIA and the FBI. In it, FBI director Hoover is quoted as saying, "More and more we are telling CIA about our domestic operations and always to our detriment. I want this stopped."[45]

Other events that occupied the FBI and the CIA in the early '60s were investigating a "high-priced Hollywood call girl" who supposedly had information about sex parties involving "then-Sen.

---

43 "In J.F.K. Files, a Peek Back at an Era of Secrets and Intrigue," by Peter Baker, *New York Times*, October 27, 2017; https://www.nytimes.com/2017/10/27/us/politics/jfk-files-cuba-castro-cold-war.html?mwrsm=Email.

44 "Strippers, Surveillance and Assassination plots: The Wildest JFK Files," by Michael E. Miller, Washington Post, October 27, 2017; https://www.washingtonpost.com/news/retropolis/wp/2017/10/27/strippers-surveillance-and-assassination-plots-the-jfk-files-wildest-documents/?utm_term=.1d1103384843&wpisrc=nl_az_most&wpmk=1.

45 Ibid.

John F. Kennedy; his brother-in-law, actor Peter Lawford; Frank Sinatra and Sammy Davis Jr."; searching for a stripper named "Kitty," an associate of Jack Ruby, the Dallas nightclub owner who killed Lee Harvey Oswald; investigating "a committee organized to kill Oswald"; determining the validity of the accusation that President Lyndon B. Johnson was in the Ku Klux Klan; investigating "an alleged plot to bribe a U.S. congressman and bring deposed Cuban dictator Fulgencio Batista to the United States; running down rumors within the Communist Party about JFK's assassination; wiretapping people suspected of being on the "Hollywood blacklist"; making predictions that the Cuban revolution would soon collapse; and devising various outlandish schemes to kill Castro—by gifting him with a skin-diving suit contaminated with tuberculosis bacilli and a fungus producing madera foot, by booby-trapping a "spectacular seashell" with explosives in a place Castro enjoyed diving, and by using a ballpoint pen containing a hypodermic needle to inject Castro with poison.[46]

The race riots that began in the mid '60s continued to flare up, with occasional clashes with police and the FBI. Antiwar sentiment was escalating at a rapid pace, with more than 60 percent of Americans opposed to U.S. involvement in Vietnam, and often drew protest crowds in excess of 100,000. Hoover used both legal and illegal surveillance methods to monitor protest organizers and anyone who dared challenge him, in a division of the Bureau named COINTELPRO. The FBI's methods included infiltrating the protest groups, illegal wiretapping, spreading damaging information about the movement leaders, and committing blackmail and burglaries. On March 8, 1971, activists broke into an FBI office in Media, Pennsylvania; stole cases of documents detailing the FBI's illegal activities; and leaked them to the press. Even among his strongest

---

46   Ibid.

supporters, Hoover lost credibility, which had steadily eroded since President Nixon assumed office in 1969.

The FBI was challenged with Hoover's death on May 2, 1972, and again on June 17, when five men were charged with attempted burglary at the Democratic National Committee's headquarters at the Watergate Complex in Washington, D.C.

In the 1970s, the CIA was also extremely busy attending to three major distractions. It is well documented that the Agency had been involved with providing mercenaries to assist the military in Vietnam and surrounding countries. On June 13, 1971, leaks and the publishing of the Pentagon Papers proved that the CIA and the U.S. government had actively lied to the American people, which shook the country to its foundation. During this time, the Agency attempted to suppress the publication of a book by Victor Marchetti, a former executive assistant to the deputy director of the CIA. *CIA and the Cult of Intelligence* discusses the Agency's use of propaganda and disinformation to mislead the American public.

Adding to the stress on the FBI and the CIA was the annoying frequency of hijacking in the United States, which often required them to coordinate their investigations. The Cooper hijacking was the second of the month, and two more would follow in the next sixty days. The Bureau was clearly stretched at the time of the Cooper hijacking.

On the evening of November 24, 1971, Walt R. Peca hijacked Northwest Orient Flight 305 (the same number as his old U.S. Air Force Reserve unit), parachuted out of the plane, and vanished forever, so the story goes. Nobody was injured, the aircraft was recovered that same night in Reno, and the amount of the ransom, $200,000, was a miniscule sum when you consider how much it could have been. The U.S. Air Force started an immediate search close to

Portland, Oregon. A list of flights and aircraft deployed will show that the money spent for the search far exceeded the ransom amount.

The CIA had recently acquired an impressive supersonic spy plane, the A-12, and the Air Force had obtained the SR-71—both in the Blackbird family. The plane could cruise at speeds in excess of 2,000 miles per hour, faster than any anti-aircraft interceptors and the fastest plane ever made to that date. It could reach altitudes greater than 80,000 feet and was equipped with the most sophisticated surveillance cameras available. The plane required two different fuels, one for takeoff and one for cruising, which necessitated refueling in mid-air shortly after takeoff. The Blackbird cost the military an estimated $200,000 per hour to fly in 1970. *Interestingly, according to FBI records, the U.S. Air Force decided to use this ultra-high-speed plane on five separate occasions to assist in the search for D.B. Cooper in February 1972, three months after the hijacking.*

CHAPTER 10

"YOU WORK FOR US NOW"

U ntil November 24, 1971, Walt R. Peca was a thirty-eight-year-old man who believed in ghosts and guardian angels. As a husband, he would be rated *poor*. As a wage earner, even worse. Following his discharge from the army, he'd tacked a criminal record onto his résumé. So why, after his death-defying parachute jump, did agents of the U.S. clandestine services seek him out? For one reason: despite the bad grades I give Walt as a father and a husband, it was in covert activities where Walt had talent.

"It was the early spring of 1972," Walt told me, "two or three months after the Cooper hijacking. Something happened to me one day that I've never forgotten. I remember this more clearly than any of the D.B. Cooper stuff. I didn't know it then because it happened so quick and was so odd. I thought at first it was a trick. I wasn't sure I would go through with it, but I did, and it changed my life forever.

"It was close to quitting time when two ironworkers walked over and said, 'Hey, wanna go for a beer after work?'"

I remember asking him, "Did these guys know your name?"

"I think so. I think they called me Walt," he said.

"Anyway, after work I followed them in their car to a place I'd been to before with other ironworkers to drink beer—the Brown

The Brown Derby

Derby, I think it was. So the young lady came over, and we ordered beer. When she went back to the bar, one of these guys said, 'Mr. Peca, do you want to go to prison?'[47]

"'No.' That's all I said.

"'Then you work for us now,' one of them said.

"Then they got up and left. I sat there a couple of seconds before I stood up and looked outside. Their car was gone."

"What did you do?" I asked Walt.

"Fuck . . . what the fuck was that? And then the girl was at our table with three beers, so I paid her and I asked, 'Do you know those guys?' and I think she said, 'Never saw them before.' I sat down and

---

47   It's interesting that they called him "Peca" because at this time he had been going by "Reca" for years.

tried to figure out what the fuck had just happened. They didn't stiff me out of three beers because I still had the beers, so I started to drink one. Something about going to prison and I said no. I remember I almost said, 'Who the fuck wants to go to prison?' And then they said, 'Now you work for us.'

"I didn't sit there long, but you can't imagine how many things can go through your mind in ten minutes. Before I left that tavern, though, I had it narrowed down to two: it was a joke, or someone thought they knew what I'd done, and it was their attempt at blackmail."

The next day Walt asked the supervisor who those two new guys were, and he said, "What new guys?" Walt then called the union hall, where he knew the dispatcher, and told him what had happened.

"They're not ironworkers," dispatch told him.

"How do you know?" Walt said.

"Thousands of ironworkers have come through this hall," he said. "Thousands. I don't know one of them, let alone two, who would leave beer on the table, do you?"

"I guess not," Walt said. "Someone must be pulling a prank."

"Mind-Sculpting" in Boise, Idaho

One month later, Walt got a phone call.

"Is this Walt Peca?"

"It is."

"Mr. Peca, there is a ticket with your name on it at the Spokane Airport, 8 a.m. tomorrow morning departure. Be on that flight."

The voice was clear, precise, and professional. If it was a joke, it didn't sound like one. The next morning Walt got to Spokane Airport wearing a suit but still wasn't certain he would catch that flight. He had his ironworking gear with him. He searched for familiar faces, someone who would run up to him and say it was a joke, but when

7:45 came, he went to the counter, got the ticket, and left on that 8 a.m. flight to Boise, Idaho.

Upon arrival, Walt and a well-dressed man from two seats behind him got off the plane, until another well-dressed man approached them and shook their hands. He took them to a restaurant and began asking questions. They were then taken to a building on a college campus, where Walt was questioned for four days, none of the questions involving the hijacking or his work at the union.

This was the start of Walt's new life, if he wanted it. He knew what the alternative would be. The two men at the tavern had made that clear. The only question that remained was: Did they want him?

Over time, Walt learned what working for *them* meant. Walt told me that he was subjected to a process that he called "mind sculpting" (to me, it sounded like the CIA's top secret mind control program MKUltra—see Appendix B). Each morning, they took him into a different room of what he assumed was a college of some sort. He said his trainers were always very polite, and they never forced him to be there. Of course, he always had the knowledge that if he didn't stay, he would go to prison. That was enough for Walt.

For two years, they sent him to different locations, and all they did was ask him questions, sometimes the same questions over and over in different forms. They were searching for character flaws, something that revealed if he were ever caught, he would talk. But Walt told me that talking was out of the question. By the time Walt's training was over, he felt like he couldn't give away a secret even if he wanted to.

He was dealing with professionals, he could see that. Never "Walt," always "Mr. Peca." The sessions ended at 5 p.m. sharp. Did he want a car? Did he need spending money? "You understand you are free to come and go, but if you go, there is nothing we can do. Other people are in charge of that. Do you want to know who we are?"

"No," Walt said. He had an idea they were somehow associated with Boise College, and as days turned into weeks and weeks into months, there always seemed to be a small college nearby, as he was questioned. The questions were not personal in nature but scientific, dealing with emotional processes of human and animal behavior, traits, and the breaking of the human mind.

I asked him what kind of questions they asked, and he said, "All kinds. There wasn't any sense in it. Once they asked me, 'It's the end of the day, and you have a choice: you can clear off your desk to keep it neat and tidy or have a date with a very attractive person of the opposite sex. What would you do?'

"They asked that question or a similar one at least fifty different ways during the year and a half I was in their program," Walt told me.

"How did you answer?" I said.

"I answered like I didn't want to go to prison," Walt said.

On March 13, 1972, Walt made a trip back to Oakland, Michigan, where, despite jumping bail and violating the terms of his probation, he was discharged from probation.

In July 1972, eight months after the Cooper hijacking, Walt tried to rent a house at 1207 W. Cleveland Avenue, Spokane, Washington, from a realtor who flipped houses and sold them on land contracts to individuals.

"Carla and I had money now," Walt said, "so we were going to rent this house on Cleveland Street, and the guy said, 'Why don't you buy it?' so we did. I don't remember what month . . . When I'd put the [hijacking ransom] money in the bank in Vancouver, Canada, I kept some out, not a lot, maybe two thousand, in case I had to go on the run again. My leg was okay now. I didn't want to walk the high iron, so I took a small job just outside Spokane, a building with work for a week or two."

The realtor had offered to sell him the house for a down payment equivalent to two months' mortgage payments, which totaled $685. During this time, Walt used the last name Recca for the house purchase, which was finalized in July 1972. The realtor, now retired and living in Kentucky, confirmed that he'd sold a house to Recca on a land contract. The realtor owned several houses around Spokane and accepted only cash for the house payments. He remembered that Recca traveled around the world. Walt also used some money to buy furniture and a car. Because all of the realtor's customers paid in cash, a large deposit of $20 bills did not raise suspicion with his bank.

In a long confession Walt dictated to me in 2013, he said, "At some point after becoming Cooper, I knew I was positively being protected." He added,

> For two and one half years I labored anonymously. I always had work. I was never threatened or intimidated but always feeling like I was one wrong move from going to jail although no one had ever said that. Nor did I ever have to give an explanation to my employer as to why I needed four or five days off or did they ever ask. Often, I seemed to be employed by two or three different companies at the same time and that was never questioned. My résumé, made for me by the Consulate General of the USA in Dhahran, Saudi Arabia, lists me as an employee of the Vinnell Corporation from 1971 to 1974. It is good to remember that [in] my résumé . . . many times items were omitted so as to make me appear to be someplace that I was not.

Walt traveled the world

Another voyage for Walt

International Travels as a Covert Operative

On March 26, 1974, although he hadn't officially changed his name to Walt Richard Reca, he got his first passport under that name. On this passport, a convicted felon/petty thief/construction worker with an eighth-grade education traveled throughout the world and told me that he was admitted to some very high-security installations. The countries he traveled to included Algeria, Austria, Bahrain, Belgium, Canada, Chile, Denmark, Ecuador, Egypt, France, West Germany, Greece, Greenland, Guatemala, Indonesia, Iran, Japan, South Korea, Netherlands, Nigeria, Panama, Peru, Poland, Saudi Arabia, Sierra Leone, Singapore, Switzerland, Thailand, and the United Kingdom.

1974

In 1974, his passport indicates a trip to Scotland, which Walt called his first assignment. In April 1974, Walt started that job, ostensibly as a fabricator of offshore oil platforms. But after only a couple of months, a labor strike shut down the job, and it was canceled midway through. He flew back to the States in June 1974.

He also made multiple trips to the UK between 1974 and 1978.

JUNE 1975–DECEMBER 1975

Kharg Island, Iran—Walt's résumé lists his position as assistant supervisor of structural ironwork for an offshore oil platform. He also spent several summer months in the States in 1975.

1976

Walt said his next job was in Saudi Arabia, listed on his résumé as assistant superintendent of constructing an offshore oil platform, from May to November of 1976. The restrictions of Islam did not suit him, and the six months he spent without drinking were a test.

1977

According to his résumé, Walt worked in Indonesia from May 14 to December 20, 1977, as a supervisor in charge of expanding a cement factory. He learned to speak broken Indonesian at this time. Yet he told me that he worked as a spy while there, wore body armor, and assassinated people. He said that in Thailand, he met Neil Hanson, Jimmy Hoffa's former pilot, who Walt claimed ran a CIA flight school out of Saigon. At a spy-versus-spy bar in Bangkok, he mentioned meeting a counterfeiter named Larry Baird and said that he traded money with Baird in Holland, where they fabricated a plan to wallpaper Europe with counterfeit money. The plan was to trade the $100,000 counterfeit money for $30,000 clean money, which sounded easy enough, but Walt said it was the scariest thing he ever did. It would have been easier to kill a man for $30,000 in clean U.S. dollars than for $1 million in counterfeit dollars.

1978–1980

From March 1978 to March 1979, and again from November 1979 to November 1980, Walt worked in Saudi Arabia. He said that Phil Q acted as his handler with his work overseas. Walt, still employed by Santa Fe, said he was also part of an 800-man mercenary force on call as a last line of defense for the Saudi Kingdom of Saudi Arabia. In 1979, Walt told me that he and Phil went to Mecca to help put down the rebellion.

Walt said he was also hired to deal with the situation in Algeria. Through the rebellion, the good guys took back the government, but that didn't help the oil companies, which had deals with the previous corrupt administration. Walt said that when he went to Algeria, he killed freedom fighters—protecting oil for Aramco.

According to Walt, he worked for or with the KGB during his entire time in the Middle East, approximately ten years, and was paid in U.S. dollars from a bank in Stamford, Connecticut. Usually, his jobs were sent to a P.O. box in the form of coded letters. He spent time at the CIA base in Dhahran city, where all of Walt's passports were issued.

In 1979, Walt was issued a new passport, and he traveled to Algeria, France, Houston, and Holland.

1980

In 1980, he traveled to Poland, Toronto, Nigeria, and Saudi Arabia.

Because he spoke fluent Polish, Walt said he was sent to Poland, a communist country at the time. He started to smuggle in food and medications unavailable in Poland, as a way to curry favor with people.

En route to Poland from an airport in Egypt, Walt said he struck up a conversation with another Polish man, who introduced himself as Stanley. In fact, his name was Stanislaw Staniszewski, the leader of a top family in the Polish mob. Whether their meeting was a coincidence or part of some plan, they became friends.

Walt said that on one of his visits, Stanley's son was home sick. Walt had some penicillin in his suitcase, which seemed to cure the boy. Stanley's family was sure that Walt had saved their son's life. After that, there was nothing Walt needed that they wouldn't do for him. When Walt appeared in Poland with a job to do, Stanley was there to help. His connections to illegal activities and the black market got Walt access to information and supplies.

Walt said that he and Phil Q. remained in contact for many years, and Walt had numerous addresses for Phil throughout the world, including Saudi Arabia, Montreal, and Quebec, Canada.

Packages and mail were sent from overseas

1981

On July 27 1981, in a coffee shop in Warsaw, Walt claims he attempted to kill Abu Daoud, the architect of the Munich massacre of eleven Jewish athletes in the Olympic Village. His passport confirms his presence there on that date and his travel to Holland, where he said he was paid in francs. In 1981, he also traveled to Saudi Arabia, France, and London.

1982

In 1982, he went to Sierra Leone multiple times, Montreal, Saudi Arabia several times, and Poland.

1983

He had a new passport issued in 1983 and traveled to Sierra Leone, Saudi Arabia, London, Toronto, and Holland. (Walt sent me a 1983 monthly pay stub made out to W. Reca for $9,003.62, which equals $22,000 today. Obviously, his ironworker job was just a cover for other assignments that paid a lot more.) That year, he also had a British passport issued under the name Frank Drinkel.

Always the Charmer

Sometime during one of Walt's trips back to Michigan, he began to reestablish a relationship with his previous wife, Joni. His first move was to call her and state, "This is your husband, Walt."

Joni responded, "I don't have a husband named Walt. You son of a bitch, you said you were going out for bread and milk years ago."

Walt, the charmer, told her, "You never said if you wanted white or wheat."

Apparently, the line worked, and they spent the final years of Joni's life together.

In 1978, Walt and Carla separated for good. Despite Walt sending her money from abroad for house payments, she hadn't used the money for that. When he got back to the States after one trip, he discovered that the bank was starting to foreclose on their house.

On April 12, 1984, Joan Peca petitioned the court for a name change to Joan M. Reca.

Walt's So-Called Jewish Insurance Policy—A Wooden Building

(Yes, Walt was a racist.)

If there was a downside to all of Walt's transgressions, it was his children by Joni. Imagine your father leaving the house for a loaf of bread when you're a year old and not returning until you are sixteen. Ask him for an explanation, and his reply is, "I couldn't remember if I was supposed to get white or wheat."

Worse yet, he had remarried, and the two children of that other woman, through no fault of your own, are his favorites.

"I'll pay for everything," he said. "I'll buy you a car. I'll pay for college."

His pleas to make amends fell on deaf ears. The year was 1985. Walt's career with the agency was in its last years. Some people say, "Once an agent, always an agent," and this is mostly true because you have less overseas work and more time at home to mend fences and patch up old wounds.

So when Walt's kids by Joni said no to college, they agreed to buy a two-story, wood-frame building in Wixom, Michigan, containing an upper flat and a pizza business downstairs, where his oldest son and daughter could work. They called the shop Reca's Hot 'n' Tasty Pizza.

It didn't take long for them to realize this was a huge mistake. They found that running the shop was a much harder job than they'd anticipated, and nobody was buying their pizza. Yet Walt had covered his ass by buying a liberal insurance policy for the wood structure, so he faked some wiring problems to blame, in case the building burned to the ground. What could possibly go wrong?

You'd think burning down a wooden building would be easy, but of all the criminal enterprises that Walt excelled at, arson wasn't one of them. In his early years, he and Weldon (Willard's younger brother) had robbed a bank, armed, and were in Willard's back yard trying to destroy the evidence, the empty bank bags, by lighting match after match, then finally the whole box of matches with the bags on top. After the matches fizzled out and the bags still hadn't caught fire, Willard walked up behind his brother and Walt and said, "So you're the two guys that knocked off the Grand National. Better get a shovel and bury those bags."

So this time Walt used a candle in a dish full of gasoline, the idea being he would have time to get away—and be drinking in a bar someplace far distant from his wooden building. It finally did burn to the ground.

The building also had two apartments, which Walt rented out. Two weeks before the fire, however, he evicted the two tenants.

Then, lo and behold, the fire inspector found an accelerant in the ruins and asked, "Who holds the insurance policy on that former building?"

In the fire report dated May 21, 1985, Sergeant Michael Malloy from the Michigan State Police determined that "No accidental cause could be found," and concluded that the fire was incendiary in nature and intentionally set.

Walt claimed that prior to the fire, on March 29, 1985, someone had entered his apartment, stolen a handgun, and set fire to the headboard on his bed. Walt had filed a police report with the Westland police department, which verified the event.

A cemetery owner testified that he knew Walt's youngest son, who had told him that his father was going to burn down the pizza shop. The son originally denied this, then informed police that his father had removed a painting that he and his wife liked days before the fire and that an employee had witnessed his father practice lighting a fire.

Walt and Joni were the prime suspects, and when the police questioned the oldest son, he quickly dumped all of the blame on Walt, saying that once his father became aware that he was going to testify against him in court, the son's life could be in danger. The son further added that his father had been with the CIA and had killed people before. The son said he would need a place to hide once this case came into the open.

Prosecutor Townsend advised that the case looked good for the complaint/warrants.

Walt and Joni were arrested and charged with arson. Then word got back to Walt's former employers, who had some sort of unusual "pull" with the authorities. The son suddenly recanted his story and was arrested for perjury on November 5, 1985.

On January 3, 1986, assistant prosecutor Gary Tunis recommended to the prosecutor that "there be no prosecution on either the arson or perjury charges."

The whole case disappeared for lack of evidence, as they always did.

Semi-Retirement

In 1986, Walt traveled to Sierra Leone multiple times and to London. Other than a few small contractual work assignments, he essentially stopped working at the age of fifty-two, after the pizzeria fire. Despite no apparent income after that, Walt frequently purchased new cars and gave his two-year-old used cars to friends who needed them. He also purchased a home in Oscoda and many firearms through his friend Willard (being a convicted felon, Walt was not allowed to purchase or own firearms).

When Did Phillip Q Know about the Hijacking?

Since Phil had gotten Walt a job with Vinnell in January 1971, I wondered whether Phil could have known about the November 24, 1971, Cooper hijacking—and if so, how early?

Walt would only say that it was his, Walt's, plan alone. He had no help from anyone, except with the CIA money-laundering bank in Montreal, where Phil had previously cleared the way for him to deposit money.

Regina Scheidegger, Walt's mother, was also named on that bank account.

Once I asked an acquaintance who spoke French to call this bank, and the person who answered said, "How did you get this number? It is only available from the CIA."

Starting on January 1, 1971, with his placement at Vinnell Corporation, Walt was known to clandestine forces of the U.S. government—that's eleven months prior to the D.B. Cooper jump (and possibly longer, if you consider his 1963 application to the CIA). Approximately three to four months after the jump—that is, when two men asked him, "Do you want to go to prison?"—he was on track to be trained as a covert operative. About a month later, he had been placed by government forces in Boise for his training.

Walt knew serious material. He knew who he killed and why. He knew where to set an explosive charge to knock a foreign country out of oil for weeks. Walt seemed to have a guardian angel looking after him who had tremendous influence in the law enforcement communities. Was it Phil Q?

Walt had high praise for Phil and Mary Q. They were a major influence in the life of an orphan from Detroit who shot to the top in both the Hoffa organization and the intelligence community.

You Never Really Retire

In August 1990, according to a letter from David M. Nefores, CS2 in the Department of the Army, Walt alerted the army about risks "that existed in the Middle East beyond those belonging to the Iraqi military apparatus." Nefores went on to state, "Looking back, the information you provided was of greater concern than any of us realized at that time."

On April 26, 1991, for the actions mentioned above, Walt was issued a commendation for "Contributing unselfishly to the support of American Soldiers, Sailors, Airmen and Marines in their joint efforts to achieve freedom from Tyranny during this historic period. Signed by Lieutenant General, USA Commanding." This was for unknown work in Operation Desert Shield/Storm.

Walt followed his good friend Willard up to Oscoda, Michigan, in 1997. Walt's mother stayed with him in Oscoda until she died in 1999. During this time, Walt, a convicted felon, lived in what Jim McCusker called a fortress with more weapons than the local police.

In 2000, Walt told his sister, Sandy, that he had dreams of being in danger, due to all of the weapons in his home. He buried some of them in his back yard and kept some at his friend Willard's house.

The ATF Raid—May 2003

Walt was tipped off that he was about to be raided by Alcohol, Tobacco, and Firearms (ATF) and the Michigan State Police. He hid two machine guns in a wall of his garage before the officers arrived.

When he heard a knock at the door, Walt opened it a crack and asked to see the search warrant. He inspected it, then opened the door wider, and the room filled with officers.

The May 9, 2003, copies of a police report show that while Walt lived at his home in Oscoda Township, Michigan, a search warrant was issued for the "house and garages owned by Walt Richard Reca." The items to be seized were "any firearms and or heavy weapons, including but not limited to pistols, rifles, shotguns, hand grenades and explosive devices." They confiscated a huge arms cache—35 weapons and lots of ammunition—that included the following:

38 caliber revolver
Ruger semiautomatic pistol
357 mag pistol
Ruger M77 220 swift bolt action with bipod
30.06 bolt action Mak-90 Sporter semi auto rifle with 30-round clip
Ruger M-77 Mark II
Winchester 1300
Marlin model 60

Grenade launcher and grenades

Rifle grenades

Lots of 22 caliber rifles and pistols

Several Tasers

This case against Walt, Case 32-479, had been filed by the Michigan police under the Patriot Act, on May 9, 2003. Subsequently, all confiscated weapons disappeared, and all records of that case came up missing. Walt's guardian angel was at work again.

I have a copy of the search warrant and the list of confiscated weapons. Willard's son Mickey confirmed that he also lost some weapons in the raid. The interesting part of the story is that Walt was never arrested, although he was a convicted felon and had twice jumped bail. Even when we showed the local prosecutor a copy of the search warrant from our Freedom of Information Act inquiry, he denied that any raid had ever happened. The record had been deleted.

Fact is, when Walt's house was raided, I suspect that if they had let those guns and C-4 explosives stay put, they would have caught the buyer. But all of that blew up, so to speak, when a neighbor reported it to the police.

I believe in later years Walt was a mole for either the FBI or the ATF (Alcohol, Tobacco, and Firearms), reporting to them on large shipments of arms for clandestine use.

Swinging from the Ceiling Fan

In 2005, Carla and Walt's son—I nicknamed him "Treetop"—and Treetop's kids stayed with Walt. Carla took the "guest house" behind Walt's place, and Treetop and the kids lived with Walt. They had an old car and a few grocery bags of clothes when they came. Walt had tried to set his kids up when he had money, but they weren't interested in college or anything that might give them a future.

Now Treetop wanted money. His kids—the oldest was thirteen at the time—acted wild, throwing garbage across the room, screaming at each other, and creating chaos in the house. They literally destroyed the place, even swinging from a ceiling fan until it pulled out of its fixture.

Walt had taken care of his mom and then Joni and finally Parker before they died. Art was gone, taken by drink. His sister lived far away in Colorado, available only during their weekly phone calls. Walt had hoped he could make a family with his son, but that was clearly impossible.

Finally, Walt had had enough.

He had a fight with Carla and Treetop and drove them off with an axe handle, sending them and the kids back to Washington.

A Coded Letter

It took a long time before Walt began sending me packages, either by mail to my Florida home or wrapped up in envelopes when we met at the Billabog. They contained passports, journals, and news clippings that provided details about his work as an operative for the intelligence community. These documents opened the door to what he had been doing for foreign governments and our government. He could be vague about details.

On December 21, 2008, a month after he'd admitted to being D.B. Cooper, Walt sent me something that didn't make any sense. It was a letter in a legal envelope from someone employed by the *Detroit Free Press*. It looked official, with the *DFP* letterhead and signed with the guy's name and title. It said,

Mr. Walt Reca
28927 Manchester
Westland, Michigan 48185

Dear Mr. Reca,

After some thought and discussion, we've decided not to print the photographs from the Polish calendar you lent us. So I am returning it.

We appreciate your interest in bringing it down to the office. If you have any further thoughts on our international coverage, don't hesitate to call or write.

And if you're planning to be in Vienna let me know; our correspondent there would be glad to see you.

Thanks again.

Sincerely,

[48]

"What's it say?" Loretta wanted to know.

"Nothing. It said nothing. Walt lent this guy at the *Free Press* a calendar, and he's returning it."

So why did Walt send it to us? He didn't say. Originally, it went to Joni's place on Manchester. I didn't know why Walt kept it so long—twenty-seven years.

I read the letter once more before depositing it in the trash.

A day or two later, I called Walt. He told me Fat Willard had smashed his truck—again.

"Did you get my letter?" he asked.

"I did, the *Free Press* thing."

"What did you think?"

"We didn't," I said. "Something about a calendar. What should we think?"

"Let me read you the last paragraph," Walt said, and he read it aloud. "Paragraphs one and two are snowflakes. But that last paragraph tells me everything. Go to Vienna (gateway behind the

---

48 Name and job title withheld.

Iron Curtain), and be in touch with my handler. They use the word *correspondent*, but that means my handler in the United States."

The surprises kept coming.

Walt explained that the letter was actually a coded message to him about the next job he was expected to do: assassinate Abu Daoud in Vienna. Walt said that the *Detroit Free Press* employee was his handler and worked for the Israeli Mossad, and Walt's code name was "the Russian." But the job turned into a "dry run" because Daoud never showed up. And Walt also sent a passport showing he'd been in Warsaw at the time Daoud was shot, along with a newspaper article about the shooting. He claimed to have shot Daoud in the Warsaw coffee shop. It was as if Walt had concocted a game to make me figure out this stuff as we went along.

He was trying to show me one of the main parts of his life after the hijacking. I say "one" because there were many more. Smuggling diamonds out of Sierra Leone would be another.

This was what those years at Boise and other small colleges had prepared Walt for. He told me about the Daoud case because he said it involved Israelis, not Americans, so he felt no betrayal. Walt said that he had worked for Jews, Russians, countries in Indochina, everybody.

Despite admitting to these other misdeeds, Walt bristled when called a crook. "I'm an opportunist," he said, often forcefully.

"I have no criminal record," he reminded me years later, after I started his book. "I told you I couldn't be caught."

"You couldn't be *prosecuted*," I said. "You were caught several times."

Oddly enough, Walt had forgotten it was his record that made him eligible to be hired by the intelligence community in the first place.

I prompted him, "How about those guys asking you, 'Do you want to go to prison?' Remember that?"

Someplace, in some deep dark file, Walt's record exists but not in the public domain. The government has the option of losing or keeping records it wants or doesn't want. Once when Walt was offered an extremely well-paying job in China with a major U.S. oil company, he wasn't aware that the government had scrubbed his records. So he confessed that he had a record and passed up the best job offer he ever had.

Walt never wanted to admit he was caught for the Cooper hijacking. "That was the perfect crime," he often said. I suppose I would agree, except Walt's situation was more like that of our friend Dick Wilson, who was caught with a load of drugs. Like Walt and most of the others, they all became DEA or double agents of some sort to stay out of prison.

"What about the guy at the *Detroit Free Press*?" I asked. "Was he caught, too?"

"I don't know," Walt said, "but he was probably just like the rest of us. He has to get his information from higher up. He doesn't just sit in an office someone is paying for and make stuff up."

Walt always knew more about covert cases than the CIA case officers knew, and most of the time you could paper trail him there. In addition to being an assassin, an airplane hijacker, a gun runner, and a bank robber, he dabbled in counterfeit money, and on his days off in some godforsaken country that forbade the drinking of alcohol, he would go to Sierra Leone and risk hanging on a well-worn noose to smuggle out diamonds right under the nose of a customs agent.

Things like this were Walt's life's work. Yet he never spent a full day in jail, received a prison sentence, or had a criminal record open to the public. In 1971, after Walt pulled the biggest heist of all time, he wasn't a criminal but a legend, a folk hero, and my best friend, even though I detested those things he did—most of them, at least. That one he did early in the winter of 1971, I loved that one.

Like I told another friend of mine, I could have done that one myself.

"Why didn't ya?" he asked.

"I don't steal," I said.

FBI Stonewalling

Other than the one time Walt told me he was D.B. Cooper, he was pretty sly—partly because I was now taping his phone calls. He talked about the hijacking. He sent me information. But despite telling me intimate details of the hijacking, he avoided verbally admitting to being D.B. Cooper again until 2012. (At that time, he dictated a confession to me over the phone, and I had it typed up.)

Once I asked Walt if I could collect a DNA sample from him, but he refused. So I decided to DNA him anyway. Not long after one of the Billabogs, I spent a few days at Walt's house. It was 2009, a year after he had told me over the phone that he was D.B. Cooper.

When Walt was out of the room, I secretly used tweezers to pick up one of his Kleenexes and put it in an old prescription bottle. As soon as I returned home to DeLand, Florida, Loretta and I began looking for an attorney.

We picked a lawyer from the Daytona phone book: David Damore. We met him in person only once. All of our other communication was through his office and by e-mail (and there were only a couple of those). We paid him $1,000, plus $300 to have the lab test on the DNA sample. Damore chose the lab; Loretta and I never saw the name of the lab he used.

Damore sent the tissue in the pill bottle to the lab, and the lab said, "Perfect sample."

After we received the lab test results (which I never saw because Damore kept them in a safe), Damore sent the card to FBI agents in Seattle on July 27, 2009, for comparison with the D.B. Cooper case in Virginia. Damore never gave my name to the FBI. Agent Larry Carr told Attorney Damore that the lab test should take only a day or two.

A couple of days after the DNA was sent to the FBI, Walt called and screamed at me, "What the fuck are you doing, DNA'ing me?"

He then said, "I'm done talking to you."

From that day on, Loretta and I began hearing strange sounds during our phone conversations, as if they were being monitored. Walt never mentioned how he had been contacted, most likely by phone. I'm confident he kept in touch with his former handlers in the intelligence community because once when I spent the night at his house, I overheard a phone conversation that obviously involved some sort of covert operation.

When I'd first met Damore in June 2009, I told him that the hijacker had asked someone to pick him up after he landed. The thing is, I had never told Damore anything about Walt or revealed Walt's name. Damore and I referred to him as Mr. Blank. Damore did not know who D.B. Cooper really was. Only the FBI knew, so it had to be them who contacted Walt.

It's also odd that in a phone call, Agent Carr asked Damore for the name of the person who had allegedly picked up "D.B. Cooper" after the hijacking. I had never revealed Don Brennan's name or the location as the Teanaway Café to Damore, so he couldn't answer Carr. Yet the real question is, why did Agent Carr ask the name of the driver who picked up "D.B. Cooper" but not the name of the hijacker? Was it because the FBI already knew "D.B. Cooper's" real name?

Instead of the 1 or 2 days that Agent Carr said the lab test would require, it took 74 days. Damore e-mailed Agent Carr on October 7, 2009, inquiring why the test was taking so long.

In an e-mail dated October 8, 2009, FBI agent Larry Carr told Damore, "Today I received a call from the lab advising the DNA you submitted to me, is not a possible match with what we have on file."

In my assessment, the FBI has known from Day One who D.B. Cooper was.

I was not the first to find D.B. Cooper, you know. That would be the covert agencies of the U.S. government. I was only the first to *expose* D.B. Cooper, something they had good reason not to do. I waited until my friend was dead before I brought him into the open, so no damage was done.

How do they operate, our clandestine agencies? They lie a lot.

So when Walt called me, furious, I wasn't surprised that the FBI had been on to him. I *was* surprised at how mad he was, though I knew that all his life, one of Walt's biggest fears was going to prison. Even years later, he thought the feds could still take him in. Maybe he was right. He might not have had a lot of years left in him, but he didn't want to spend a minute of his time behind bars.

After a couple of months, Walt started calling me again, but now he initiated all of the calls and only phoned me at my house, so I couldn't tape him. Also, the phone line sounded funny. I'm pretty sure our phone was tapped and all of our conversations were recorded until Walt died.

"Hey, Charlie, it's me, Walt." The call came during dinner.

"How you doing, Walt?" I'd been worried I had lost him for good.

Walt seemed to be in a nostalgic mood, reminiscing about our jumps in Saginaw and the crazy things we did in our youth. When he signed off, I listened to the dial tone for a moment, thinking, *It's all over now but the storytelling.*

CHAPTER 11

THE AUDIOTAPES

Despite his years of absolute silence about the hijacking on November 24, 1971, until his confession thirty-seven years later, evidence suggests Walt Richard Reca wanted his story told, the whole story. Why else would he send me evidence, let me tape him discussing the entire hijacking, and then send documents verifying his years as an intelligence operative?

Walt wanted power and control, and the combination of those two became his ticket out of poverty. They would bring him recognition and constitute his legacy—but that was not the Cooper story.

My semiretirement job of running dog kennels was great, for what it was worth, but Walt's story gave me a new, much-needed project to focus on. From all of those conversations, I put together a pretty good account of the hijacking. At times, it was like pulling teeth from a chicken, but I was driven by the need to figure it out, to discover the truth.

Some people might ask, "Out of all the writers in the world, how did you get this story?"

One day I asked Walt, "Can you think of any reason why you're telling me this now?"

"Probably because we got into it gradually. I mean, this has been going on for a couple years now. I never told nobody. You're the only one, and that's because I trust you."

There were others who knew Walt as well as I did: Bill Parker, Fat Willard, Art and his brother Mike, Bob Sinclair, and quite a few more. Remember, Walt never told us anything. Yet I was determined to uncover the truth.

"We almost settled in Atlanta," Walt said on an audiotaped phone call one night. "It seemed like it could be a nice life. I got a job, earned some money, and we got the car fixed. Carla liked it there."

Loretta motioned for me to walk the dogs. I waved back to her, indicating it was Walt.

"He sure likes to talk," she said.

"I'm trying to get his story," I whispered to her, covering the mouthpiece of the phone.

Walt paused. I think he could sense I was distracted.

"Why'd you leave Atlanta?" I asked, to prod him on.

"Once again, a guy I knew from Flint showed up on the job. I didn't know if he saw me or recognized me, but I wasn't going to take a chance. Anyway, Carla put up a fuss. 'Can't we live like other people, settle down, and grow flowers? I hate this running all the time.'" Walt said the last part in his version of Carla's voice, high-pitched and nasal. "She was like any woman, looking for something stable. Finally, I offered a compromise right there. I told her within a year we would buy a house. Just the idea of settling down someday seemed to soothe her nerves, and she moved with me one more time, back to Washington."

Crash Landing in Cle Elum

I steered the topic of conversation back to the hijacking.

Walt laughed. "I just was hoping the pilot wasn't like Art; it would be a kamikaze flight. One time I asked Art what would happen if someone hijacked him. Art said, 'That guy would be in a lot of fucking trouble.'"

"Were you worried about the jump?" I asked.

Walt brought up an even more dangerous jump. "The night I jumped in Saginaw, that was my third jump that night and the wind was blowing 45 mph and gusting, so it never bothered me because I made *that* one and survived it."

Coming back to the "Cooper" jump, I asked, "Did you see the tree before you hit it?"

"No. I hit the tree first. . . . The only fuckin' dead tree in the forest, and I happen to get to it."

He mentioned that on the way down, before landing, he'd noticed two cars' headlights along a road and lights from what looked like a bridge. He also noticed a bright light off to his left prior to landing.

"Holy mackerel, that's amazing," I said. "If you'da jumped two minutes before you did, you would have been right in the middle of a huge forest."

"I woulda been in somethin'."

After landing, Walt knew his leg was broken.

"So then, you buried your chute," I said.

"No, I just gathered it all up and put it in the backpack and left it there with the broken trees. Threw a few branches on top of it." He described walking toward a small knoll.

"So you walk out of the woods up a slight grade to where you thought you saw car lights."

"Yeah."

"So now," I said, "when you're walkin' out, is the money still around your chest and your raincoat on?"

"No. I had to clean myself off, took the raincoat off, put the money in the raincoat. . . . Had like a bundle."

"And were your pants or anything torn from hitting all those tree . . . dead limbs?" I asked.

"No," Walt said.

"So you walk out and you get to the road."

"Yeah. I was carrying the money in my raincoat under my arm and spotted more car lights, so I was walking that way."

"And you could see a road? What luck!"

"I couldn't see it yet, but I could hear the tires on the concrete, and that there."

"Then what?"

"That's when I saw the one light quite far off. I was hoping it was a truck stop. It's dark, but you can tell it's not a town or anything. . . . Maybe a quarter of a mile away. Possibly more. My leg hurt like hell, but I started walking. I was freezing to death. . . . I couldn't stop now."

"Okay," I said, "and when you get there, do you just find a door and go in?"

"Yeah," Walt said. "I go in. I order a cup of coffee. My hand's shaking real bad. It's spilling right there, so I didn't want nobody to see it. . . . You know when you peel a beet, how red it looks? That's the way my face was when I looked in the mirror. After it all happened, right, with that fuckin' —that rain hitting me in the fuckin' face."

"You mean . . . you looked that way when you got to the truck stop?"

"That restaurant. Yeah."

"Did anybody say anything?" I asked.

"Yeah. I think they said, 'Your face is real red,' you know? And I didn't pay any attention. I mean—it's a question you don't answer. . . . You can't say, 'Well, I jumped out in the fuckin' rain,' or something."

"And then what did you do?"

"I got some change from the waitress, and I asked her where the telephone was, and I called up Don. And I said, 'I done it.' He said, 'You done what?' I had discussed it with him before."

"Did you have to go to the bathroom or anything?"

"Oh, fuck yeah. I mean, I was pissing in the woods coming out."

"But you had to get directions from somebody in the restaurant—the truck stop. You had to get directions to tell Don where to come and pick you up."

"I gave the phone to the only guy there. The dump truck outside was his. He gave Don the directions. . . . That's how come I remember him good, too, with his fuckin' guitar, cowboy hat, Western gear—"

"How come he was by the telephone?"

"'Cause I called him over," Walt said. "Because I didn't know where I was. He knew where we were."

"So you sat there and drank coffee for two and a half hours."

"Yeah, right about that. It could have been two and a half hours." . . .

"Did you see Don pull up outside . . . or did he actually have to come in the place and look for you?"

"He come in the place," Walt said. "He seen me and come walking over to me. . . . I was just staring and numb. You know what I mean? Staring at the menu overhead. You know, like hotdogs, hamburgers, or whatever, and I was like mesmerized by just staring at that sign."

"You said you didn't know where you were."

"Not until you told me years later. If you'd have said if I'd kept going on that road fifty more miles, I'd come to Blewett Pass, then I'd have known. But as it was, no one told me, so I didn't know until later that night, and that there. Remember, about forty years later when we would talk, and you kept saying, 'Portland,' and I told you I was nowhere near Portland, even though I didn't know where I was?"

"Yeah," I said. "I remember."

"Blewett Pass is why. After Don picked me up, and we got to Blewett Pass in just a few minutes, I knew I was nowhere near Portland. Portland has got to be two hundred and fifty miles from Blewett Pass. No way could I have been anyplace close to Portland."

Secrets Breed Paranoia

One day, during another audiotaped phone conversation, Walt said, "Don Brennan called me yesterday."

"No kidding," I said.

"Yes. He calls me about once a month. We talk."

"You never did ask him where you were, did you?"

"No," Walt said. "We don't even talk about that. 'Cause if I did, he'd never call again."

"Really?" I said.

"Yeah."

"He's that paranoid?"

"Yeah," Walt said.

"Well—God, he ought to know better because you're not gonna do anything to put him in hot water."

"He calls me once a month. We talk about some of these guys we worked iron with together, and that's about it."

"I'll be darned," I said. "He won't even talk to you about that?"

"No."

"I've never heard of anybody being so scared of anything in all my life."

"Yeah," Walt said. "He's very cautious."

"You know, I've often thought about calling him, but you told me, 'Well, you can call him, but don't mention that, or he'll hang up on ya.' So I just figured what's the point?"

"He's a tough old man," Walt said. "He's a year older than I am."

Potential Blowback

During another audiotaped phone call, I said to Walt, "I gotta ask you this, and I need the absolute honest answer."

"Yup."

"Are you D.B. Cooper?"

"I ain't saying nothin'."

"Okay," I said. "Here's the problem. There's another guy writing a book. I just found this out yesterday. If you're not, we gotta find out because it's gonna destroy us."

"No," Walt said. "I'm not admitting to anything."

"Okay. So we really don't know, then."

"If they wanta claim anything," Walt said, "let them claim everything they want to. I don't care."

"I know, but that's the problem. Put yourself in the agent's place or the publisher's. We're just another couple of guys . . . coming up and saying this stuff. We really don't have any proof. You know, we're just—"

"I understand that," Walt said, "but I'm not gonna go to prison just to prove a point to a publisher and to an agent."

"Okay, I understand that."

"That's how come I said, 'Okay, go ahead and print it,' because if anybody come up to me afterwards, I'd deny everything. I'd say that's the imagination of the author, the publisher, or whoever, you know."

"Okay," I said. "But knowing that it's going to destroy us if we're wrong, should I keep going on with the book?"

"That's your choice, Charlie."

"I know."

"My choice is I wanna be free of everything. . . . I don't want nothin' hanging over my head."

"I understand," I said. "Are we the only guys that know pretty much your story? You've never told this to anybody else in the past?"

"Never told anybody anything," Walt said. . . .

"Okay," I said, "so what do you want us to do with this book? Do you want us to hold it until a certain time because— Let me just give you an example. Right now, if they said, 'We're gonna put that book out tomorrow,' even if I didn't talk to you, I'd say, 'Don't do it. I want that book held. I don't want that book put out right now.' I've talked to different people—I didn't tell 'em what we're doing or nothin'—but [they] said, 'Well, hijacking is a federal crime, and I'm sure that there's no statute of limitations on it.'"

"Let me think this over," Walt said.

"Yeah, well, nothing's gonna happen within a month anyway, but this is a big deal. But it isn't so big to me. It isn't so big to me that I would want you to go to jail over this thing."

"Michael's got publishers, and they've got attorneys," Walt said. "They can decide what to do about that situation."

"Okay," I said, "but I wanna make sure that we're covered on this thing. This thing doesn't get out of our hands. It's gone on a long time, but you kept the secret for thirty-seven years, give or take a week or two. I still find it hard to believe that we are talking about it."

"Yeah. Me, too."

"I thought there had to be some health reason or something like that, that you're talking about it."

"Well," Walt said, "I gotta go Monday for nuclear medicine. They gotta check my heart, all sorts of shit."

"That's this coming Monday?"

"Yeah. 'Cause my valve's not working right, in my heart. And so they got all sorts of stuff to do, tests going on."

"But did that have anything to do with you finally fessing up?"

"No. I don't think so," Walt said. "Talking to you is different than talking to somebody else, you know? I don't feel that I'm exposed talking to you, where I do with somebody else."

"Well, but don't forget— . . . Sooner or later, if we write this in a book, it gets out there, you know what I'm saying? Sooner or later, if a book goes out, it's just like you reading the *Detroit News*, it's there. And people see it. And I mean, the FBI'll see it, everybody will see it."

"I figure you'll know what to do about that, Charlie."

"The only thing that we can do is sit on it. Is tell 'em we just can't publish this thing at this time."

The Jump

Walt, the person the world now knew as D.B. Cooper, jumped out of Northwest Orient Flight 305 shortly after 8:05 p.m. Pacific Time via the airplane's back stairs, after takeoff from Sea-Tac Airport at 7:36 p.m. Flight 305 was at 10,000 feet, with the outside temperature less than –10 degrees Fahrenheit. The plane was clearing the highest mountains on its flight by just 1,000 feet, so Walt waited only 2 seconds to pull the ripcord and was under full canopy by an altitude of 9,600 feet. The ground under Walt was approximately 1,945 feet, so Walt, in an unsteerable canopy on a night too dark to steer anyway, drifted with the wind in a northwesterly direction at approximately 10 miles per hour. Unable to see because of blowing sleet, Walt couldn't know the wind was blowing him to a friendly place just a football field in length from Highway 97, the road he would take to Cashmere. Had there been no wind, Walt would have come down in a forest too thick to walk through, and the outcome, significantly different.

Walt's first contact with earth was a dead pine tree. He crashed to the ground, shearing off limbs and breaking one leg as he did. He lost his wraparound sunglasses and lost all track of time, but an estimate of the time within two minutes would put it at approximately 8:15 p.m. Pacific Time.

Walt whispered, "I made it."

By about 8:20 p.m., Walt had placed the ransom money in a bundle made from the money bag and his raincoat and secured it with the belt from his pants. Using a tree limb as a prop, he got to his feet. He packed the parachute into the backpack and tossed branches over it. With the ransom under his arm, Walt limped with his broken leg toward State Highway 97 about 100 yards away. Standing within inches of a two-lane highway, he looked west into blackness. To the east, he saw one light. Seconds later, a dump truck erupted from the darkness going west to east, nearly hitting him. He crossed to the other side and walked in the direction of the light. The rain had soaked him, and he recognized the onset of hypothermia. As he closed the distance, he saw the dump truck parked by some gas pumps.

Again, he said, "I made it."

He entered the café at approximately 8:45 p.m. and sat a seat away from a man in Western attire, with his cowboy hat and guitar case on the counter. That man said, "Hello."

Walt nodded.

The lady behind the bar said, "Your face is beet red."

Walt said, "Coffee, black."

Walt cradled the coffee in both hands, trying to get his frozen fingers to move. Minutes later, he nudged some coins into his left hand, as he held the ransom money tightly with his right arm.

He walked away from his coffee cup to a pay phone in the back and rang a number, then seconds later came back to the counter.

"Mister," Walt said, "can you help me?"

The guy in the cowboy outfit could see the man behind him in the mirror. "Sure," he said.

"My car broke down," said the man, dripping water and holding the bundle. "Can you tell my friend where I am and how to get here?"

Cowboy followed Walt back to the pay phone. Walt stood in front of Cowboy, holding the bundle under his arm, still dripping water, as Cowboy gave Walt's friend directions.

One more time Cowboy looked down at the water accumulating at Walt's feet, then said, "I've got to go. I've got a gig to play a couple of miles down the road."

He finished his coffee, picked up the guitar case, and said, "Good luck." Then he got into his dump truck and drove east into the night. It was approximately 8:53 p.m. Pacific Time.

Aftermath of the Hijacking

One day I asked Walt, "What did you think when it was over?"

"Never gave it a second thought," he said. "It was done."

"Was there a time in life when you nearly forgot you were D.B. Cooper?"

"Right afterward. I put the money in the bank. It was no big deal. It was done, and I lived through it." . . .

"Have you read any of the stuff that's out there about the hijacking?" I asked him. "Did you follow it in the news after it happened?"

"I would have no interest in reading it."

"There's a bunch of reports out there. A whole conglomeration of people have been following the story and have written their accounts. Gobbledygook. It just keeps coming at ya."

"I'm quite sure I haven't followed it," Walt said. "It was over, and it out was of my mind. The government itself investigated this and put out a lot of disinformation.

"After I got home, I put the money under my bed. And then I went back to work on Monday after the holiday weekend. I had a limp, but I could get around okay. They sent me to the company doctor to put a cast on my broken leg.

"Then I decided to go to Vancouver. I went through Sumas—there were no custom agents at that crossing. Only locals knew about it."

Walt deposited the money in a Canadian bank.

Yet there was more to come, and it was even more interesting than what he had already revealed.

At the time I didn't realize this would be the start of something bigger. I would spend the next fifteen years trying to unravel the mystery and reconstruct the life of my friend, using whatever information he gave me and what I could dig up myself. In doing so, I uncovered a life of clandestine activity.

I thought I knew my friend, and maybe I did know him deep down for who he really was. I knew he was generous, but he could be brutal. Yet the details of his life were a mystery. As he sent me packages in the mail, I started to piece together the person he was.

As we approach the last stage of our lives, everyone struggles to make sense of it. I tried to picture Walt as a young boy and thought about how much of life happens for reasons beyond our control.

CHAPTER 12

FINDING COWBOY

I was fixated on the hijacking, but my story about Walt had come to a dead end—at least, that part of the story. He would answer my questions, but then he'd get wily, and I'd have to change the subject. I kept track of his answers, though. Then, during our next conversation, I prodded him about what happened after he landed.

For years, people had talked about whether D.B. Cooper could have survived the jump. They said he would have to be a superman. I knew different, but I needed the full story. I either had to quit or find Cowboy; he was the key.

Then, in June 2013, for the first time, Walt told someone other than me that he was D.B. Cooper. He described to his niece Lisa Story the part about walking from the woods and meeting Cowboy. By June of that year, I had accumulated Walt's passports, journals, newspaper articles, letters, and many other documents that proved what kind of life he'd led, that he most certainly worked as a government operative for our government and other governments. This was when I realized that what had started as a curious pastime, following Walt as he stumbled from one debacle to the next, had turned into a serious investigation.

But the hijacking, although a good story, had the least number of documents to support it. Walt always spoke reluctantly about the hijacking, and I had to work backward from his story. We knew approximately where he jumped by his description of things, such as a bridge, railroad tracks, lights in the distance, and other landmarks.

Yet I knew the first thing people would ask me was, "How do you really know your friend was Cooper?"

As bad as I hate to travel, I seriously thought about going to Washington State in search of more evidence and the man who played music by night and most likely drove a dump truck by day. Yet the idea seemed too far against the odds. Cowboy obviously was not his name, and he could have been a drifter and moved to another continent by now or even died. Even so, my own life has been a life against the odds. Some of those odds were greater than this, so I decided that if my wife, Loretta, didn't mind, I'd do it.

The idea of leaving the farm, a place that fits my comfort zone, to go to Washington State and look for a parachute and a man who might or might not still exist was not borne from logic but from desperation.

I sat down and took notes on all the things Walt had told me.

"I didn't know where I was," Walt kept saying, so Loretta got online and compiled a list of small towns and villages in the area. I pored over maps to find a location that matched everything he mentioned. The next time I talked to Walt, I slowly went down the list and asked him if any sounded familiar.

I mentioned ten or twelve before reading, "Teanaway."

"Say that again," he said.

"Teanaway."

"I've heard that name," he said. "I think that's it."

I then said, "Describe anything you saw as Don drove you home, road signs, anything."

"Blewett Pass," he said, "and Cashmere, a small town on Highway 2."

"Did you then know where you were?"

"I'd been to Blewett Pass before. I did some drinking at a tavern there one day. You have to go through Cashmere to get to Seattle, so I'd been through there a lot."

"Anything else?" I said.

"Yellow street lights." Walt said he'd never seen lights like those in his life.

"They were a warning for something," I said. "Maybe railroad tracks?"

"I didn't see nothing."

I asked him, "Was your leg throbbing?"

"Oh, everything, yeah. My leg, my head. My hands are shaking. My sore leg, as I could feel it swelling up."

"Did you have to take your shoe off, or would it still be on?"

"No," Walt said. "I never took my shoe off because then I couldn't get it back on. . . . Then you draw a lot of attention, walking around barefooted in November."

Something else Walt told me, another piece to the puzzle, was approximately how long it took him to walk from where he'd started on the road until he got to the truck stop café. It was far from exact, but it gave me some parameters to work within. It took him more than ten but less than thirty minutes.

Later, when I pinned down the actual place he'd walked to, it became less than twenty minutes because of the proximity of the town of Cle Elum. He never saw a town, meaning he couldn't have been that far south on Highway 97, the highway that the yellow lights and Blewett Pass were on.

The things Walt remembered about the café where he met Cowboy gave me enough information to help me locate it before I left on my search. He remembered the café was open until midnight and didn't serve beer.

Loretta went online and found a list of cafés and restaurants near Cle Elum, so I could narrow down which one it was. The first one I called was in the middle of lunch rush, and I asked a lady, Gerry Snyder, a server at the Liberty Café, if I could call back. She graciously said yes. I contacted her two hours later and repeated part of what Walt had told me.

"This place was not only a café but had gas pumps," I said. "It had a large menu, full meals, did not serve beer, and was open to midnight."

"Teanaway Junction Café," Ms. Gerry said.

"Are you sure?" I said.

"It was in 1971," she said. "It burned down several years back, and now it's a fire station. Can I ask you something?"

I said, "Sure."

"Where did you say you were?"

"Florida," I said.

"Oh." She paused. "It's such a long time ago and so far away."

"You're right," I said, "but I'm writing a book."

"Oh, dear," she said.

"Yeah, kind of a 'who done it,'" I told her, "and your information is most helpful."

Finding where Walt had actually landed, in Teanaway, close to a café, close enough to walk to with one fractured leg, proved to me that our discussions were finally getting someplace.

I needed hip surgery, so I thought I could walk pretty much like a person with a broken leg. From the corner to the end of my property was exactly a quarter of a mile. I walked it, dragging my leg as Walt would have done, to get a sense of how long he would have taken. From his description, I located what would have been his landing site, and it was a mile and a half from the Teanaway Junction Café. It took me four minutes to walk the quarter mile, and from that, I figured it took Walt twenty-four minutes to walk to the café. If he'd landed at the time he said, he would have gotten to the café at the time Cowboy saw him, right before Cowboy left for his nine o'clock gig.

Before traveling to Washington, I did have hip surgery and waited a few months for it to heal. Then on June 7, 2013, my friend John Clark and I left for the airport. After my new stainless steel hip set the TSA's metal detector squealing, we boarded a plane to Seattle, armed with Loretta's blessing and our own, much smaller, metal detector.

"Maybe I'll have some peace around the house," Loretta said. "Don't let the bears gitcha."

In Sea-Tac Airport, we rented a car and drove east from Cle Elum, close to where Walt said he landed.

He figured that out from the route he took home in Don's car. They drove north on Hwy 970 and 97 and went through Blewett Pass, a place they were both familiar with, then Cashmere, and, from there, home to Hartline. In previous conversations, Walt had mentioned strange yellow lights. Before I left, Loretta and I Google-mapped the area Walt had mentioned, and, sure enough, there were the strange lights. My son in-law works for the Florida Highway Department, and we asked him what the lights were. He said they were yard lights. Sometimes people use them in remote areas.

Tracking Down Forty-Year-Old Clues

We got to Cle Elum, a charming small town in mid-state Washington, the following afternoon. We picked up a free road map and drove to the firehouse that used to be the Teanaway Junction Café, which burned down, and worked our way west. We knew where Walt had landed within reasonable bounds, a strip around fifty yards wide by a half-mile long, more than a foot deep. I had a metal detector, in hopes of locating the metal on the chute. Yet the area was so dense, we couldn't even walk in there. It was overgrown with bushes and trees up to eight feet high, plus it was private land. My hopes for the search turned to frustration when my friend started bellyaching to go home at every turn. This was before I realized the FBI must have picked up the parachute.

"This is not the place," John said.

"This *is* the right place," I said. "I wanted to see the terrain."

"And now you've seen it," John said.

Then it dawned on me. John was afraid of bears. When we'd parked at the airport, John had a gun he'd asked me to put into my carry-on luggage.

"Are you crazy?" I said. "I get searched every time because my hip sets off those metal detectors."

He'd tossed the 9mm back into his trunk, and now he didn't have a gun to protect himself from the bears. So he wasn't going into the woods, those woods with a thousand trees and a bear behind every one of them. We gave up, but I knew I still had to find Cowboy. The bellyaching from my friend continued.

We made our way to the small town of Cle Elum, three miles away. Remembering that Cowboy had driven a dump truck, I went to a garage with a sign that said, "Truck repair."

"That guy ain't gonna tell you anything," John said.

Ignoring him, I walked across the street. The grumbling from my friend intensified. There I met a young man named Steve and asked him if he knew about a man who lived in town about forty years ago, drove a dump truck, wore cowboy garb, and played music in a band. I'm thinking, *This has to be a million-to-one odds that he'll know, especially since he's so young.*

"You need to talk to Wayne Willett," he said. "He owns a gas station downtown, and his father, Tom, used to own the Teanaway Junction Café."

This was incredible luck. Despite John's whimpering and squealing, it resulted in a solid lead on Cowboy.

At the Shell gas station, I found Wayne busy repairing a car. I said, "I'm looking for a guy who was an eyewitness to something very big that happened here forty years ago. Something that happened in this town. He was a Country Western singer who wore Western clothes, like Gene Autry or Roy Rogers would have worn back in the day. And he drove a dump truck during the day."

Without hesitating, Willet said, "D.B. Cooper."

"Why do you say that?" I asked, surprised, because Walt felt pretty sure that nobody would remember him from that night. Even if they did, the FBI had reported that the hijacker jumped over Portland, 225 miles away.

"Because that's the only thing that happened here that would bring a person all the way from Florida."

I didn't admit or deny it. I gave Wayne Willett my phone number and asked for his.

A week later, Willett called and gave me the name of the band leader who often played at the Grange Hall. I asked if he drove a dump truck, and Willett said he didn't think so. He promised to keep asking around.

Remembering the "Drowned Rat"

A few days later, Willett called again. "I got your guy. We went to school together. He was a member of the band, and his son works at the auto parts store across the street."

I called the son, who gave me the phone number of his father, Jeff Osiadacz. I now had Cowboy's real name.

I then called Jeff and asked him if he remembered a man coming into the café the eve before Thanksgiving forty years ago, asking to give his friend on the phone directions to pick him up.

He said, "Yes, I do, as a matter of fact."

Jeff Osiadacz a.k.a. "Cowboy"

Stunned, I couldn't believe what he'd said. "What would make you remember something from such a long time ago?"

"First, I passed him on the road," Cowboy said, "but I couldn't pick him up because it was against company policy, and they'd removed the passenger seat. When he came in the café, I apologized for not picking him up. He was dripping wet and had his raincoat wrapped around a bundle. I hoped it was dry clothing because he looked like a drowned rat. He had on a dark suit, white shirt, no hat, slicked-down dark hair. He ordered a coffee and drank it black."

"Anything else?" I asked.

"Yeah, he had on penny loafers."

"Penny loafers? You remember penny loafers, why?"

"I always wanted my parents to buy me some, but they never did."

Finding Cowboy was huge. This was when I realized I had it, something I could develop, a time line for the Cooper hijacking. Not every answer but some answers: nearly the exact spot where he walked out of the woods, his time of arrival at the café, the phone call Walt said he made to Don Brennan, and what happened after the hijacking. All of which, in my mind, was more exciting and dangerous than the hijacking, probably because it happened over a much longer time frame and involved many more people than the Cooper hijacking.

I haven't met Jeff Osiadacz in person yet, but I talked to him many times on the phone. Jeff recalled the meeting with Walt, due to the very unusual circumstances: Walt was soaking wet and freezing, with an overcoat bundled and tied together on his lap, and Jeff took the phone to give some man driving directions for a person who had no idea where he was. Jeff learned that Don would drive down from Seattle and instructed him to go over Stevens

Teanaway Junction Café—Cowboy and Walt met here

Pass, rather than on the other available route. Walt had called Jeff "kid" and paid for his coffee.

After Cowboy said, "Good luck," to the drowned rat, he left the café at 8:52 p.m. and hopped into his dump truck. He drove to Grange Hall Ballard, and when the music started at 9 p.m. sharp, Cowboy was there and on key.

(As an aside, Jeff Osiadacz was named "King Coal 2017," after working long years in Washington State coalmines, following in the footsteps of his father and his Croatian grandfather.)[49]

An Unwitting Accomplice

Meanwhile, Walt—usually a cordial man—was silent, as he drank one black coffee after another and waited for our friend Don to take him home to Hartline.

Sometime before midnight Don arrived. Walt grabbed his bundle and limped from the café to Don's car.

Don, a petty criminal his entire life, said, "What the fuck have you done now, Walt?"

During the drive, Walt showed Don the contents of his overcoat—bundles of $20s—and explained the hijacking. He handed Don two or three bundles.

Don told him, "It's people like you and me that the penitentiaries are full of."

When they reached Walt's house, he said to Don, "Remember what you said about prison back there? We're in this together now. Don't say a fucking word to anybody."

Walt put the money in an old Air Force B-4 bag and slid it under his bed, along with the clothing he'd worn during the hijacking.

---

49   For more biographical details on Jeff Osiadacz, see Jim Fossett, "Jeff Osiadacz Named King Coal 2017: In the Mines It Was a Risky O-Dark-Thirty All Day Long," *Northern Kittitas County Tribune*, September 21, 2017.

Jeff Osiadacz's band

Thirty years later, he sent me his socks and insulated underwear bottoms. His throbbing leg and worry about getting his car home from Spokane kept him awake the rest of that night. Soon Carla and the kids would be home from her sister's.

In the morning Walt called another ironworker who lived nearby—Jerry Grady—and got a ride to Spokane. Walt explained that his wife and kids were near Seattle for Thanksgiving and would be home shortly.

Grady said, "You got your days mixed up, Walt. We got lots of time. We celebrate Thanksgiving tonight. Carla and your kids likely won't be back until sometime tomorrow."

And they weren't.

On Monday, Walt showed up on the Grand Coulee Dam Project, limping badly.

"Wait a minute," his supervisor shouted, as Walt hobbled toward the iron. "Go to the infirmary."

219

[51 THURSDAY, SEPT. 21, 2017 · NKC TRIBUNE

Jeff Osiadacz named KING COAL 2017

In the mines it was a risky 0-Dark-Thirty all day long

CORONATION CANCELLED

Author's Note: King Coal 2017 Jeff Osiadacz was to be crowned in Roslyn on Sunday, Sept. 3, but the event was cancelled due to smoke, heat, concerns for public safety and the need to keep roads open for firefighters assigned to the Jolly Mountain Wildfire. The ceremony was rescheduled for Saturday, Sept. 30, 5 p.m., at Hawthorne Hall in Ronald – but due to an unforeseen booking conflict at Hawthorne Hall the coronation was cancelled last week for good. Heritage Club officials said Osiadacz would be crowned and recognized in a private, informal ceremony at some point in the near future. The following story pays tribute to Osiadacz, his family, and to Upper Kittitas County coalminers.

by Jim Fossett
jim@nkctribune.com

SOUTH CLE ELUM – It is a tragedy so many died in the mines or died later in life because of them. It is a miracle some did survive the terrible ambushes awaiting miners in deep, dark places where the cry for help was easily smothered. King Coal 2017 Jeff Osiadacz began his story with the blows the mines dealt him, his father and his grandfather a thousand feet or more below the grounds where today we build our homes, work our jobs and mow our lawns. They are the grounds on which Upper County mothers and fathers raise their children.

Rockfall, cave-in, explosion

"My dad and I were down 1,200 feet or so," Osiadacz began, "about halfway to the bottom of the shaft, when a big rock broke shook it off and went back to work.

"My dad came back to the mines because he didn't want me to be down there alone. He worked in the No. 3 and Patrick's Mines. It was in the No. 3 he got caught in a cave-in. It crushed his left hip and pelvis.

"There were two other miners with him at the time. One of them took off running. The other, Sam Craven, told dad he wouldn't leave him behind.

"Sam was a big man, a giant at over six-feet tall.

"He got some jacks to free my dad from the rubble, then he carried him out.

"The Cravens: I got nothing to say but good things about that family."

Osiadacz's grandfather worked in the Shaft Mine behind Roslyn City Hall, 200 yards from the turnoff to Carek's Meat Market. The slag piles there are

KING COAL 2017 Jeff Osiadacz with the miner's helmet and lamp, like the one he wore back in the day. This one is on display at Swiftwater Cellars Winery, site of the old No. 9 Mine, where he worked.
Photo courtesy of Osiadacz Family

Cowboy: "King Coal 2017"

Walt did.

"This looks like an old break," the doctor said. He questioned whether it was work related, but he set it anyway.

For the next few weeks, Walt was assigned to a desk job in Spokane, until he had healed sufficiently to return to the dam project.

I didn't know Don Brennan well—not the way Walt, Bob Sinclair, and Art knew one another from their days in Alaska. In May 2011, Walt asked me, "Do you want to talk to Don?"

"You and Don still talk?" I asked.

"All the time. Just never about that night."

"Sure," I said. "Call him."

Walt was right. Don never would admit to anything, but I wouldn't either, if I were Don. Interestingly enough, he never gave any denial, like I would have, such as, "What the fuck are you talking about, Charlie? I never had anything to do with any hijacking."

Then Don said, "I was questioned, you know, right here in my house by the FBI, not about picking up D.B. Cooper but for being D.B. Cooper, but I'm too tall. I'm six foot, five inches."

(FBI agent Larry Carr stated that more than a thousand parachutists in the Northwest region were interviewed after the hijacking. Don Brennan happened to be one of them because he was a fire jumper, but his height ruled him out as a suspect.)

Don Brennan died that same year, November 10, 2011, almost forty years to the day after Walt said Don picked him up at the Teanaway Junction Café and drove him home to Hartline.

The D.B. Cooper Money

"You're damn right I kept the money," Walt said, when I asked him.

"How did you arrive at the figure $200,000?"

"The number come off the top of my head, and if it was so much I couldn't carry it, I'd throw it out of the plane, just to have everybody wonder how I carried it."

I laughed.

"It was never meant to be a cure-all," Walt said. "I would continue to work, but it would always be there, and I would never have to worry like poor people all do. If my car broke down, I'd be able to fix it or send my kids to college, you know. Not just never work again. Problem was, after I got it, I didn't know what to do with it. I knew sooner or later either the kids or Carla would find it, so I decided to put it in a bank in Canada, not here."

"What about that CIA bank in Montreal?" I asked. "I know you put some there in two accounts, yours and your mom's."

"Later I did," Walt said, "but I was uncomfortable with that. They might not know what I did wrong, but they'd know I did something wrong, and what if they decided to keep it? Who could tell? I didn't want any investigation and that there. I didn't leave it there. I took it out and put it in a Channel Island account and bought counterfeit money with some of it. I had money all over the place, Charlie. I bought Canadian mining stocks, too. One time after I bought this gold mine stock, the Canadian government put a road right through the middle of it, and the mine paid me several times what I bought it for. I had all that stock in a garbage can, I had so much of it. I was now making money doing everything legal. I opened a second banking account in Canada, in case I was ever investigated. That one, I only put a little bit of money in. That way, I didn't have to lie. If anyone investigated me and asked, 'Do you have any bank account in Canada?' I'd say yes and show them that one."

Walt snickered and said again, "Fuck, I had money all over the place."

And then he said something I had nearly forgotten about: "If you and Art hadn't taught me to parachute jump, I'd still be the Royal Oak barber, flat busted."

CHAPTER 13

CONTROVERSIES & CONFLICTING REPORTS ABOUT THE D.B. COOPER HIJACKING

I don't have all the answers, but I have most of them. And what I did, by finding Cowboy—rather, Jeff Osiadacz—was better than anything the FBI had managed.

It's unbelievable today, but it took the FBI until December 8, 1971, to distribute the serial numbers of the bills given to Cooper, so that banks could trace them.[50] The FBI sent the information by U.S. mail, and it might not have reached some banks for a couple of weeks. The Reno police, instead of the FBI, conducted the search of the plane when it landed, and they botched it, not even collecting the magazines Cooper had thumbed through or some of the other evidence.

50　When the FBI began to circulate the serial numbers of the hijacked money, they were at a distinct disadvantage. The bills were previously circulated $20s, most of them minted in 1968. The serial numbers were not sequential, and without computers, each bill would have to be examined individually and manually matched up to the pages and pages of bills used. In addition, the life expectancy of a $20 bill is two to three years. When the bills are taken out of circulation, they are not examined for serial numbers, only to see if they are counterfeit. Only if someone makes a large purchase using only $20 bills would banks be likely to check them against the extensive list.

The Flight Path

There are mistakes everywhere in this case. The FBI first stated that Cooper had jumped near Portland—whether they believed that or simply wanted the public to believe it, who knows? In addition, First Officer Bill Rataczak, who took over from Captain Bill Scott for that leg of the flight, said that the hijacker jumped close to Portland. I believe that Rataczak was coerced into giving that information.

In his 1971 FBI report, "Rataczak stated that approximately 5 to 10 minutes after the last contact with the subject at 8:05 p.m., they heard and felt an oscillation of the aircraft and commented at the time that the hijacker could have departed, causing the unusual vibration since there had been no change in altitude, speed or any other external force which would account for this sudden oscillation. They telephoned the company representative, Paul Soderlind, in Minneapolis shortly thereafter, and stated that the oscillation, which could have been the hijacker's departure, would have occurred between 8:05 p.m. and their call to Soderlind 5 or 10 minutes later, the exact time which would be recorded in the company log. Rataczak stated that they had not yet reached Portland proper but were definitely in the suburbs or immediate vicinity thereof."[51]

Then in a 2012 speech, Rataczak said, "Tina comes into the cockpit. She said, 'I told him how to open the door and lower the stairs.' . . . at about 20 miles, 28 miles north of Portland—well, a little before that. First of all, he started jiggering with the door, he got the door open, and he was trying to get the stairs down. So he called up front and said, "I can't get the stairs down." And I said, "Well, stand by for just a minute.' So I called Paul [Soderlind] and said, 'Paul, he can't get the stairs down. . . . we're limited by speed at about 175

---

51   From FBI eyewitness report of First Officer William John (Bill) Rataczak on December 1, 1971, by SAC Harold El. Campbell Jr. and SA H.E. Hinderliter Jr., File LV 164-60-158.

knots, pretty close to 200 mph, because that's what he wanted. . . . What can we do to help him get out of here?' And he said, 'Slow the airplane down to your approach speed . . . and that'll give you a little less wind flow, air flow, back there, and then he'll be able to open 'em.' So that's what we did. . . . We saw the 'door open' light come on in the second officer's panel. . . . We were operating unpressurized, and there's a light there that when that needle goes to 10,000 feet of rapid descent, you get the same feeling, and it's analogous to when you've driven down the road at highway speed, 60–70 miles an hour, and you lower the window and then raise it and you feel that bump in your ears. That's the same thing we got. I got on the horn to air traffic control and I said, 'I think our friend just took leave of us. Mark it down on your . . . radar screen.' Why was this important? Because once Paul Soderlind figured out the winds prevailing at that time, he could track out an area where the hijacker would've or could have landed. . . . And that could be a pretty big area. The area would take into consideration when he jumped, did he open the chute immediately, which would take a longer float-down time, and he would cover more distance, or did the chute not open at all and he bore a hole in the ground somewhere? Paul did all the math on that, with his abacas and his slide rule."[52]

Then, in 1980, after a small portion of the money was found at Tena Bar—an area not on that flight path—authorities started changing their tune. Years later, the lead FBI investigator is on record saying they had searched the wrong location—this after defending the initial location reports for many years. No wonder it's a mystery that's never been solved.

Although I personally believe the FBI already knew the identity of Cooper and that they planned to feed misinformation to the public

---

52   See the videotape of a speech given to Northwest employees by First Officer Bill Rataczak at the Northwest Airlines Museum in Minneapolis in 2012.

as a diversion, I'm open to another possibility: maybe the FBI was simply inept, succumbing to the "corporate think" that's endemic to every large organization. At the time, the FBI was an agency in disarray. Their director and the agency at large were under attack for their complicity in how they investigated antiwar activities, the Pentagon Papers had been leaked earlier that year, and the agency was involved in trying to quell the civil rights movement. In baseball, it's easier to hit a fastball than a curveball. The FBI was still hitting fastballs, but this case was the ultimate curveball. It was unlike any other hijacking in history.

As an example of poor decision making, on the night of the hijacking two jets and one helicopter were scrambled to follow the plane. But the jets they chose could not fly slow enough to keep pace with the plane, and the helicopter was too slow. It was like bringing both an atomic bomb and a knife to a gunfight: overkill or underkill. Neither was effective.

In addition, the FBI has a command structure that sometimes prevents the truth from being told. So they either know more than they are saying, or they were ill-equipped to conduct this particular investigation. There has to be a reason they are still defending a route that was approximately sixty miles from where the plane actually flew.

Here's my take on this—there were only two ways the plane got to Cle Elum: either someone told First Officer Rataczak to fly there, or the crew decided to go there. No amount of confusion in the cockpit would lead them east. Rataczak was the pilot and knew where he was the entire time. The only logical explanation is that the diversion by the intelligence community had to happen immediately, while the plane was at Sea-Tac. Walter Cronkite reported the route to Portland that night.

I recently interviewed a commercial airlines pilot, Jeff Wierenga, about some inconsistencies in the D.B. Cooper case. I asked Wierenga why Sacramento would dictate the flight route, as FBI agent Larry

Carr stated.[53] Wierenga said that this wouldn't make any sense because Seattle was the regional FAA hub. He further explained that the Sacramento airport has a very restricted air control, unless you're talking about the huge U.S. Air Force base located there. When I worked for Zantop, I routinely flew into that base.

Jeff Wierenga brought up another interesting point: that with radar being "line of sight," a plane flying out of Seattle at 10,000 feet would get lost, on and off, from the radar screen. This would mean the airplane was lost several times during the fifteen minutes or so after takeoff it needed to find its Victor.[54]

I went to Washington State on June 8, 2013, in search of Cowboy and the Cooper parachute, but I now have reason to believe the FBI recovered the chute on the morning of November 25th, 1971. I have no direct evidence that the FBI found it, but it was lying in plain sight, covered by only a few branches and able to be seen from the air within a half-mile of the airport at Cle Elum. Maybe it's better to ask, "How could it *not* be found?"

Of course, it's possible a local person found it: a kid snatching it to build a fort, an adult who wanted to use the material for a household project; even someone who wanted the chute as a souvenir.

Yet if I play devil's advocate, even with my own theory, then why would the FBI insist that Cooper landed near Portland, if they'd found the parachute at his actual landing spot? Was this all part of the diversion to keep Walt's identity secret?

---

53 January 28, 2008, 11:13 a.m., Post #1473: "Neither requested Victor 23. The pilots and NWA flight operations wanted to fly out to the coast and were waiting for clearance to do so. It was not until just before takeoff that they were cleared through Sacramento via Victor 23." (From a series of messages Carr posted to a skydiving group, www.dropzone.com, under the name CKRET.)

54 Victor airways are like highways in the sky. Before GPS, all planes followed Victor (pronounced "vector") airways and virtually flew from radar tower to radar tower. This was what kept planes from colliding (most of the time).

Finding Cowboy helped me focus on the plane's route, and the route is the whole enchilada. The D.B. Cooper airplane actually flew east out of Seattle. That is how Walt landed near Cle Elum. That route was deemed the safest place to drop a hostage, had Walt taken one—but Walt said that was never in his plan. Still, the FBI, the FAA, and Northwest Orient had to consider the possibility. They also had to account for the bomb on board. The east route toward Cle Elum avoided all population centers, unlike the southern route, which passed over Tacoma, Olympia, Vancouver, and Portland. The crew, who lived in Washington, stated that they had the final say, and I maintain that they took the east route over Cle Elum, then later gave erroneous information by saying the flight path went over Portland.[55]

The alleged route to Portland was never a possibility. To tell everyone that they flew directly south to Portland, the FBI should have the parachute in their possession. In 1971, all airliners were equipped with DME, Distance Measuring Equipment, which tells you right where you are or, in this case, where the hijacker jumped. That's not to say they knew where he landed, but if they knew the way the wind was blowing, thus the amount of drift, they could come very close to determining the spot. I suspect that the FBI, with the aid of one or two search planes, had that parachute by 10 a.m. the next morning. They're smarter than we are. That's why we haven't found D.B. Cooper yet. Well, at least you haven't.

I had a secret weapon. D.B. Cooper helped me out.

---

55 From FBI eyewitness report of First Officer William John (Bill) Rataczak on December 1, 1971, by SAC Harold El. Campbell Jr. and SA H.E. Hinderliter Jr., File LV 164-60-158. Also, in the interview my publisher conducted with commercial airlines pilot Jeff Wierenga on September 15, 2017, Wierenga says that the only direction flights travel out of Seattle is east, unless they are headed due south, generally over the ocean. He sees no other logical route to Reno than the one I discovered. Wierenga has been flying with major airline companies for thirty years, and he is convinced that Walt Peca was D.B. Cooper.

When Did the Authorities Identify Walt as Cooper?

Over the decades, my theory changed about when the authorities actually knew Walt had pulled off the Cooper hijacking. During one early phone conversation, Walt and I talked about what I called his "dark years."

"When those two guys met you in that bar and said, 'You work for us now,' I was always under the impression that they got you from the Teamsters, rather than for the other thing you did, you know?" (I was trying not to spook Walt so avoided the word *hijacking*.)

"Yeah," Walt said.

"I mean, I couldn't prove either one of 'em, but I just always thought that it would be easier to catch you for the Teamster thing because there were a lot more people involved with the Teamsters, where the other was a one-man deal."

"Yeah," Walt agreed.

"And if they didn't catch you right there doing it, there was nobody to rat on you, nobody to squeal. That's just my thinking, you know. In other words, if they didn't catch you when you did that other one, then how the hell would they catch you? . . . You know what I'm saying?"

"Yeah."

"How would they trace—"

"I don't even think about it, Charlie. . . .That's the problem. If you start thinking about things like that, you'd never go to sleep at night."

Yet as time passed, I began to suspect that the FBI had known much earlier that Walt was D.B. Cooper.

Why was Walt, now D.B. Cooper, never caught? I'm not sure. The bank in Vancouver should have been suspicious. An American stranger, limping, putting a very large sum of money (into an account or a safe deposit box) in a Canadian bank. It also could have been his CIA friend Phil Q who suspected it was Walt, and his tip was escalated to a level of authority that could insist on letting Walt go. Phil personally knew Walt, knew what he looked like. I think Walt had been identified as D. B. Cooper pretty quickly.

Walt told me he used his real name to put the money into a Canadian bank, but which real name? His only traceable name was "Walt R. Peca," but at this time he was doing everything he could to avoid using it. He experimented with using Reca, Recca, and Pecca and eventually decided on Reca. Back in 1971, maybe banks didn't do extensive background checks on their depositors, and this was in the pre-digital age, when they had little technology.

Yet somehow, I think the intelligence agencies found out Walt was the hijacker and then sent operatives who threatened him with going to prison.

His plane ticket to Boise, Idaho, was the start of two years of training and interrogations. For example, they would have Walt walk through a room, then afterward be required to describe the location of exit openings, hiding places, possible weapons, and so on.

After his first assignment in Scotland, Walt returned to the States, to Carla and his kids in their new house. He continued to work iron at various sites in the United States and Canada. His training ended in June 1975, when he was sent to Kharg Island, Iran. He worked there until December 1975, then he returned to the States just one day before Iran took hostages and held them for one year.

I think it's very possible that someone in the intelligence community, probably Phillip Q, actually knew Walt was the hijacker before the plane left Sea-Tac (Seattle-Tacoma International Airport). The disinformation that the authorities made public about this hijacking started immediately with the wrong flight path. I believe that the intelligence community decided they needed Walt free so that he could be fully indoctrinated into their projects. We all know that the FBI, the CIA, or the ATF routinely "call off" police actions on small criminals in order to track larger targets. Joe Koenig calls it interfering for the "Common Good." Joe Koenig, CFE (Certified Fraud Examiner), is the owner of KMI Investigations and the author of *Getting the Truth*. He was the lead investigator on the Jimmy Hoffa case for the Michigan police. Similar to "Common Good," I've read about incidents where the CIA overruled the FBI for the "greater good."[56]

The Common Good would explain why the actual flight path selected was dictated from Sacramento, California, overriding the flight crew and Sea-Tac. I have no idea why the orders would come from Sacramento—except for the fact that Mather Air Force Base was located 12 miles east of Sacramento.[57] Otherwise, it's a very odd location because the FAA control towers in Portland and Sea-Tac are much larger.

Phil Q had already been heavily involved in getting Walt a job with Vinnell Corp in January, prior to the hijacking. Phil was certainly Walt's handler in whatever agency he worked for. Walt was already on the payroll of a known front corporation for the intelligence community. This provides a line of logic that he was being monitored for possible placement well before the hijacking. There is good reason to think that he was being watched pretty closely, if they had the intention to use him in the near future.

---

56   Joe Koenig, *Getting the Truth* (published 2014; 2016 Montaigne Medal Award Finalist, 2016 Indie General Non-Fiction Award Finalist). Also see *Wedge: The Secret War between the FBI and the CIA*, by Mark Riebling, which describes one case in 1969 where the FBI confronted a man, Ne'eman, with evidence that he'd been spying in the United States. Quoting from the book: "Horrified, Ne'eman contacted Mossad's station chief in Washington, D.C., and asked for help. The station chief decided to circumvent the FBI by appealing to the CIA. A few days later, Angleton suggested to William Sullivan that it would be in the U.S. national interest if the Bureau left Ne'eman alone. Angleton was negotiating an expanded U.S.-Israeli intelligence cooperation deal, he said, and he didn't want the Bureau's hounding of Ne'eman to put that arrangement at risk. Papich relayed the message and the FBI backed off, but Hoover was furious."

57   Mather Air Force Base was closed in 1993.

He was probably acting erratic, possibly depressed, and drew their attention by buying weird clothing and items, renting a typewriter, and sending his family away for the holiday. Walt couldn't exactly hide from view in tiny Hartline. Or perhaps his supervisor at Vinnell suspected something, and when he heard news of the hijacking, he made a report to his higher-ups.

Maybe the hijacking made the CIA or the FBI move quickly to get Walt fully integrated. The misdirection of the flight path makes no sense whatsoever without the intervention of the FBI or the CIA.

I do believe that Walt went rogue on them with the hijacking. I don't have any evidence, except for the fact that according to Special Agent Larry Carr, the course was dictated from Sacramento, which, according to the pilots we spoke with, was highly unlikely because the flight path barely entered the Sacramento air space on either route, if it did at all.

Carr said, "Neither requested Victor 23. The pilot and NWA flight operations wanted to fly out to the coast and were waiting for clearance to do so. It was not until just before takeoff that they were cleared through Sacramento via Victor 23."[58]

Using Victor 23 is contrary to the normal flight path around Sea-Tac, where planes typically arrive along the route from Portland and depart east around Mt. Rainier, then proceed to their destination.

According to my calculations, the flight initially headed on the routine flight path east toward Ellensburg on Victor 2, which passes directly over Cle Elum. The plane then continued on V25 toward Yakima.

---

58 In 2008, Agent Carr opened up a dialogue with a group of primarily skydivers on an online public forum/message board, with the theme of solving the D.B. Cooper hijacking. On December 28, 2008, Carr responded to a question by giving the above information about Victor 23. (From a series of messages Carr posted to a skydiving group, www.dropzone.com, under the name CKRET.)

The remainder of the flight path is based on my experience as a pilot, which is confirmed by other commercial pilots and matches the notes contemporaneously written by Northwest Orient employee George Harrison from the tower at Sea-Tac on the night of the hijacking.

The flight crew was informed by the FBI profiler that he believed that Cooper would take a hostage with him and would detonate the bomb as he exited. As a pilot in that position, I would be worried about avoiding any mountains in excess of 9,000 feet so that I could remain at the 10,000 feet required by Cooper, finding a safe drop area for a potential hostage, and locating a possible landing airport for my 727 in the event of an emergency.

My preferred route would be to go straight to Yakima, then head directly south; however, there are no airports on the flight path between Yakima and Reno where I could land a plane the size of a 727.

My choice—and the choice of most other pilots—would be to put as many airports in my path as possible, while considering the other restrictions.

This route would direct me on a familiar Victor used by general aviation flights to Portland, V448. Once near Portland, I would take V23 south through Medford directly to Red Bluff, then head to Reno via V332 and V200.

The route from Portland to Reno matches the path handwritten by Harrison and confirmed by multiple radar "pings" that night.

Agent Carr came on the case years after the hijacking, so we don't know whether he was misinformed or still trying to convey the FBI's original statement to the public: that the flight followed Victor 23, as dictated by Sacramento.

I discovered the *actual* flight path along Victor 2 from my interviews with Walt: the route that Walt said Don Brennan took to pick him up, the route they drove back to Walt's house in Hartline. And locating Cowboy finalized the connection to that route out of Seattle.

My theory on *why* the flight path was diverted to Victor 25 considers the circumstantial evidence: the parachute not being recovered, the slow release of the serial numbers, the FBI not being involved in the crime scene, and so on. And why was that route dictated by Sacramento significant? Maybe to ensure that their man survived?

For me, this all points to immediate misdirection by the FBI.

What other explanation would seem reasonable for misleading the public about the route, if they really wanted to catch him?

Yet I'll offer the opposite theory just to be balanced: it's possible the pilots made a decision on their own to veer from the designated flight path. Back then, pilots did this all the time, as proved by the number of mid-air collisions that occurred. If you look up the FAA investigations of these crashes, you'll see that they relied on visual identification by pilots. This implies that the FAA's system of tracking planes had a lot of flaws, if they blamed many air crashes on loss of visual identification by pilots. I think the whole Victor system had problems, especially because pilots in the cockpit were allowed to change their course under special situations. According to the FAA, "At all times, whether in the air or on the ground, whether at the gate or taxiing, the pilot-in-command (PIC) has final and ultimate responsibility for the safe operation of the aircraft. Per ICAO Annex 2 [with similar statements/definitions by individual civil authorities]." In other words, the pilots ultimately decided which path to take.

While the FAA could track from the ground, the technology of the era (and even now) is not as precise as they say. Note how many airliners go down worldwide and are never found. If they were that good at tracking flights, they would never lose an aircraft's location—

that is, no airliner would ever be difficult to find after it crashes. This has been proved time and again to be totally false.

So, yes, the FBI might have dictated the flight path, but that decision might also have been made by a flight crew—or maybe the flight crew was so distracted trying to prevent the airplane from crashing while keeping it under 10,000 feet that they flew by the seat of their pants to keep from hitting a mountain, thus wandering into the ultimate drop zone where Walt landed. Yes, it could have been a conspiracy, but it also could have been a pilot trying to save his plane and paying little attention to his exact location at all times. These are all theories I offer but don't necessarily believe.

Yet this still doesn't explain why First Officer Rataczak said in his 1971 FBI report that the hijacker jumped near Portland.[59]

As a pilot, I sometimes try to imagine what Rataczak experienced when flying Flight 305 from Seattle to Reno. Only a minute or two after takeoff, he would have realized he had a problem other than D.B. Cooper: that problem was ice. In spite of a modern bleed air system to remove ice, enough of it was sticking to the aluminum to make a difference.

And the configuration the hijacker requested was even worse. He ordered that the airplane be flown with the gear down. The good thing was, the airplane was empty, or what we refer to as empty, when it had just five people and four parachutes. Climbing to 10,000 feet, even with the gear down, takes the 727 only minutes, but First Officer Rataczak made a wise decision. As Rataczak leveled off at 10,000, per Walt's request, he was hand-flying, not on autopilot as usual. The temperature at 10,000 feet was 17 degrees F, with rain moderate to heavy. That meant ice to an airplane already in a dirty

---

59   See FBI eyewitness report of First Officer William John (Bill) Rataczak on December 1, 1971, by SAC Harold El. Campbell Jr. and SA H.E. Hinderliter Jr., File LV 164-60-158.

configuration.[60] Pretty soon, Walt would be lowering the stairs for his exit, and that would increase drag on that airplane, which was already in a precarious situation. The crew's main concern was a stall, not Walt with his bomb. In addition, First Officer Rataczak later said he was skeptical that it was a real bomb and often repeated that the bomb actually consisted of dynamite or road flares.[61]

First Officer Rataczak said, "Paul [Soderlind] had the chief test pilot and the chief design engineer on the hotline from Seattle all the way to Minneapolis . . . and we wanted to know . . . what is gonna happen when those stairs come down in flight? . . . Jack Wydell, the chief pilot, said, 'What's going to happen is your nose is going to lower about 3 to 5 degrees. . . . And he wanted us to go at 10,000 feet—now that's near sea level. [He gestures.] This is sea level, this is Sea-Tac, and this is the Cascade Mountain Range. So 10,000 feet above sea level is not 10,000 feet above the ground. And any map will show you that we were probably anywhere from 5 to 7 or 8—9,000 feet above the mountains, but we were in a safe area because it was an airway, and there's so many miles on each side that are protected."[62]

Rataczak did whatever he could to prevent the worst thing that could happen: an outright stall, which would be fatal. The only possible survivor then would be Cooper, because he would already be standing outside on the stairs, prepared to jump. Had that airplane gone into a full stall, which the crew tried their utmost to prevent, it would have whipped upside-down, violently throwing Cooper off the stairs. But if he managed to pull his ripcord, he probably would have survived. Not the crew, though, no matter who was flying, and

---

60 A dirty configuration refers to flying with the gear down, the flaps down, the slats up, the landing gear down, and in this case, toward the end of the flight, even with the aft stairs down. That creates a lot of drag on the plane.

61 See videotape of a speech given to Northwest employees by First Officer Bill Rataczak at the Northwest Airlines Museum in Minneapolis in 2012.

62 Ibid.

Rataczak knew that. Thus, the hand-flying, so he could feel that first shake of the stick or the wheel. At that point, it would be nose down, full power, gear up, save the airplane, and don't worry whether the bomb is real or fake. All of that would be of no consequence if the airplane crashed.

First Officer Rataczak confirmed that their biggest concern once the plane was airborne was icing—and not the hijacker—because his demands meant they had to fly in dirty air.[63] Rataczak said, " . . . we went to 10,000 feet. And unfortunately, that was where the cloud layer was. Now temperature reduces about 3 degrees per 1,000 feet. . . It was 38 degrees on the ground, I think, so at 10,000 feet the temperature's gonna drop about . . . 30 degrees. So we were certainly below the freezing point. . . . One of the ways we were able to tell how much ice was building up on the wings was what's building up on that center post between the captain's . . . windscreen and my windscreen. And we were getting . . . about two inches of rime ice. And that doesn't do much for the smooth flow of the way the wing was designed. So we were concerned about that. But he wanted to be at 10,000 feet, so we had all the de-icing and what have you on."

In 1980, Rataczak changed his story about the plane's route: he told the lead FBI investigator (at the agent's retirement party) that the FBI had the wrong flight path and that they were east of the FBI's drop zone— thus contradicting the testimony he gave in his 1971 FBI report.[64] To further muddy the waters about who decided Flight 305's route from Seattle, in 2012 First Officer Rataczak said in a speech before a packed house at the Northwest Airlines Museum in Minneapolis that the crew contacted the head of the airline to state that they, not the FBI, were in

---

63   Ibid.
64   FBI eyewitness report of First Officer William John (Bill) Rataczak on December 1, 1971, by SAC Harold El. Campbell Jr. and SA H.E. Hinderliter Jr., File LV 164-60-158.

charge of the airplane. In other words, there was far more confusion during the hijacking than the FBI admits. Yet this claim about being in charge could be bravado on Rataczak's part because if the FBI tells you to go someplace, you go there.

First Officer Rataczak said, "Paul Soderlind, director of flight path operations, he put things in action. Paul set up a command base in [Bill? Phil? Hochman's] office. . . . [the hijacker] never came to the cockpit and that was a break for us because we could openly discuss what we wanted to do or what we think we should do, what's his demeanor—his demeanor was generally pretty calm. There were a couple of times when he got very upset and threatened to touch the two wires [of the bomb]. . . . So we felt like we had somebody that we could deal with, and whatever he wants, we're gonna give it to him. So I called Minneapolis again and I asked Paul Soderlind, 'What I want from you, Paul, is to tell Mr. Nyrop that we want his word that he will not allow any outside intervention—FBI, county sheriff's deputies, whatever.' We wanted to handle this our own way. And if we needed help, we'd call for it. [Note: Nyrop was the CEO of Northwest Orient and went on to become head of the predecessor agency of the National Transportation Safety Board (NTSB).] Paul said, 'Mr. Nyrop is here, and he heard what you said, and you've got his word that they will not interfere.' So, they did anyway."[65]

I include all of the previous statements to show that there are multiple versions of who made the flight selection. I can make a case for the opposing comments of both sides: the FBI and the only remaining survivor of the in-flight cockpit crew, First Officer Rataczak.

But if the FBI is so cocksure of their route, why haven't they been able to find any evidence along an eight-mile-wide path after

---

65   Videotape of a speech given to Northwest employees by First Officer Bill
      Rataczak at the Northwest Airlines Museum in Minneapolis in 2012.

forty-six years? Is it a misdirection on their part, incompetence, or something else? If they were right about the flight path, they would have solved the case within days of the hijacking.

I am an ex–airline pilot who flew mountainous routes in the Western United States. You will never convince me that the flight crew flew at 10,000 feet in an area of mountains higher than 10,000 feet and one as high as 14,000 feet, without knowing their position at all times. That's what the FBI wants us to believe. As soon as that airplane touched the runway in Reno and everyone knew Cooper had jumped, the FBI would have taken the "flight plan" of Flight 305 on Northwest Orient Airlines, a standard form, so they would know where to search for D.B. Cooper. That would have been the time to get that information, not one month or five years or thirty years later. No other explanation works for me.

What do I believe? I believe 100 percent that the FBI did get the flight plan and told the crew never to tell. And I believe that the FBI found the D.B. Cooper parachute the very next day. With that chute in their possession and knowing that D.B. Cooper had survived, the FBI knew that nobody could challenge any route they announced or dispute whether D.B. Cooper was dead or alive—except D.B. Cooper himself.

The real reason the FBI claimed the plane flew directly south toward Portland was that it fit their narrative. They could not let a million people with high-powered rifles run through the woods looking for a man with $200,000 in tax-free dollars, so they had to divert the public's attention to another location.

I think that the intelligence community had already designated Walt as potentially being useful to them, so they didn't want to "out" him. I'll even go out on a limb and say that his successful hijacking of Flight 305 added an impressive accomplishment to his résumé. It showed that he could take on this daring feat without cracking, losing control, failing, or getting caught—exactly the type of person who would excel as a covert operative.

I estimate that Walt jumped around 8:10 p.m. and landed near Cle Elum about a half mile from Teanaway Junction Café. This was along Victor 2 airway, which goes east 88 degrees out of Sea-Tac. The plane's actual path was a difference of only 2 degrees from due east (due east is 90 degrees)—a long way from the route the FBI *claimed* the plane took. This route quickly passes over the Cascade Mountains and arrives at a flat high plains area before crossing over the U.S. military training center. The FBI obviously believed that Walt had a bomb on board and that he was taking a hostage because he ordered four parachutes. This is the only route that makes sense, meets the time line, and passes over where all the people meet—the Teanaway Junction Café. And it's the only place where Cooper's parachute could have been recovered.

Professional pilots tell me that the first option with a bomb on board would be to go over the ocean, never over a heavily populated area; however, the possibility of landing this aircraft partly disabled from a detonated bomb would dictate flying near larger airports. With the threat of a hostage jumping, too, the ocean would be out. Getting the plane away from a populated area and toward a flat landing area for a jumper would be a priority. The FBI's stated route, Vector 23, did neither.

According to First Officer Bill Rataczak, when the plane approached Sea-Tac, the airport initially wanted the plane to go into a holding pattern five miles out, over a residential area. This implies that at first, the authorities didn't understand the magnitude of having a live bomb aboard an aircraft, and the crew alerted the tower that it would be best to circle over water. So, instead, they went into a holding pattern over Puget Sound for more than an hour.[66]

---

66 Videotape of a speech given to Northwest employees by First Officer Bill Rataczak at the Northwest Airlines Museum in Minneapolis in 2012.

Rataczak also revealed that all of the airways (his word for Victor) had been cleared of other traffic. Rataczak said, "So we kept going to Reno, and we had to make a long, slow descent because we were unpressurized. And, uh, we had the run of the airways. . . . We got into Reno, approached control, and we got clearance to descend and land. [Note that Captain Scott took over for the landing.] . . . [When the stairs came down] I was hand-flying it at the time. . . . You don't want to see my flight path because it looked like connect the dots. But we weren't concerned about that because we knew we were at a safe altitude and air traffic control was watching us."[67] That leads to him saying that they didn't need to be as concerned about where the airplane was at any one time and this allowed them to concentrate on meeting the hijacker's demands, along with the immediate concerns of icing.

So if it wasn't a diversion by the FBI to switch from Victor 23 to Victor 2, then the pilots in the cockpit, knowing the dangers of flying over mountains and population centers such as Portland, might have taken it upon themselves to modify the route. There are two possibilities: one arguing for diversion and the other arguing for logic. The reader can choose from two explanations.

The FBI agent assigned to the case from Portland, Ralph P. Himmelsbach, wrote in 1986 that the drop zone where Cooper should have landed had been wrong, possibly by as much as eighty degrees. "We'd probably spent a hell of a lot of money and manpower searching the wrong area."

It was estimated that the temperature was less than –10 degrees F at 10,000 feet, with heavy cloud cover and freezing rain on the ground.

Is it not illogical to say that Flight 305 took off from Seattle Sea-Tac at 7:36 p.m. flying south toward Portland, Cooper jumped out a little

---

67   Ibid.

after 8:10, and was first sighted at 8:25 on Highway 97 around 225 miles away from the Portland area in a different direction? By 8:50, Walt had been seen by two people, one still living and one dead.[68] The living one, Jeff Osiadacz a.k.a. "Cowboy," told Don Brennan by phone where to pick up Cooper and what route to take. Don drove to the junction of Highway 970 and Highway 10, picked up Walt, and took him home. Only Don knew Walt was D.B. Cooper. They'd first met in Fairbanks, Alaska, in 1958. Both were ex-airborne paratroopers. Both worked for a time at Zantop Airlines, where Walt got Don a job. Both were ironworkers and very good friends, as well as drinking buddies. So Don would not have needed a picture of Walt to know he was D.B. Cooper. Don knew Walt as well as I did. I flew for Zantop for ten years, all of the time both Don and Walt worked there. The FBI said there are no pictures of D.B. Cooper. I've got lots of pictures of D.B. Cooper.

"You don't have any pictures of D.B. Cooper," is what the FBI should have said. I'll guarantee that they have his picture as well. The U.S. government put lots of Walt's photos on his passports after 1974.

Truly, though, Helen Chambers, the waitress, and Cowboy did not know the identity of the stranger they both met the night Walt fell into Cle Elum and sat in the Teanaway Junction Café, waiting for Don to pick him up. Helen died never knowing, and Cowboy identified D.B. Cooper by a picture I sent him. I actually sent two pictures, but one was D.B. Cooper at age seventy-eight. Cowboy never would have been able to identify Cooper by that one.

Conflicting Eyewitness Testimony

Although many facts about the hijacking have been confirmed by multiple sources, conflicting reports exist about some details. Eyewitness reports are notoriously unreliable. Probably because

---

68 The waitress, Helen Chambers, is deceased.

the Flight 305 stewardesses were under such stress, some of their testimony conflicted with other crewmembers'—and with what Walt told me.

For example, the FBI reported certain evidence being left behind by the hijacker: a towel from the back of the hijacker's seat with a brown limb hair, a clip-on tie and a tie pin, the contents of an ashtray (eight cigarette butts, Raleigh 8mm filter tips), but only two parachutes: one intact main parachute and one orange chest (reserve) parachute with three of the *shrouds* (an old term for "suspension lines") being cut, apparently by the hijacker. The reserve chute had been opened and removed from its packing. What happened to the second reserve chute, the one Walt discovered was a dummy? In a phone conversation, Walt told me he threw it out of the plane.

In 2012, during the Q & A period after a speech by First Officer Rataczak, someone asked what happened to the other three parachutes. Rataczak said, "He opened up one of the parachutes and took the shroud line and apparently tied the money bag around his waist or somewhere around him, and so that parachute was inop. But it was inop in the first place because it was a training chute. The fellow at McChord Air Force Base had used it—you know those long tables they put parachutes on—and he had used it as an example, how to pack a parachute. He had sewn all the panels together, so it would have been 32 feet per second per second [Rataczak repeats 'per second'] when Cooper decided to jump out of the airplane. . . . Terminal velocity. . . . So they did in fact send a bad parachute." A follow-up question asked, "Did McChord intentionally send a bad parachute and why?" Rataczak said, "I can't tell you for sure, but my gut feeling is that they did it on purpose. I don't know that for sure, but I'm guessing they did."[69]

---

69   See the videotape of a speech given to Northwest employees by First Officer
     Bill Rataczak at the Northwest Airlines Museum in Minneapolis in 2012,
     which conflicts a bit with Agent Carr's explanation of the dummy chute in the
     following note.

Rataczak's 2012 statement conflicts with a comment made years after the hijacking by FBI agent Larry Carr, who said, "The good reserve he tore apart was found on the aircraft along with another back pack. The dummy reserve was not found." And, "The agent who originally interviewed Cossey mistakenly reported it was sewn shut. It was not sewn shut, the canopy was cut in half and the panels then sewn together. This was done so that when students practiced deploying the emergency canopy, they could easily gather it and quickly stuff it back in the container for another practice throw."[70]

In another taped phone conversation between me and Walt, he mentioned that after landing, he partly stuffed the parachute into the backpack and covered it with branches. This refers to the backpack he wore that contained the chute he jumped with. Yet he didn't mention what happened to the bank bag after he landed. Personally, I think he kept the money in it and then bundled his raincoat around that, before walking to the café. It would have been too hard to keep loose bundles of money together with only the raincoat holding them together—much easier to leave the money in the bank bag. Which means he probably disposed of the bank bag somewhere after he got home. I regret that I didn't think to ask Walt about this when he was alive.

Another issue was the ransom note. Walt told me in several phone calls that he'd rented a typewriter from a stationery shop and typed one note and wrote the other in a calligraphy style that he had practiced. Stewardesses Flo and Tina described a handwritten note, which made me believe that he either used the calligraphy note or, more likely, wrote a third note after he found himself sitting alone in the back row with few passengers around. So he needed to instruct a stewardess to sit next to him.

---

70   From a series of messages Carr posted to a skydiving group, www.dropzone. com, under the name CKRET.

Theories about the Money Found on Tena Bar

In 1980, $5,800 of the ransom money (290 bills) was found on Tena Bar, a sandy shore of the Columbia River near Vancouver, Washington, more than twenty miles from Lake Merwin. The money, though deteriorated and water logged, was still bundled together. More than $194,000, or 9,700 bills, from the ransom have never been recovered.

A big question remains: how did the packets of bank money show up on Tena Bar, still intact, bundled in rubber bands that were unbroken and barely corroded? I never could drag any info out of Walt or Don Brennan about this. What happened to the money Walt said he gave Don on the night of the hijacking? Don refused to talk about that night for the rest of his life, afraid he'd end up in the penitentiary.

If Walt gave the money to Don Brennan, as he told me, then maybe Don, either with someone else or by himself, drove the eighty or so miles down I-5 from his home in Olympia to bury the money in Tena Bar, the place where it was found—which was really close to the highway. First Officer Rataczak mentioned that Dwayne Ingram, the stepfather of the boy, Brian, who found the money, was a fugitive.[71] I tried to track down whether he was a friend of Don's, but no luck. With Don being such a shady character, though, it seems plausible.

Two ex-FBI agents, Bernie Rhodes and Russell P. Calame, presented an alternate theory in a book called *D.B. Cooper: The Real McCoy*.[72] In it, they state that Cooper was really Richard McCoy, the man who had also hijacked United Airlines flight 855 on April 7, 1972, and parachuted out of the plane near Provo, Utah. Karen McCoy, the

---

71 Videotape of a speech given to Northwest employees by First Officer Bill Rataczak at the Northwest Airlines Museum in Minneapolis in 2012.
72 Bernie Rhodes and Russell Calame, *D.B. Cooper: The Real McCoy* (Salt Lake City, Utah: University of Utah Press, 1991).

slain hijacker's widow, admitted in court that she had helped her husband prepare for the UA hijacking. Yet she and her family denied that her husband had committed the 1971 hijacking of Northwest Orient Flight 305, and when these two FBI agents published their book, she filed a lawsuit against the authors, saying that their book defamed her.

There are a few similarities between Walt and Richard McCoy, who also was an army veteran and an avid parachutist. Someone might jump to the conclusion that McCoy had done both hijackings, as Rhodes assumed. But even more likely is that McCoy was a copycat: he read about the Cooper hijacking and realized that with his skill set, he could do the same thing—with the United Airlines flight a few months later, which had also been designed with a rear door stairway near the tail.

Central to Agent Rhodes's theory was the idea of the Cooper hijacking money floating unprotected downstream and being discovered nearly nine years later with rubber bands on it. Yet when Tina, the stewardess, first saw the money, she said it was in bank bands (which are made of paper). In addition, a 1971 FBI memorandum stated that the packets of bills "were banded with Seattle First National Bank or Federal Reserve Bank bands."[73] And in his 2012 speech to the Northwest Airlines Museum in Minneapolis, First Officer Rataczak also said that the money was in paper bank bands. So, how did the money found at Tena Bar get rebound in rubber bands? The FBI has no answer for this.

And how was the money still pretty much intact? These FBI agents believed it was not possible, unless the money was protected by the bank bag. They thought the bank bag disintegrated shortly before the money was found, but, of course, they didn't know anything about the fact that Walt tied the bank bag around his neck

---

73   FBI memorandum dated December 2, 1971.

(so the found money couldn't have been in that bag) and that Walt said he had been picked up at the café by Don Brennan and he had paid off Don. Given that evidence, my case for Don burying it at Tena Bar is very strong. The FBI's theory of the money floating down the river in the bank bag is not credible.

The FBI says the bank bag was crucial to the money surviving the river waters. They brought in a geologist, Dr. Leonard Palmer of Portland State University, who analyzed the sand where the money was discovered. Between the 1971 hijacking and 1980, when the money was found, the Columbia River had been dredged and sand deposited on Tena Bar in 1974. This sand was a sterile layer that would have preserved the money once it floated downstream and landed on Tena Bar. Photos of the rounded edges of the money bundles suggest that the money had tumbled in the river before reaching Tena Bar. This is possible, yet the FBI's conclusion that the bank bag was part of the equation is flawed. If the money had been in a bank bag, the bundles' edges wouldn't be rounded. Agents Carr and Himmelsbach also stated the hijacker was probably killed in the jump, and the rest of the money was lost.

First Officer Rataczak said, "And the parachute he took was a 28. . . Then I can tell what I think. And I got this from Ralph Himmelsbach, who was the FBI agent in charge of the whole hijacking, and we've become good friends through the years. . . . So we trade secrets once in a while. . . . He [the hijacker] took a 28-foot-diameter parachute— that was called a skill chute or something else. It's one of these kind that you kind of float down . . . and there's never been anything found. They put the troops out, the National Guard, civilians, and everybody in the mountains. And . . . anyone who's ever lived in the Seattle-Tacoma area . . . you know that there's . . . blackberry bushes . . . they've got thorns like this high. You can't get through them unless you have a . . . flame thrower or a machete. So what he landed in was that kind of undercover. Did he ever make it? Ralph Himmelsbach and I both agree, although we have no substantive evidence, that he never lived through the landing."[74]

But maybe this was just the story they needed to spread, to steer the public away from the truth.

Walt always told me he gave a few bundles of money to Don Brennan on the ride home. If this is true, then I believe that Don later buried the money on Tena Bar, but it's also possible he threw the bundles into the river. However, then the money had to land in that sterile layer of sand deposited by dredging the river, during just the right time frame, so that it would be preserved. It would have required a "perfect storm," a rare confluence of events—which, even so, doesn't totally defy logic.

But whether he buried it or tossed it in the river isn't important. The crucial detail is that according to Walt, Don was afraid to spend the money and he got rid of it, after he took the bribe (which it really was—a way for Walt to buy Don's silence). Remember, Walt said Don told him, "It's people like you and me that the penitentiaries are full of."

Agent Carr's Smokescreens

FBI agent Larry Carr corresponded online with a group of skydivers about the Cooper case, and he got a lot of his speculations wrong simply by not knowing that Walt gave some of the money to Don Brennan.

Agent Carr said, "Since there is nothing that reasonably points to someone planting the money, we can rule out any jump point that could not put Cooper near a tributary. . . . As I posted, there are very few probably [sic] ways the money got there in its condition. . . . There

---

74 See the videotape of a speech given to Northwest employees by First Officer Bill Rataczak at the Northwest Airlines Museum in Minneapolis in 2012.

would be no logical reason for someone to come back and plant the money there 8 years after. It would not have cooled the investigation or thrown it off a subject. No matter where the money is found the subject list would have stayed the same. Plus, at this point who ever [sic] Cooper is, he got away with it. The investigation was dying, why would someone fan the flames and $5,800 was a large sum in the late 70's and 80's, if you got away with it, you wouldn't give it up for no apparent reason. . . . Remember, the money was found bundled with the rubber bands around the bundles. They crumbled to the touch but where [sic] still in place. This tells us the money had to have been protected from the weather for the majority of the time it was missing, most likely in the bag."[75]

I think Carr was also throwing up a smokescreen about other details of the case.

Smokescreen Number One: As I previously mentioned, Carr later contradicted First Officer Rataczak's initial statement from the 1971 FBI report about the flight path.

Smokescreen Number Two: Carr said the hijacker never requested a flight path, and Carr concluded that Cooper had little idea where he was when he jumped. "Cooper never requested a flight path, he never requested an update from the flight crew and no one reported he even had on a watch that he could have timed wheels up. Also, V23 was not the only low altitude route south from Seatac. Conclusion, Cooper had little idea where he was when he jumped."[76]

However, Cooper did make multiple demands in choosing a destination, per the FBI interviews with the flight crew, conducted

---

75   From a series of messages Carr posted to a skydiving group, www.dropzone. com, under the name CKRET.

76   February 1, 2008, 8:47 a.m., Post #1607. From a series of messages Carr posted to a skydiving group, www.dropzone.com, under the name CKRET.

right after the hijacking. This shows he attempted to control the direction the plane took. These interviews mention Walt first asking for Mexico City or anyplace in Mexico (having stewardess Tina Mucklow write this in a note).[77] Years later, First Officer Rataczak said, "He wanted to go to Mexico City. . . . He wanted the gear down, the flaps down, he wanted the cabin lights out STAT—in other words, right now. He wanted no one after first class; wanted the curtains drawn." First Officer Rataczak said that initially the hijacker wanted the flaps at 15 degrees, and that he himself knew nothing about flap settings, but he knew that there was a flap setting for 15 degrees. It showed that Cooper was familiar with 727s.[78] Re: gear down and flaps down—"That's called a dirty airplane. You dirty it up by putting the flaps down, the slats up, the landing gear and so forth. Plus, we may have the stairs down. So there's lots of drag on that airplane. We were not going to be able to go nonstop to Mexico City, even if it was clean. And so I told Tina to tell him that, and so now I'm thinking, This guy is threatening our lives and, to a point, thirty-five other people and, to a point, the flight attendants."[79]

The flight crew said there wasn't enough fuel for that and suggested San Francisco for refueling, but Walt then said Phoenix. The crew still said not enough fuel and gave the options of either Yuma, Arizona, or Reno, Nevada. Walt finally settled for Reno.[80] The 1971 FBI interviews describe this discussion in detail, and both Mucklow and Rataczak reported it.

---

77 FBI report of interview with stewardess Tina Mucklow, dated November 24, 1971. Report by SA H.E. Hinderliter, Jr., and SAC Harold E. Campbell, File LV 164-60-139.

78 Videotape of a speech given to Northwest employees by First Officer Bill Rataczak at the Northwest Airlines Museum in Minneapolis in 2012.

79 See the videotape of a 2012 speech First Officer Bill Rataczak gave to Northwest employees at the Northwest Airlines Museum in Minneapolis.

80 Ibid. And see also the FBI eyewitness report of First Officer William John (Bill) Rataczak on December 1, 1971, by SAC Harold El. Campbell Jr. and SA H.E. Hinderliter Jr., File LV 164-60-158.

As for "Cooper" having no idea where he would land, technically that's true. But he made sure to jump not too long after takeoff, and I think he planned it so that he would land within a reasonable driving distance of Don Brennan's house, so that he could call Don to come pick him up. Maybe the real question is, why would Agent Carr want the public to *believe* the hijacker didn't try to determine the route?

In 2012, First Officer Rataczak gave an account of this discussion of the flight plan that varied slightly from both his initial FBI report in 1971 and Tina Mucklow's, also in 1971.[81] Rataczak claimed that he really wanted to follow the coastline and suggested to Cooper that they refuel in San Francisco. He then said that Cooper rejected that destination by saying it was too big. Rataczak said he next suggested L.A., then San Diego, both of which Cooper rejected.

Rataczak said, "So we started talking about where are we gonna refuel? I said, 'How about San Francisco?' 'Too big an airport,' he [Cooper] said. 'Well, then, how about Los Angeles?' The refrain became 'Too big an airport.' 'San Diego?' 'No, that's too big an airport. I don't wanna go there. You have to pick a smaller airport.' So we told Paul [Soderlind], and Paul said, '. . . Bill, we've got it set up to go to Reno.' So that was my objective. We took off out of Seattle, and we headed to Reno. We went down over Portland, about

---

81   In an interview with commercial airlines pilot Jeff Wierenga, September 15, 2017, my publisher asked Wierenga about the roles of the captain and the first officer. Wierenga thought that First Officer Rataczak exaggerated his importance in the hijacking, when retelling the story for Northwest Airlines employees at the Northwest Airlines Museum in 2012 (but Rataczak would have been involved in the diversion). Wierenga said that if he were in that situation, he would tell his first officer to fly the plane, which he routinely does. The captain should be more worried about communicating with the various towers, airline headquarters, and the FBI. The captain is in charge, and the first officer only performs tasks that are assigned by the captain. Wierenga believes the videotape of Rataczak at the airlines museum is way off base: that he was never in charge and was given only one task, flying the airplane, so that the captain could stay engaged with communications and managing the others on board the plane.

28 miles north of Portland he jumped out of the airplane. Scotty said, 'I wonder if I should go back and see if he's there?' I said, 'What difference does it make?'"[82]

It's hard to believe they could make it to San Diego with the amount of fuel they had. Also, suggesting L.A. after rejecting San Francisco for being too big was very strange. In fact, Rataczak's suggestion to fly into the Bay Area, one of the most densely populated areas in the United States, or to L.A. with a bomb on board contradicts Rataczak's fear of flying over the Seattle suburbs.[83] I can't explain these inconsistencies.

Smokescreen Number Three: Agent Carr said, "Cooper never gave instruction to the positioning of the fuel truck."[84] This contradicts the original 1971 FBI interview with First Officer Rataczak, who was on duty during the hijacking. As was mentioned in Chapter 8, Rataczak said, "It was further established that hostess Mucklow was to act as intermediary between the hijacker and the individuals meeting the plane to supply his demands. The chief pilot for Northwest Airlines and one other individual were to be in the first vehicle with the money. The second vehicle was to carry the stairs so that the hostess could exit from the front of the plane with only one driver designated for that vehicle, with a third vehicle being a fuel truck containing a driver only which was to remain in a 10 or 11 o'clock position from the plane in order that all would be in full view of the hijacker at all times."[85]

---

82 See the videotape of a speech given to Northwest employees by First Officer Bill Rataczak at the Northwest Airlines Museum in Minneapolis in 2012.

83 Videotape of a speech given to Northwest employees by First Officer Bill Rataczak at the Northwest Airlines Museum in Minneapolis in 2012.

84 From a series of messages Carr posted to a skydiving group, www.dropzone. com, under the name CKRET.

85 From FBI eyewitness report of First Officer William John (Bill) Rataczak on December 1, 1971, by SAC Harold El. Campbell Jr. and SA H.E. Hinderliter Jr., File LV 164-60-158.

252

Rataczak also stated that while at Sea-Tac airport, the FBI purposely held up the refueling to buy more time and the crew finally had to demand that they stop delaying and fuel the plane.

First Officer Rataczak said, "We were ready to go, except we waited for fuel, and Harold Anderson, 'Andy,' the second officer, of course he's mentioning the fuel going on the airplane—he's mentioning the fuel gauge. And they went up. And they stopped. Just barely off the needle, off the empty mark. And he said, 'Bill, we're not taking any fuel.' And I thought, 'They're trying to intervene here.' So I called downstairs where the refuelers had their own interphone, and I said, 'What's going on down there? We're not getting any fuel from that truck.' 'Well, uh, we ran out of fuel from that truck.' Now I'd only been flying for five years, but I had quite a few hours, and I never ever had a fuel truck run out of fuel when they knew what the loading was supposed to be. . . . We go by pounds of fuel, and that airplane holds about 50,000 pounds . . . it comes up to around 7,500 gallons of . . . jet fuel. I said, 'Get that truck out of there and get one here that can pump.' So they brought in another one, and Andy said, 'Oh, we're getting fuel now.' And I said, 'That's good.' So Andy and I are going back to doing our own thing, talking to the company, and all of a sudden Andy says, 'It stopped fueling again.' So I got on the horn and I swore at them . . . I said, 'What in holy hell is going on down there?' 'Well, the fuel valve froze up on us.' Well, I have the original fuel slip right here, and it says it's Type A jet fuel with a freeze point of minus 40 degrees. And it was 32 or 34 degrees outside. And, uh, that was strictly bogus. I said, 'Get that truck out of there and quit delaying. We need to get this show on the road.' So, finally they did."[86]

I can't figure out what Agent Carr would gain by saying Cooper didn't give instructions about the fuel truck or why Rataczak would

---

86 Videotape of a speech given to Northwest employees by First Officer Bill Rataczak at the Northwest Airlines Museum in Minneapolis in 2012.

add this to his story if it weren't true, but one person is clearly incorrect.

Smokescreen Number Four: Now the FBI is saying they doubt that Cooper was a skydiver. When I read this, I laughed out loud. The online article features a photo of Agent Carr, and it states:

> "Evidence of absence," a term the FBI uses to show that a claim is unlikely or false, is often invoked when there is an absence of evidence when evidence should be present. Sometimes what didn't happen can reveal considerable information. No one has found any evidence that D.B. Cooper was a skydiver. In fact, Cooper does not appear to have had much familiarity with skydiving equipment. He chose to jump an older, unsteerable parachute; he jumped without a helmet and with slip-on loafers on his feet; and he jumped without a reserve. . . . based on "evidence of absence," one theory about Cooper has changed from the initial investigation: Authorities now state that D.B. Cooper probably was not an experienced skydiver since he made so many "amateurish mistakes" and since no evidence indicated that he was a regular jumper.[87]

Agent Larry Carr claimed that the FBI delivered two chutes to Cooper, one being more "steerable" than the other. He then stated that an experienced parachutist would have picked the more steerable one. Yet in fact, for an overcast night jump, you can't see anything until you hit the ground. It's like falling down a tunnel. Steering the chute would be worthless, and with steerable chutes the path is more horizontal across the ground, which would have been

---

87 "The Secrets of D.B. Cooper, Part Two—Evidence of Absence," http://parachutistonline.com/feature/secrets-db-cooper-part-two-evidence-absence.

worse when landing in trees. Most important, in a situation with so much stress, Walt picked something familiar. He was familiar with the round chute he selected, having used that type for many years.

Cooper had to be satisfied with the parachutes the FBI gave him; his only choice then was to use them or throw in the towel. The FBI was stalling for time, using three different fuel trucks. I've flown for 12,000 hours, and I never had three fuel trucks break down. Never once. Walt swore when he saw those four chutes, but, as I would have done, he took one and jumped, with no reserve. That really was his only choice. Walt told me it was what we used to call an aerobatic chute. The chute itself was not aerobatic, but it was the type of chute we wore if we did aerobatics, with no reserve and no accommodations (that is, D-rings) to wear a reserve. They were also worn by the first fighter pilots, without a reserve. They usually held a 28-foot round canopy. Early models held a 24-foot one. *Leg-busters*, we called them. We used the leg-busters for water jumps. The FBI sourced the parachutes from McChord Air Force Base, which primarily used chutes designed for military fighter planes, with no reserve—thus no D-rings to hook a reserve onto them. When ejecting from a fighter jet, pilots get only one shot with a chute deployment. Plus, fighter jet cockpits are too confined for pilots to wear both a main chute and a reserve. In Walt's world, he knew of only one chute: the type worn by paratroopers in the military, which was essentially the same type we adopted for our parachute team back in the Saginaw days.

First Officer Rataczak said that the hijacker ordered two backpacks and two fanny packs. Rataczak said he'd take the backpack, and Captain Scott (Scotty) said, "Fanny pack." And, "Oh, that was one of the times when we really got concerned. Four parachutes. If I do the higher math—one for the hijacker, then there were Scotty, Rataczak, and Anderson up front. So we figured this guy is no dummy; he ordered four parachutes with the idea that 'if anybody gets wise about trying to get a bad parachute in there, if I order four of them, they're gonna send good ones.' They didn't."[88]

I don't know what to make about one strange comment Carr made: "Given the facts surrounding the tie and DNA, DNA in this case could not 100% rule anyone out or in as being DB Cooper, that would not absolutely make him DB Cooper."[89]

Yet one thing that Agent Carr said *does* agree with the facts as Walt reported them. Carr said, "There is no indications [sic] Cooper would have known where he was when he jumped, or knew to the point he would have been able to link at a predetermined spot, which would preclude him from having help on the ground." This was confirmed by our interviews with Jeff Osiadacz, a.k.a. "Cowboy," who said that Cooper had no idea where he was when he landed, and he, Jeff, assisted him with directions.

The Bank Bag

Even minor details varied in the FBI eyewitness reports, such as the size of the bank bag. One passenger, Cord Harms Zrim Spreckel, testified that it was about 2 feet by 1½ feet by 1 foot. However, SAC J. E. Milnes stated that he saw the white canvas bag at the Operations Office of Northwest Airlines, and it was about 1 foot by 1 foot by 8 or 9 inches, and FBI agent Carr also says 12 inches by 12 inches by 9 inches. First Officer Rataczak mentioned in his 2012 Northwest Orient Museum in Minneapolis that it was a drawstring bag.

---

88 Videotape of a speech given by First Officer Bill Rataczak at the Northwest Airlines Museum in Minneapolis in 2012, to Northwest employees.
89 From a series of messages Carr posted to a skydiving group, www.dropzone.com, under the name CKRET.

Cooper's tie, left behind

Analyzing the Tie

In January 2017, three amateur scientists working for a group called Citizen Sleuths announced that the clip-on tie the hijacker had left on the airplane seat contained valuable evidence. They used an electron microscope to identify rare earth particles (e.g., titanium) that pointed to the tie's owner being either an aerospace engineer or manager, possibly at Boeing.

"A tie is one of the only articles of clothing that isn't washed on a regular basis," reads a section on the Citizen Sleuths website devoted to the tie. "It picks up dirt and grime just like any other piece of clothing, but that accumulation never truly gets 'reset' in the washing machine. Each of those particles comes from something and somewhere and can tell a story if the proper instruments like electron microscopes are used."

Yet their theory has one big problem: Walt bought the entire outfit he wore from a thrift store. So the previous owner of the clothing, not Walt, is the man who worked in the aerospace industry.

Conflicting Descriptions of the Hijacker

As for a description of the hijacker, most of the eyewitness testimony is conflicting. One plane passenger, George R. Labissoniere, said the hijacker was about 5'10', 150 pounds, and about 35 years old. Another passenger, Robert Gregory, who happened to be seated closest to the hijacker, stated that he was white, Caucasian but possibly of Mexican or American Indian descent, short (about 5'9"), about 165 pounds, with wavy jet-black marcelled hair that had a greasy patent leather sheen. A third passenger, Cord Harms Zrim Spreckel, said the hijacker was 5'10", medium heavy, and 50 years old.

Stewardess Florence Schaffner said he was a white male, 6 foot, 170–175 pounds, average build, mid-40s, brown eyes, straight black hair, olive complexion, and appeared to be of Latin descent.

Stewardess Tina Mucklow described him as a white male, 5'10" to 6 foot, 180–190 pounds, medium to dark complexion, medium build, dark straight hair, narrow sideburns, eyes not observed due to his wearing wraparound sunglasses.

In short, they did agree on his dark complexion and dark hair, but some said the hair was straight, others wavy; his height varied from 5'9" to 6'; his weight ranged from 150 to 190, and his age from 35 to 50. Good luck identifying someone based on those stats.

One item of information was included in the 1971 FBI reports, and First Officer Rataczak elaborated on the meals: he mentioned that Cooper ordered steak dinners for the entire crew, and they were delivered.[90] That would make sense; otherwise, the crew wouldn't have had anything to eat from approximately 1 p.m. to 10 p.m. However, Rataczak said that the German shepherds searching the plane ate all of the filets. I'm not sure whether he was joking.

The Richard Tosaw Book

In his 2012 speech at the Northwest Airlines Museum, Rataczak recommended a book written by Richard Tosaw, *D.B. Cooper, Dead or Alive*.[91] According to an *L.A. Times* article, Tosaw conducted a lot of his own interviews with the flight crew and passengers. Yet he didn't cite sources or dates for some quotes, and he provided no references or footnotes throughout the book. Tosaw was an FBI agent for five years, then he went into the law. He lived alone, had no memorial when he died in 2009, and was buried in Iowa, where he grew up. The *L.A. Times* article described Tosaw as being obsessed with using divers to try to find Cooper's body in the Columbia River. He obviously assumed the FBI's (later revised) flight route was correct. As FBI agent Larry Carr said, "This would have put Cooper landing in an area that could have fed into the Columbia and a good reason why he was never found, because he landed in an area out of the search grid."[92]

Rataczak admitted to having a lot of input in the Tosaw book, and he thought it was an accurate account of the hijacking. Some of the information conflicts with the FBI reports, and other statements support my case. I'll list some of them here.

---

90 See the videotape of a speech given to Northwest employees by First Officer Bill Rataczak at the Northwest Airlines Museum in Minneapolis in 2012.

91 Tosaw's book was self-published in 1984. There is an interesting article about Tosaw's D.B. Cooper obsession in the *L.A. Times*: http://articles.latimes.com/2005/aug/28/nation/na-dbcooper28.

92 January 21, 2008, at 8:03 a.m., Post #1225, from a series of messages Carr posted to a skydiving group, www.dropzone.com, under the name CKRET.

Tosaw claimed that the hijacker handed Florence a white envelope that contained the hijack note written with a felt tip pen and letters neatly drawn. I know for a fact that Walt had studied calligraphy.

Bill Mitchell, a twenty-year-old student, sat in the middle seat in row 18 across from Cooper. He stated that "the man's socks or long underwear or whatever it was that was showing didn't match his shoes or trousers." Walt claimed that he wore long underwear bottoms, and decades after the hijacking, he gave me the actual pair he wore that night.

In Mitchell's testimony to the FBI, he said that "Cooper's hair was black and a little shiny, which caused him to think that perhaps it was dyed. . . . He said that Cooper wore a business suit, white shirt, tie and raincoat. He said that he was well dressed except for the long underwear, or whatever it was that was showing over his socks."

Tosaw claimed that the Northwest employee stationed in Minneapolis (Paul Soderlind, former director, Flight Operations-Technical Northwest Airlines) selected the route. The route selected totally ignored the concern for population centers because "It stayed fairly close to Interstate Highway 5 (I-5) and went over or near Tacoma, McChord AFB and Vancouver, all in Washington. It then continued south across the Columbia River at Portland and down Oregon's Willamette Valley, flying close to Eugene and Medford and then to Red Bluff where it turned east to Reno." I find it interesting that they said Soderlind was in Minneapolis (which Rataczak also mentioned in his 2012 speech to the Northwest Airlines Museum) because it contradicts both Rataczak (who claimed it was the crew that decided the flight path) and Agent Carr, who said the order about the flight path came from Sacramento.

Here, Tosaw described the money: "Around each packet was a Federal Reserve paper band. Some of the individual packets, in addition to the paper band, had a rubber band around them." This contradicts both Tina Mucklow's FBI report and Bill Rataczak's testimony.

He went on to say, "The 100 packets were put into a plain, gray canvas sack that had no zipper, drawstring or other way to close it." This strays from Rataczak's testimony that it was a drawstring bag.

Tosaw also contradicted Agent Carr by saying that "the bills were in $2,000 packets, each packet containing 100 bills." Carr said that the bundles varied in the number of bills.

On the two F-106 all-weather search planes that were assigned to follow the 727, he said that the pilots decided to "pass by on top of the 727 and then circle back underneath." This didn't work, as he stated, "But their orders were to not get too close and with the poor visibility they weren't able to see anything."

He also stated that the pilots reported "that they were unable to see any falling objects on the screens of their five-mile radar." Maybe they couldn't see anything because they were sent on the wrong route.

Tosaw's book had some other interesting quotes. After the plane landed, the FBI began looking for evidence. "Tina was contacted and stated that Cooper, after he had finished drinking, had placed the two empty bourbon bottles in his empty glass." And, "The agents were hopeful that they would find some fingerprints on the aluminum staircase railing on the handle that lowered the stairs. But the prints that they found were too smeared to be identifiable and the agents found nothing on Cooper's glass and empty bottles, except for the prints of the two stewardesses." This supports Walt's claim about how the glue worked.

In the book, Tosaw gives a lot of credit to Rataczak and Agent Ralph Himmelsbach, who was placed in charge of the Cooper case in Portland. Rataczak and Himmelsbach became very good friends

Almost $6,000 found in a picnic area

following the hijacking, as Rataczak often repeated in the video. From my view, conspiratorial friends.

Tosaw stated that the FBI believed that Cooper had flown that same flight previously. When they circulated the composite pictures of Cooper, he said, "No one working at the airport remembered having seen the man, but the agents were not disappointed because they realized that the drawing was generally a poor method of identification."

Tosaw included some details about the Ingram family. Stepfather Dwayne, mother Patricia and their eight-year-old son, Brian, had recently moved to Vancouver, Washington, from Oklahoma, looking for work. In subsequent interviews, Dwayne appeared to be a rather disreputable character. He seemed like the kind of guy Don Brennan would befriend at a bar.

The family went to a remote sand bar owned by the Fazio family, at the recommendation of a "friend" for a family picnic. After gathering wood for a fire, Dwayne said that he asked Brian to smooth out some sand with his forearm. In doing so, Brian uncovered three bundles of money slightly covered with mud right where Dwayne told him to dig. On brushing it off, Dwayne discovered that the muddy bundles were money.

"The Fazios said that the beach gets constant use. They commented that they use it all the time in connection with their farming operation, including the movement of cattle, and that during the year hundreds of people come there for recreational purposes. They were of the opinion that if the money had been there very long, even under a layer of sand, someone would have stumbled over it."

FBI "Loses" Key Evidence

And finally, this bit of information is just too good to be true and proof that the FBI really doesn't want to *publicly* solve "the only unsolved hijacking in U.S. history." In 2011, there were news reports of a new suspect who had been dead ten years. The FBI hoped to prove his guilt by using DNA from the saliva on the eight Raleigh cigarette butts that the hijacker had left on the plane. However, soon after this, a headline announced "D.B. Cooper: FBI Lost Key Evidence That Could Identify Thief."[93]

Apparently, bureau agents in Reno had sent the cigarette butts to Quantico for testing, which then sent them back to Las Vegas for safekeeping, and they somehow vanished. The disappearance of such conclusive DNA evidence is a little too convenient, if you ask me, and confirms that Walt was too "valuable" to arrest, after his years of working as a clandestine operative for intelligence agencies.

---

93   See http://www.thedailybeast.com/db-cooper-fbi-lost-key-evidence-that-could-identify-thief.

CHAPTER 14

"IT'S BEEN ONE HELLUVA RIDE"

We kept losing members of the Michigan Parachute Team, one by one. Yet considering the risks we'd taken in our youth, most of us lived surprisingly long lives.

Parker (Wilbert Luther "Bill" Parker, Jr.), the oldest among us, died on May 5, 2004. At the time, he lived next door to Walt in Oscoda. During the last years of his life, he wasn't right in the head and acted a bit crazy.

The Billabogs lasted from 1998 to 2009. The guys planned to have the next one at a motel nearby because by that time, Art Lussier had passed away. He died in 2010 at his home in Pinconning, where we held the Billabogs.

Summer 2010

Loretta and I usually had Sunday dinner with our daughter, Suzie, and her husband each week. Suzie had been a stewardess for years, so I revealed to them what Walt had confessed about the hijacking. At that time, I was still trying to put together the stories about Walt. He and I talked on the phone regularly, and I had started to record those conversations. I had files full of newspaper articles and letters Walt had mailed to me.

Always a Salesman

In 2013, or possibly late 2012, I visited Walt. His health was not good. He could walk but required oxygen. We had just returned from dinner, so it was sunset. We heard a quick knock on the door, and a man known to Walt entered. He was carrying a hand grenade. He came to the kitchen table where Walt and I sat. I stood to give him a chair, and we all said hi.

Walt chuckled when he saw the hand grenade, then said, "German, three seconds."

I saw it and knew it was real.

"How much?" Walt asked.

The man gave a unit price, I forget how much, then he stopped cold and looked at me as if I had just walked into the room.

"He's okay," Walt said, so the man continued.

I questioned my friend after that man left, as to the wisdom of the risk he was taking. Yet after I said, "You know, the government has people looking for illegal gun sales," I realized I was the fool, not Walt, because Walt was one of those people.

"I can't be caught," Walt said, so I knew what that meant.

2013

In the summer of 2013, Walt and a friend drove to Windsor, Ontario, to make a withdrawal from the bank account where he'd stashed the hijacking money.

Saving Walt

"Willard, have you talked to Walt lately?" I asked over the phone line. I had called him because I couldn't get in touch with Walt. "Was he in bed or was he up? Think hard. When was the last time you saw him walk?"

"I don't think he *can* walk," Willard said. We discussed Walt's situation for a few minutes, then I hung up and turned to Loretta.

"I'm worried about Walt."

"Then you should go up there," Loretta said. She made plane reservations and arranged for a car rental at the airport in Detroit.

The entire life story of my friend Walt is a superlative tale not because it was so well planned, but because it was not. Nothing ever seemed to go as planned, unless you dug deeper and you saw that all of those bad plans worked in spite of themselves.

Walt died on February 17, 2014, at the age of seventy-nine, but he'd intended to die five months earlier.

I should have realized from his phone conversation that Walt wanted to die. Between everything he told me and what I figured out on my own about the man, it should have been obvious to me, of all people, but it wasn't. Maybe I did know but hadn't yet come to grips with the idea that the man who was responsible for taking so many other lives was now doing the unthinkable: taking his own.

The month was September, and the year was 2013. I was driving north to save Walt. I had traveled this road many times in the past, especially in my youth. Saginaw, the first big town north of Flint, was where all of us developed into skydivers and batwing jumpers and where Art and I taught the man who later became D.B. Cooper most of what we knew about parachuting. Several years later, Walt took parachuting to a new level when he executed his famous hijacking of Northwest Orient Flight 305.

Seventy miles north of Saginaw lies the almost ghost town of Pinconning, and fifteen miles west of Pinconning on land suitable only for frogs and white-tailed deer was where Art retired and built his cabin on the Billabog.

Driving this familiar road, I remembered one night when we gathered in Art's cabin and someone said, "How in hell did so many people get so screwed up, and how in hell did everyone survive against such severe odds?"

Then Art's younger brother Mike, the only one who went to college out of the nine or ten of us sitting around the potbelly stove, said, "I don't know, but somebody ought to write a book."

This was how I remembered it, even after most members of our team were now dead, as I passed the road to the Billabog on my way to save Walt.

I turned onto Seminal Street around sunset. Walt's house screamed 1970s architecture, square and functional, with concrete steps leading up to a small front porch. Walt had always been a vital force, but this place felt like it could drain the life out of the entire universe. It had the feeling of a house where a sick person lived.

I entered through the passage door in the garage and called out, "Walt, are you here?"

Walt shouted, "Come on in, Charlie!"

The door was unlocked. When I walked into the bedroom, Walt was half in and half out of the bed because his dogs had chewed up the mattress. I saw thousands of chunks of cotton all over the floor. The smell of dog poop and urine almost knocked me out. Walt's seven little poodles crowded around my legs, barking their yippy barks. They followed me as I walked through the house. Walt had told me he was concerned about who would care for his dogs if he died.

Even though Fat Willard had just gotten back from visiting Walt, he hadn't grasped the seriousness of Walt's condition. Anyone else would have looked around at the dog feces and the ripped-up mattress, with Walt hanging over the side, and realized something was seriously wrong.

Walt loved his dogs

That first day, I cleaned Walt's house and tried to convince him to go to the hospital. He wanted to wait until the next morning. We talked about the Cooper case on and off, and he cleared up some details.

The next morning, during the two-hour drive to the VA hospital, we continued to discuss the case.

At one point, he repeated something he'd told me years ago: "Remember that story you wrote about me? You gave me way too much credit. I never did no planning. That's all I'm going to say right there."

The truth was, Walt liked to say he had no plan, but the more he revealed to me, the more I realized that he denied planning it to absolve himself of guilt. He'd laid the groundwork by making a fake bomb, renting a typewriter to type a note, going to the thrift store to buy the clothes he wore, and using rubbing alcohol and glue to disguise his fingerprints. Yet all the while, he kept telling himself he didn't have to do anything if he didn't want to. It was like the time he robbed the Big Boy, an impulse, a compulsion to take action and get it over with. Then, after it was all over, it became unreal to him, and he tried to forget, to convince himself that nothing had happened.

At the hospital, I grabbed a nurse and a gurney and got Walt into bed. I told the nurse, "My friend is dying. He quit taking his water pills."

After some initial treatment to stabilize him, she called a doctor.

Later I phoned Loretta and told her the doctor said, "If you hadn't brought him in today, he would have died."

Walt was in the hospital for four days. He had congestive heart failure. During his hospital stay, they drained a lot of water off his chest, so he was in much better shape by the time he was released.

"You saved my life. I owe you," were the first words out of Walt's mouth.

"I'm just glad I decided to come up," I said. "I had a feeling."

"There's nothing more the doctors can do," Walt said. "I'm supposed to get some home care and be more careful about my heart."

I stayed another day to make sure he would be okay. Then I called the guys, the ones who were still left, and updated them on Walt's condition.

Guardian Angels

Earlier, I mentioned the book my friend Michael Abrams wrote about the world's biggest risk takers.[94] He'd accidentally discovered that the majority of them were orphans. The explanation for that makes no sense to me. People say, "They have nothing left to lose." What the hell does that mean? I don't want to die any more than you do. Yet even when I seemed to be heading for certain death, I never considered the possibility that I would die. I never worried about dying—even now, at age eighty-three. I know I'm going to die, but it's something I've never considered.

I know I have a guardian angel, and so did Walt. We only talked about it to each other. Walt saw ghosts, whereas I never did. People's explanations vary. I'm getting out of my element here, but I'm positive of this. The guardian of some sort—the term *angel* is most often used—never made a sound, never gave a whisper, but every time I obeyed, I'm glad I did.

I will leave people to their own thoughts, as I move off the subject of orphan life, but I'm glad I was one, an orphan. I have only love for those who gave me life, no regrets.

Losing your sense of fear altogether is a bad thing. Let's say there's an 18-wheeler barreling down the road straight at you. Step back to safety. If you don't believe me, ask the person who stood his ground and let that 18-wheeler run him down. On second thought, ask his next of kin. Losing your sense of fear altogether would be a devastating thing.

Orphans are the worst, or the best, however you define fear. Art was not an orphan, but Walt and me make it two out of three.

---

94 *Birdmen, Batmen, and Skyflyers: Wingsuits and the Pioneers Who Flew in Them, Fell in Them, and Perfected Them,* Michael Abrams (Harmony Books, 2006; Amazon Kindle edition 2007).

Best friends—Charlie and Walt

That said, our experiment with death might have started as army paratroopers. Everything has a simple beginning, like the tightrope walker who crosses from one skyscraper to another while a thousand feet in the air. That feat began with an old rope in his backyard tied between two trees, not far off the ground. Parachuting in the military started for us with a tower and a rope much like the modern-day zip line.

But don't ask Art, Walt, or me about the loss of fear. All of us lived to be old men after it appeared we had lost all fear—or had we? We had lost most of our fear but not all, yet even losing some is dangerous. We learned to conquer fear of death, but that was not absolute. Walt, for example, feared getting caught smuggling diamonds, which would mean death by hanging without a trial.

"I feared being hung in some godforsaken country, then thrown into a dump where I'd be devoured by jackals," he told me.

"But you did it anyway," I said.

"That's because I feared being poor more than I feared death," he said.

Thus his legendary D.B. Cooper jump in 1971. Walt told me and his niece Lisa Story about it, as Lisa confirmed in a letter to me. She said it was the nearest Walt came to a deathbed confession for why he did it.

"Better dead than poor," was Walt's answer. That was his simple explanation for his complex airplane hijacking. After that Northwest Orient Flight 305 hijacking, Walt spent his years working for the U.S. government, other governments, and covert entities doing things more dangerous than his Cooper hijacking. Walt had to conquer those fears as well.

The things nobody knows about are more exciting than the ones we know about: Walter's years of smuggling diamonds, his years with Jimmy Hoffa and why they called Walt "Little Jimmy." Walter knew things from being inside, but he warned me, "Never tell."

I think Walt moved back to Michigan when he retired to be near Willard and Art. He still had his mom and his sister, who would forgive him for anything, even for the years he'd disappeared, and two wives, one who still loved him and one who was batshit crazy, and a few kids who either rejected all his offers or only cared about him for what they could get.

The friends who knew him to the core knew he was good and generous, though hardened and determined, and knew he was crazy in good ways and bad. They were the family Walt stuck with until the end.

Joni was the love of Walt's life

Willard died on September 26, 2014. He and Walt had shared a long history and were best friends. After a rowdy youth, Willard became a family man and had a career in the auto industry. He loved to drink (but mainly later in life, after his wife died in the 1990s). His family and friends adored him. Earlier in life, he was quite a fighter. He and Walt solved countless conflicts with their fists. Yet despite their closeness, Walt didn't tell Willard about the Cooper hijacking—because when Willard drank (which was all the time after he retired), he couldn't be trusted to keep the story confidential.

Walt's niece Lisa Story and her mother were with him before he died and shortly after his death. She told me that Walt had always been looking for a father figure, since his father had died when he was so young. Lisa knew Walt's softer side, unlike most of his male buddies, who didn't talk about such things. I do know, however, that Joni was the love of Walt's life. Walt is buried between his mother, Regina, and Joni.

Walt's grave

Walt and His Women

The mysteries of Walt's marriages were hard to unravel. Only as late as 2017, when his niece provided me with documents, was I able to sort things out a bit. When Walt first joined our parachute team, he was going through an annulment from his first wife. Then he started dating Joni (b. March 17, 1939). He married her on November 3, 1960. His first child, a daughter, was born on February 19, 1962. His second child, a son, was born in 1963. Sometime in early 1964, as I mentioned previously, Walt told Joni he was going out for some bread and milk, and he didn't come back.

On October 2, 1964, Walt and Joni got a judgment of divorce. Next, Walt took up with Carla and returned to Michigan.[95] Carla herself, born on February 8, 1938, had a questionable history. On December 7, 1953, at age fifteen, Carla had married her first husband, Rupert P. F__ using the name Florence L. E__.[96] She divorced the first husband on July 1, 1963. In September 1965, she and Walt began living together. Walt's third child, a son (whom I nicknamed "Treetop"), was born on February 14, 1967. On September 30, 1974, still using the name Florence F__ E__, she married Walt Reca (even though he didn't legally change his name from Peca to Reca until 1976). On July 9, 1978, Walt and Carla both signed a petition for dissolution of marriage in Spokane, Washington, but nothing came of the petition because they were unable to agree on terms. Sometime in the mid to late 1970s, Walt and Joni got back together.

Then, apparently "forgetting" to get divorced from Walt first, on February 8, 1989, Carla married Floyd C__, under the name Florence Carla M__, and gave her date of birth as February 8, 1940.[97] The last name M__ indicates that she might have married another man before Floyd C__, despite still not being divorced from Walt.

So there was a marriage license between Carla and Walt, but the marriage wasn't exactly legal because he'd used a fake name. For a while, it seemed like he had both women and then neither of them. Then Walt's mother and Joni went to live with him in Oscoda. His mother passed away in 1999. On January 23, 2001, Joni Reca died at Tawas St. Joseph Hospital.

Walt finally had the marriage to Carla legally dissolved in 2002. In addition, Walt and Florence Reca were granted a default judgment of divorce on February 4, 2002, in Tawas City, Michigan.

---

95 Both last names withheld.
96 Last name withheld.
97 Both last names withheld, and, as mentioned, Carla is a pseudonym.

POSITION OBJECTIVES
Direct Field Management/Quality Control Inspector/Heavy Horizontal/Vertical/ Undergroung Structural Steel, Rigging, Erection, and Welding, Superintendent Supervisor.

FOREIGN LANGUAGES: Speak Comprehensive Polish, Russian, Ukranian (Working Knowledge) German, Philippino, Thai Iranian, Indonesian, and Arabian.

Walt spoke many languages

On August 18, 2005, Carla and her son by Walt moved into his house, along with the son's kids, until Walt kicked them out in December 2005.

"Oh, yeah," he said, "and I had this girl in Antwerp who sometimes came along on diamond runs."

"Was she your girlfriend or another wife?" I asked.

Walt just smiled.

"I Work for All of Them!"

Walt and I had much in common: size, weight, age, hazel eyes (not brown), and hair color dark brown. Walt's was actually blond, but he kept it dark brown. You might think he dyed it brown for the D.B. Cooper job, but no, it was much earlier. He started dying it in the mid-sixties, to avoid being recognized by the ironworkers' union. He kept dying it until his hair started to turn gray.

Walt and I both were expert paratroopers. He was exceedingly polite to women, addressing them as "young lady," and was always the gentleman. He'd introduced me to Loretta, my wife of fifty-three years.

277

Walt was the most intelligent eighth-grade graduate I've ever known. He spoke perfect Russian, Polish, and English by age six. He also learned a fourth language, Indonesian, and these languages came into play later in life, after the D.B. Cooper jump in 1971. These languages were absolutely essential in helping him avoid a prison sentence, by placing him behind the Iron Curtain, where he saved some lives and ended others.

The 1970s and '80s were tumultuous times throughout the world, with numerous murders, assassinations of politicians and public figures, and government-led coups. Walt claimed to be either directly involved or complicit in a few of these on behalf of various agencies.

People often wonder, *Who was behind these events, and how did they find people to carry out these acts?* Intelligence organizations are known for recruiting paratroopers and ex-military personnel, and Walt fit both categories.

During one of our conversations, I mentioned Walt working for the CIA, and he corrected me.

"I don't work for one of them, I work for all of them!" he said, almost yelling at me.

This time, I listened, and Walt was right. By all accounts, he worked for the multinational Vinnell Corp, which had interests all across the globe. As his passport and identification documents indicate, at various times he worked for or with numerous intelligence agencies and countries. How else could you explain his KGB identification badge, his British passport under an assumed name, and entrance into some of the most dangerous countries in the world?

The Confession

On November 24, 2008, my old friend Walt Peca first confessed to me that he was "D.B. Cooper." During the next few years, he filled in the details of his life, and in the fall of 2012, he dictated a long confession to me in a phone call. He intended to sign and notarize the typed copy in 2013, but his health was failing, and his niece refused to drive him to the notary. She and her mother, Walt's sister, persuaded him not to sign, fearing that he might spend the final months of his life in prison.[98]

In this document, Walt said, "There are three events that had great influence upon my life: my father's electrocution, meeting my best friends Art Lussier, Bill Parker, and Carl Laurin (Charlie). Had I not met them, I probably would never have become D.B. Cooper. And getting caught by the agency was the third. That influenced all of my life after my D.B. Cooper hijacking. Following being caught after the Cooper event, erased any possible chance for normalcy."

Although law enforcement authorities never revealed to the public that the hijacker had been found, intelligence agents confronted Walt a few months after the hijacking and threatened him with prison if he didn't begin working for them in covert operations. He spent the next few decades in the world of espionage, largely in the Middle East, in Asia, and behind the Iron Curtain.

He said, "In 1974, I was forty-one years old. For the next several years, I was tracked by Interpol and for good reason. During this time, I worked for several different agencies throughout the world doing the same type of work. Exposing what I did creates a great element of danger for the recipient of this information, even following my death."

In his confession, Walt described his motives for carrying out the hijacking. The death of his father resulted in a childhood of poverty and desperation. He said, "Warmth, religion, and security were replaced by a life in unheated tenements, and always

---

98   Although Walt Peca's confession remains unsigned, these events are corroborated in a video interview of Walt's niece Lisa Story, in the documentary titled *D.B. Cooper: The Real Story*.

hungry." To save himself and especially his sister from hunger, he committed petty crimes, ended up in "juvie hall," met his lifelong friend Willard there, and formed a gang. Of this time, Walt said, "I was very young and had little choice of my actions, as I did as an adult. Having said this, if I hurt anyone, which I tried never to do, I'm sorry." He summed up that period by saying, "I was just trying to survive."

On his seventeenth birthday, Walt enlisted in the paratroopers, the U.S. Army's Eleventh Airborne.

After an honorable discharge, Walt met Art and me and joined the Michigan Parachute Team. He said, "I saw things being done with parachutes I never dreamed of. All the things the military told us could not be done, these guys were doing. They jumped throughout the winter in winds over forty miles an hour onto frozen ground undaunted by broken bones. It was from these guys jumping in Saginaw that I learned the limits of parachuting, or maybe I learned there were no limits."

A few years later, Walt was on the run "from both the Union and the Law." Worried about getting money to support his family, he committed robberies, sold guns on the black market, worked as an "enforcer" for Jimmy Hoffa's Local 51 Teamsters, and later sued the ironworkers' union to get the pay he thought he deserved. The resulting federal investigation cost the union billions of dollars.

Walt said, "The law wanted to put me in jail, and the Union wanted to kill me. . . . I was on my third marriage and had four children and never had enough money. The plan to hijack an airplane was concocted while I was drunk in a bar and desperate. . . . It was not the cold, loneliness and hunger that I felt, it was the fear of that for the children I were [sic] now responsible for and that is what drove me to the hijacking."

Help us remember

One of the last, great adventurers

WALTER PECA "RECA"

Join Sandra Peca Griffith; Lisa, Kaili and Sydney Story; and Vince Griffith as they celebrate the life and adventures of their brother and uncle. Stop by for stories, drinks and refreshments.

Saturday, July 19 – 2 to 6 p.m.

Hilltop Bar and Restaurant
431 W. Mill St., Oscoda, MI

Memorial flyer

He explained, "The D.B. Cooper hijacking was not a complex job. The plan would fit on one side of a post card. What was complex were the lies the FBI put out with their version of the hijacking. First they said I died from the jump—I did not. Secondly they said the ransom money was never spent—it was, and third, they said that Flight 305 flew over Portland reroute[d] to Reno— not even close."

When I first told Walt I thought he was D.B. Cooper, he didn't want to admit it, but he realized that I'd figured it out. Walt later told me, "I was never a liar; I was a robber, a thief, and a hijacker, but never a liar. But I lied that day: I said, 'I am not.'"

He described feeling guilty: "I had lied to one of my very best friends, something I cannot remember ever doing in my seventy some years. It took about a month for me to call him back. I gave no apology, I just said, 'I am D.B. Cooper.'"[99]

I remember that conversation so vividly. Right away, we changed the subject and talked about other things, but before we hung up, I asked him, "Why now, Walt?" He just said, "Because it's time."

"I am D.B. Cooper." He said those words and then wrote them in his confession. "The plan and execution of the hijacking, November 24, 1971, was mine alone." He elaborated:

> On the morning of November 23, 1971, I left my home in Hartland Washington with the intention of hijacking an airplane after takeoff from Portland Oregon en-route to Seattle, Washington. The weather at Hartland was decent that morning. I wore clothing I had purchased from the thrift store in Spokane. A dark suit, clip on tie, white shirt, dark penny loafers and dark raincoat. In a dark brief case I carried a look alike bomb I fashioned from a

99   Actually, Walt had denied being D.B. Cooper the first few times I asked him, starting in 1999. So it would be more truthful to say that Walt had never lied to me about anything during our friendship except being D.B. Cooper, before he finally confessed.

lantern battery, wire and six road flares. I wore insulated underwear bottoms, the ones I wore on cold work days and hand carried a dark rain coat. I had in my pockets eight packs of Sire [sic] Walter Raleigh Filter tip cigarettes, a lighter, a pocket knife and two notes, one type written and one printed in Calligraphy. I also had paper money for a bus ticket from Spokane to Portland, food and hotel and taxi in Portland plus a ticket for air fare to Seattle.

Nobody knew what happened to the hijacker after the jump. The media and the FBI said it was unlikely anyone could have lived through it. Walt did his best to forget, saying, "It had become an event that to me was lost in time."

Walt began this long confession by saying, "Approximately one year ago a friend of mine asked, 'If you had your life to live over, what would you do different?' I said, 'Everything.'"

Later, he told me this was an exaggeration because he treasured his time with his friends and family.

He ended the confession with these words: "In spite of this, I thank my God and friends for the life I had, and for those I've hurt, I am sorry. By the time people read this, I will be with old friends, Art Lussier, Bill Parker, and from the old team only Jim McCusker, Willard Stahl, and Charlie are with you. In the final years I have studied the Bible and embraced the true God. This is my testament, every word True."

Final Days

In August 2013, Walt's niece Lisa and his sister, Sandy, visited Walt to help prepare him for hospice care.

In November 2013, Lisa, her daughter Syd, and Sandy came to see Walt in the nursing facility.

In February 2014, Sandy made one final visit, days before Walt died on February 17.

In March 2014, Lisa and Sandy went to Walt's house to go through his possessions, dispose of unwanted items, and ship his papers back to their home in Las Vegas. A party was planned at a local tavern to memorialize Walt, but it was canceled, due to no one attending.

Walt's Diary

Walt's niece Lisa sent me the following quotes, sources unknown, which he had written in his diary. Some, I recognized as previously published, so Walt probably heard or read them; others he might have made up. Either way, they rang true with him, enough to prompt him to write them down. I think they epitomize his out-of-the-box way of looking at the world.

It's pretty hard to tell what does bring happiness; poverty and wealth have both failed.

> The art of being wise is the art of knowing what to overlook.

> Thanks to the interstate highway system, it is now possible to travel from coast to coast without seeing anything.

> The ordinary acts we practice every day at home are of more importance to the soul than their simplicity might suggest.

> Usually, terrible things that are done with the excuse that progress requires them are not really progress at all, but just terrible things.

FBI wanted poster of D.B. Cooper

Associated Press file

A hijacked Northwest Airlines jetliner sits on a runway for refueling at Seattle-Tacoma International Airport on Nov. 25, 1971. D.B. Cooper vanished out the back of the Boeing 727 wearing a business suit, a parachute and a pack with $200,000 in ransom money.

40 years later, skyjacker's identity remains a mystery

By GENE JOHNSON
ASSOCIATED PRESS

SEATTLE — It's been a rich year for students of D.B. Cooper, the mysterious skyjacker who vanished out the back of a Boeing 727 wearing a business suit, a parachute and a pack with $200,000 in ransom money 40 years ago Thursday.

An Oklahoma woman came forward to say Cooper may have been her uncle, now deceased. A new book publicized several theories, including one that Cooper was a transgendered mechanic and pilot from Washington state. A team that includes a paleontologist from Seattle's Burke Museum released new findings this month that particles of pure titanium found in the hijacker's clip-on tie suggest he worked in the chemical industry or at a company that manufactured titanium — a discovery that could narrow the field of possible suspects from millions of people to just hundreds.

Nevertheless, no one's been able to solve the puzzle, or even determine whether Cooper survived his infamous jump.

"This case is a testament in a way to our enduring fascination with both a good mystery and a sense of wonderment — mystery because we still don't know who this guy was, and wonderment that a guy could do something this bold — or stupid," says Geoffrey Gray, whose book, "Skyjack: The Hunt for D.B. Cooper," came out in August.

On Nov. 24, 1971, the night before Thanksgiving, a man described as being in his mid-40s with dark sunglasses and an

COOPER

olive complexion boarded a Northwest Orient Airlines flight from Portland to Seattle-Tacoma International Airport.

He bought his $20 ticket under the name "Dan Cooper," but an early wire-service report misidentified him as "D.B. Cooper," and the name stuck.

He sat in the back of the plane and handed a note to a flight attendant. She was so busy she didn't read it until after takeoff: "Miss, I have a bomb and would like you to sit by me."

He opened his briefcase, displaying a couple of red cylinders, wires and a battery, and demanded $200,000 in cash plus four parachutes. His demands were granted at Sea-Tac, where he released the 36 passengers and two of the flight attendants. The plane took off again at his direction, heading slowly to Reno, Nev., at the low height of 10,000 feet. Somewhere, apparently over southwestern Washington, Cooper lowered the aircraft's rear stairs and dove into a freezing rainstorm — a jump so daring that even some of the police who scoured the area reportedly said they hoped he got away.

No sign of Cooper has ever emerged, but a boy digging on a Columbia River beach in 1980 found three bundles of weathered $20 bills — Cooper's cash, according to the serial numbers.

A few events are planned for Saturday to mark the anniversary, including a Cooper symposium (http://huntfordbcooper.com/) at a Portland, Ore., hotel, where sleuths will present their latest findings and theories — and serve as jurists for a Cooper-themed poetry contest.

Carol Abraczinskas, a scientific illustrator at the University of Chicago, said she plans to present the results of her three-year study of the French comic "Dan Cooper," a series about a test pilot in the Royal Canadian Air Force which may have been the source of the hijacker's pseudonym.

In one issue from 1963, she noted, the character boards an airliner wearing a dark suit and a mask over his eyes and sits in the back of the plane. He demands to be given a briefcase that's in the cockpit, and then, wearing a military parachute, he jumps out of the plane — over a wooded area, at night, in the rain.

"I'm looking at this as, are these comics a possible blueprint for the hijacker?" Abraczinskas says.

Also among those planning to attend is Marla Cooper of Oklahoma City, who disclosed this year that she had provided a tip to the FBI about her deceased uncle. Relying on childhood memories, she recalled that her uncle Lynn Doyle Cooper had arrived at a family home in Oregon with serious injuries and that she overheard him talking about the hijacking.

Cooper says she's optimistic the FBI will be able to match her uncle's fingerprints to those involved in the case.

Associated Press article by Gene Johnson

Laziness is nothing more than the habit of resting before you get tired.

When you're in love, it's the most glorious two and a half days of your life.

There's more to life than increasing its speed.

Getting old is not for sissies.

One never knows what each day is going to bring. The important thing is to be open and ready for it.

To believe everything or doubt everything, both save us from thinking.

There are lots of ways of being miserable, but there is only one way of being comfortable, and that's to stop running around after happiness.

Freedom is not worth having if it does not include the freedom to make mistakes.

A lot of people mistake a short memory for a clear conscience.

Anger is the feeling that makes your mouth move faster than your mind.

Learning to ignore things is one of the great paths to inner peace.

Walt and I had been very good friends for a very long time. Before he died, our last words to each other were "I love you, Walt." "I love you, Charlie."

I miss our almost daily conversations.

On the last line of the diary, Walt wrote, "All human beings should try to learn before they die what they are running from, to, and why."

In the end, Walt was running toward redemption, and, if I'm right, he thought that in death, as in life, he had a fifty-fifty chance of making it.

THE VINNELL CORPORATION

T he Vinnell Corporation was founded in 1931 as a Southern California construction firm, specializing in civilian projects, such as parts of the Los Angeles freeway system, the Grand Coulee Dam, and Dodger Stadium. The firm became involved with military and intelligence work at the end of World War II, gaining U.S. government contracts to ship supplies to Chiang Kai-shek's Nationalist army in China and build military airfields in Pakistan, Okinawa, Thailand, Taiwan, and South Vietnam during the 1950s and 1960s.[100]

At this time, Vinnell also established a close association with Central Intelligence Agency operatives. Company founder Albert Vinnell offered the CIA the services of his staff, and various CIA agents used their alleged employment with Vinnell as cover for operations in the Middle East and Africa. Former CIA operative Wilbur Crane Eveland describes this in his memoir *Ropes of Sand*.[101] To reciprocate, the CIA helped Vinnell obtain construction contracts on oil fields in Iran and Libya.

Vinnell's corporate headquarters are located in Fairfax, Virginia.

---

100 See https://www.sourcewatch.org/index.php/Vinnell_Corporation.
101 Wilbur Crane Eveland, *Ropes of Sand: America's Failure in the Middle East* (Norton, 1980).

After World War II, Vinnell expanded its construction business into Asia. During the war in Vietnam, Vinnell became directly involved in military and intelligence operations, at one point having more than five thousand employees in Vietnam. Their official jobs consisted of repairing U.S. military equipment and constructing military bases and airfields, but U.S. military officers have disclosed that Vinnell also ran several secret intelligence programs. A Pentagon source described Vinnell as "our own little mercenary army in Vietnam . . . we used them to do things we either didn't have the manpower to do ourselves, or because of legal problems."[102]

In February 1975, the Pentagon helped Vinnell win a contract to work with King Fahd to train the Saudi Arabian National Guard (SANG), the military arm of the House of at-Saud. SANG's members are descended from the Bedouin warriors who helped the Saud clan take control of the peninsula in the early twentieth century.[103]

Vinnell Corporation is known for hiring ex-military personnel. A *Newsweek* article at the time described the company's first efforts at recruiting with the help of "a one-eyed former U.S. Army colonel named James D. Holland" in a small office in the Los Angeles suburb of Alhambra to put together "a ragtag army of Vietnam veterans for a paradoxical mission: to train Saudi Arabian troops to defend the very oil fields that Henry Kissinger recently warned the U.S. might one day have to invade."[104]

"We are not mercenaries because we are not pulling triggers," a former U.S. Army officer told *Newsweek*. "We train people to pull

---

102 Sourcewatch, http://www.sourcewatch.org/index.php/Vinnell_Corporation. See also "The VINNELL Corporation," research by Gregory Burnham, November 8, 1999, http://www.prouty.org/vinnell.html, accessed June 16, 2017.

103 See William D. Hartung, "Mercenaries Inc.: How a U.S. Company Props Up the House of Saud," *The Progressive* (April 1996): 26–28.

104 Vinnell Corporation: "We Train People to Pull Triggers," by Pratap Chatterjee, Special to CorpWatch March 20, 2003, http://www.corpwatch.org/article.php?id=6029.

triggers." One of his colleagues wryly pointed out: "Maybe that makes us executive mercenaries."[105]

Today, Vinnell advertises itself as "providing a broad spectrum of professional and technical services to government clients in multiple areas of management and training. Client requirements have led Vinnell to a vast array of challenges, from Malaysia to Mexico to the Middle East, often to the very heart of international conflict areas." (In 1992, BDM International bought Vinnell, and BDM was acquired by TRW Inc. in 1997.)

Saudi Arabia nationalists are aware of Vinnell as a link between the Saudi and U.S. governments, thus targeting the Vinnell building with a car bomb on November 13, 1995, which killed five Americans and wounded thirty more. Then on May 13, 2003, three coordinated explosions in Riyadh hit Vinnell Corporation and killed nine workers.[106] Later sources put the number of dead much higher— May 12: "35 are killed and over 200 wounded during a suicide attack on the Vinnell Compound in Rihadh."[107]

In a 1996 article in the *Progressive*, William D. Hartung lays out Vinnell's role in propping up the House of Saud:

> President Clinton tried to paint the [1995] bombing as just another senseless act of terrorism perpetrated by armed Islamic extremists, but the target was chosen much too carefully to support that simple explanation. The Saudi National Guard is a 55,000 man military force whose main job is to protect the Saudi monarchy from its own people, using arms from the United States and training supplied

---

105 Ibid.
106 "Vinnell Corp., Targeted in Riyadh Before, Loses 9 More Workers," James Gerstenzang, *LA Times* staff writer, May 14, 2003, http://articles.latimes.com/2003/may/14/news/war-vinnell14.
107 Wikipedia, https://en.wikipedia.org/wiki/List_of_terrorist_incidents_in_Saudi_Arabia.

by roughly 750 retired U.S. military and intelligence personnel employed by the Vinnell Corporation of Fairfax, Virginia. . . . The November bombing . . . was certainly brutal, but it was far from senseless. As a retired American military officer familiar with Vinnell's operations put it, "I don't think it was an accident that it was that office that got bombed. If you wanted to make a political statement about the Saudi regime you'd single out the National Guard, and if you wanted to make a statement about American involvement you'd pick the only American contractor involved in training the guard: Vinnell."

The story of how an obscure American company ended up becoming the Saudi monarchy's personal protection service is a case study in how the United States government has come to rely on unaccountable private companies and unrepresentative foreign governments to do its dirty work on the world stage, short-circuiting democracy at home and abroad in the process.[108]

During the 1979 rebellion, Saudi opposition forces occupied the Grand Mosque in Mecca. *Counterspy* magazine "reported that when the initial National Guard assault failed, Vinnell personnel were brought to Mecca to 'provide the tactical support needed to capture the Mosque.'"[109]

Vinnell Corporation also had an indirect role in the Iran/Contra intelligence scandal.[110]

---

108 "Saudi Arabia: Mercenaries, Inc.," William D. Hartung, *The Progressive,* April 1, 1996.

109 Ibid.

110 Steven Emerson, *Secret Warriors: Inside the Covert Military Operations of the Reagan Era* (G.P. Putnam's Sons, 1988).

The company was previously owned by a partnership that included James A. Baker III and Frank Carlucci, former U.S. secretaries of state and defense under presidents George H. W. Bush and Ronald Reagan, respectively.

Yet beyond military ties, Vinnell "operates deep in the back-channel world that characterizes the U.S.-Saudi relationship, experts say."[111]

"They're definitely one of the top hooked-in companies in the United States" that provides services in Saudi Arabia, said Deborah Avant, a professor of political science at George Washington University, who wrote a book on private security forces overseas.[112]

---

111 Ibid.
112 Ibid.

MKULTRA

Project MKUltra, a top-secret CIA mind control program, conducted clandestine (and at times illegal) experiments on human subjects, often without the participants' knowledge or consent. Headed by Sidney Gottlieb, the program attempted to identify and develop drugs and procedures to use in interrogations, torture, and intelligence gathering, to weaken a person and force a confession using mind control. The project was designed and organized through the Scientific Intelligence Division of the CIA and coordinated with the Special Operations Division of the U.S. Army's Chemical Corps. The CIA poured millions of dollars into funding the program.[113]

The program began in the early 1950s and was halted in 1973, but details about it didn't become public until 1975, during a congressional investigation into illegal CIA activities within the United States and globally.[114] MKUltra aimed to develop mind-controlling drugs to use against the Soviet bloc, in response to alleged Soviet, Chinese, and North Korean use of methods to brainwash U.S. prisoners of war in Korea.[115] The CIA attempted to produce a "truth drug" to use when

---

113 Wikipedia, https://en.wikipedia.org/wiki/Project_MKUltra. "One of the Most Shocking CIA Programs of All Time: Project MKUltra," 2013-09-23. Retrieved 2016-08-18. See also: Advisory on Human Radiation Experiments, July 5, 1994, National Security Archives, retrieved January 16, 2014, archived July 13, 2013, at the Wayback Machine, *archive.org/web/*.
114 "History of MK-Ultra," http://www.history.com/topics/history-of-mk-ultra.
115 Ibid.

interrogating suspected Soviet spies during the Cold War. The CIA also desired to manipulate foreign leaders with these techniques and later devised several schemes to drug Fidel Castro.[116]

To influence people's mental states and alter brain functions, MKUltra used drugs (especially LSD and, most egregiously, combining intravenous barbiturates with amphetamines) and other chemicals, as well as hypnosis, electroshock therapy, isolation, sensory deprivation, verbal abuse, sexual and physical abuse, and various types of psychological torture.[117]

Project MKUltra conducted research at eighty institutions, including forty-four colleges and universities, as well as hospitals, prisons, and pharmaceutical companies. The CIA used front organizations to operate through these institutions, although sometimes higher-ups at the institutions knew the CIA was involved.[118] As the U.S. Supreme Court noted in *CIA v. Sims*, 471 U.S. 159 (1985), MKUltra was:

---

116 Wikipedia, https://en.wikipedia.org/wiki/Project_MKUltra. "Advisory Committee on Human Radiation Experiments Final Report. Archived from the original on November 9, 2004. Retrieved August 24, 2005. "MKUltra, began in 1950 and was motivated largely in response to alleged Soviet, Chinese, and North Korean uses of mind-control techniques on U.S. prisoners of war in Korea." Also see: Church Committee, p. 391, "A special procedure, designated MKDELTA, was established to govern the use of MKUltra materials abroad. Such materials were used on a number of occasions." And see Church Committee, "The congressional committee investigating the CIA research, chaired by Senator Frank Church, concluded that '[p]rior consent was obviously not obtained from any of the subjects.'"

117 Ibid. See also Kalee Brown, "What the History Channel Left Out about the Declassified CIA Program: 'History of MK-Ultra,'" June 25, 2017; http://www.collective-evolution.com/2017/06/25/what-the-history-channel-left-out-about-the-declassified-cia-program-history-of-mk-ultra/.

118 Wikipedia, https://en.wikipedia.org/wiki/Project_MKUltra. *United States Senate, 95th Congress, 1st session (August 3, 1977). Project MKUltra, The CIA's Program of Research in Behavioral Modification (PDF). Joint Hearing Before the Select Committee on Intelligence and the Subcommittee on Health and Scientific Research of the Committee on Human Resources (Report).*

concerned with "the research and development of chemical, biological, and radiological materials capable of employment in clandestine operations to control human behavior." The program consisted of some 149 subprojects which the Agency contracted out to various universities, research foundations, and similar institutions. At least 80 institutions and 185 private researchers participated. Because the Agency funded MKUltra indirectly, many of the participating individuals were unaware that they were dealing with the Agency.[119]

The Supreme Court validated the existence of MKUltra to be used in future court cases and confirmed that the CIA had performed clandestine experiments on human behavior for fourteen years.

A 1955 MKUltra document indicates the size and range of the program, describing the study of assorted mind-altering substances as follows:

1. Substances which will promote illogical thinking and impulsiveness to the point where the recipient would be discredited in public.
2. Substances which increase the efficiency of mentation and perception.
3. Materials which will cause the victim to age faster/ slower in maturity.
4. Materials which will promote the intoxicating effect of alcohol.
5. Materials which will produce the signs and symptoms of recognized diseases in a reversible way so that they may be used for malingering, etc.

---

119 Ibid.

6. Materials which will cause temporary/permanent brain damage and loss of memory.

7. Substances which will enhance the ability of individuals to withstand privation, torture and coercion during interrogation and so-called "brain-washing".

8. Materials and physical methods which will produce amnesia for events preceding and during their use.

9. Physical methods of producing shock and confusion over extended periods of time and capable of surreptitious use.

10. Substances which produce physical disablement such as paralysis of the legs, acute anemia, etc.

11. Substances which will produce a chemical that can cause blisters.

12. Substances which alter personality structure in such a way that the tendency of the recipient to become dependent upon another person is enhanced.

13. A material which will cause mental confusion of such a type that the individual under its influence will find it difficult to maintain a fabrication under questioning.

14. Substances which will lower the ambition and general working efficiency of men when administered in undetectable amounts.

15. Substances which promote weakness or distortion of the eyesight or hearing faculties, preferably without permanent effects.

16. A knockout pill which can surreptitiously be administered in drinks, food, cigarettes, as an aerosol, etc., which will be safe to use, provide a maximum of amnesia, and be suitable for use by agent types on an ad hoc basis.

17. A material which can be surreptitiously administered by the above routes and which in very small amounts

will make it impossible for a person to perform physical activity.[120]

Project MKUltra experiments included administering LSD to mental patients, prisoners, drug addicts, and prostitutes. In one case, LSD was administered to a mental patient in Kentucky for 174 days. The Office of Security used LSD in interrogations, but Dr. Sidney Gottlieb, the chemist who directed MKUltra, wanted to use it in covert operations—for example, giving it to high-ranking officials and influencing important meetings, speeches, and so on. He began a series of experiments in which researchers gave LSD to people in "normal" settings without warning, in order to study their reactions—usually without the subject's knowledge or informed consent. This violated the Nuremburg Code that the United States was supposed to follow after World War II. "At first, everyone in Technical Services tried it . . . As the experimentation progressed, . . . outsiders were drugged with no explanation whatsoever and surprise acid trips became something of an occupational hazard among CIA operatives. Adverse reactions often occurred."[121] The objective was to elicit deep confessions or wipe a subject's mind clean and program the person as "a robot agent."[122]

Adverse reactions often occurred. Yet the experiments continued even after the 1953 death of Dr. Frank Olson, a U.S. Army biochemist and biological weapons researcher. The CIA first called it an accident, then years later began calling it a suicide, saying he became depressed after he was unknowingly administered LSD for the first time, and he jumped out of a tenth-floor hotel window.

Others, including his family, say he was murdered because in the aftermath of his LSD experience he had become a security risk.

---

120 Ibid.
121 Ibid.
122 Ibid.

The CIA feared he might divulge state secrets about highly classified programs.[123] A few days before his death, Frank Olson resigned as acting chief of the Special Operations Division at Detrick, Maryland (later, Fort Detrick), due to a severe moral crisis about his biological weapons research.[124]

> Among Olson's concerns were the development of assassination materials used by the CIA. The CIA's use of biological warfare materials in covert operations, experimentation with biological weapons in populated areas, collaboration with former Nazi scientists under Operation Paperclip, LSD mind-control research, and the use of psychoactive drugs during "terminal" interrogations under a program code-named Project ARTICHOKE.[125]

According to one source, "The family of Frank Olson decided to have a second autopsy performed in 1994. A forensics team found injuries on the body that had likely occurred before the fall. The findings sparked conspiracy theories that Olson might have been assassinated by the CIA."[126]

And another source states, "Later forensic evidence conflicted with the official version of events; when Olson's body was exhumed in 1994, cranial injuries indicated that Olson had been knocked unconscious before he exited the window."[127] The medical examiner

---

123 See the 2017 six-part Netflix docudrama *Wormwood*, directed by Oscar-winning filmmaker Errol Morris, which depicts Eric Olson's lifelong search for the truth about his father's death.
124 Ibid.
125 Ibid.
126 "History of MKUltra," http://www.history.com/topics/history-of-mk-ultra.
127 Wikipedia, https://en.wikipedia.org/wiki/Project_MKUltra Wikipedia.

termed Olson's death a "homicide."[128] "There is no indication that any investigation of foul play, particularly by the CIA officer (who was both responsible for the experiment and alone in the hotel room with Olson) was ever conducted."[129]

Declassified MKUltra documents from the early 1950s demonstrate the study of hypnosis to create "hypnotically induced anxieties," to "hypnotically [increase the] ability to learn and recall complex written matter," influence polygraph examinations, "hypnotically [increase the] ability to observe and recall complex arrangements of physical objects," and to learn the "relationship of personality to susceptibility to hypnosis."[130] The CIA conducted experiments with drug-induced hypnosis and with anterograde and retrograde amnesia while under the influence of drugs.

According to Kalee Brown, "Many other claims have come to light regarding the destroyed CIA documents, thanks to whistleblowers who have come forward who were involved in the actual experiments. A 1954 document allegedly stated that two hypnotized women were forced into conflict, with an agent telling one of the women to 'fly into a rage and shoot her,' which she allegedly did. . . .

"Of course, test subjects reacted negatively, with many ending up permanently comatose. Anton Chaitkin explains in his essay 'British Psychiatry: From Eugenics to Assassination,' under the MK Ultra section: 'Cameron would drug his victims to sleep for weeks on end, waking them daily only to administer violent electric shocks to the brain. . . . Patients lost all or part of their memories, and some lost the

---

128 Ibid. See also H. P. Albarelli, Jr., *A Terrible Mistake: The Murder of Frank Olson and the CIA's Secret Cold War Experiments* (TrineDay Publishers, 2010).

129 "Project MKUltra: One of the Most Shocking CIA Programs of All Time," http://gizmodo.com/project-mkultra-one-of-the-most-shocking-cia-programs-1370236359

130 Wikipedia, https://en.wikipedia.org/wiki/Project_MKUltra Wikipedia.

ability to control their bodily functions and to speak.' . . . Chaitkin explained: 'For the CIA, Cameron tested the South American poison called curare, which kills a victim while simulating natural heart failure.'"[131]

"At his retirement in 1972, Gottlieb dismissed his entire effort for the CIA's MKUltra program as useless."[132]

Although the CIA claims it has abandoned MKUltra-type experiments, some CIA observers say these likely continue today under different acronyms. Victor Marchetti, author and fourteen-year CIA veteran, stated in several interviews that the CIA regularly conducts disinformation campaigns and that CIA mind control research is ongoing. "In a 1977 interview, Marchetti specifically called the CIA claim that MKUltra was abandoned a 'cover story.'"[133]

131 Kalee Brown, "What the History Channel Left Out about the Declassified CIA Program: 'History of MK-Ultra,'" June 25, 2017; http://www.collective-evolution.com/2017/06/25/what-the-history-channel-left-out-about-the-declassified-cia-program-history-of-mk-ultra/.
132 Wikipedia, https://en.wikipedia.org/wiki/Project_MKUltra Wikipedia.
133 Ibid.

ACKNOWLEDGMENTS

For my wife, Loretta, who put up with a dining room table full of clutter for twenty years.

To our publishers at Principia Media, Vern and Irene Jones, who believed a total stranger.

To Dirk Wierenga, an iron man among documentary film producers, and Patti Waldygo, our book doctor and editor at Desert Sage Editorial Services.

And to Jeff Osiadacz, a.k.a. Cowboy, once a stranger but a stranger no more.

I would take a bullet for all of them.

For Art, Parker, McCusker, Fat Willard, and Sherm Reed of the Michigan Parachute Team, who kept me in stitches and broken bones I would not trade for the world, and Walter, my friend. Walter, who never quit talking about making a getaway by jumping out of an airplane and then finally did it—the orphan who came from so little and accomplished so much. My friend, who kept a misunderstood promise to his country, and his country was the better for it.

To all my friends, thank you. What a great privilege!

PEOPLE WHO PLAYED SIGNIFICANT ROLES IN THE LIFE OF D.B. COOPER

ART LUSSIER

A founding member of the Michigan Parachute Club. One of Walt's very closest friends. Big personality. Art Lussier was also a pilot who flew munitions shipments into Africa during the Biafran war.

BILL "COLONEL" PARKER

A member of the Michigan Parachute Club (MPC); a gun-loving eccentric.

WILLIAM JOHN (BILL) RATACZAK

First Officer of Flight 305, the hijacked plane. Was given the job of flying the plane in the difficult flying configuration Walt required.

CARL "CHARLIE BROWN" LAURIN

Former military paratrooper. Daredevil parachutist who was slightly more cautious than his friends. Best friend to Walt. He first suspected Walt was D.B. Cooper on the night of the hijacking. Years later, in

1998, he realized that Walt really was D.B. Cooper at a gathering of the Michigan Parachute Club. He spent the next twenty years uncovering the details of that night and beyond. Married to Loretta.

CARLA

Walt's third wife (married September 30, 1974). According to Carl, Walt "should have known better" when it came to Carla.

DAVID LAURIN

Son of Carl and Loretta Laurin. According to his father, "the gears in his head never stop turning."

DON BRENNAN

One of Walt's best and most trusted friends. He was a smoke jumper and a member of the ironworkers' union. Don Brennan helped provide Walt with a fake ID and a place to stay when he was on the run. Brennan was the first friend to see Walt after the infamous jump, and he drove Walt home after the hijacking. That night Walt gave him a few bundles of the hijack money to keep him quiet. Brennan was not involved in planning the hijacking.

FLORENCE SCHAFFNER

Stewardess aboard Flight 305. Received the note from Walt and put it in her pocket, believing it was another come-on from a male passenger. She was very attractive and often wore a wig to downplay her looks. When she finally read the note, she dropped it, and it was picked up by Tina Mucklow. Stewardess Mucklow took over in interacting with Walt, and Flo stayed in the cockpit to take notes on radio discussions between the crew and airline authorities, as well as between the cockpit crew and Mucklow, who relayed Walt's demands.

JACK "STEEPLEJACK" CLAPP

A member of the MPC; a steeplejack by trade. Fearless and made from scrap iron, as tough as they come.

JEFF "COWBOY" OSIADACZ

Was the first person to see Walt walking down the side of the road in the dark after the infamous jump. Saw him again at the café where Walt stopped to warm up and call Don Brennan. Walt asked "Cowboy" to talk to Brennan over the phone to give directions to the café. Truck driver, a talented musician, and a native of Cle Elum, Washington. His career also included law enforcement, which assisted in his recall of the events of November 24, 1971.

JIM MCCUSKER

A member of the MPC. A decorated commercial pilot. He won first place at the Fort Bragg Parachute Championship in 1964.

JOAN "JONI" PECA/RECA

Walt's second wife (married November 3, 1960) and one of Loretta's best friends. Walt and Joni got back together in their later years, and she changed her name to Reca, even though they never remarried. She was the love of Walt's life.

LISA STORY

Walt's niece, the daughter of his sister, Sandy, and one of two people to whom Walt confessed the hijacking.

LORETTA LAURIN

Carl's wife, married on September 5, 1961. Often listened to the phone conversations while Carl and Walt discussed the hijacking.

MICHIGAN PARACHUTE CLUB

A ragtag group of reckless young men with no fear and no boundaries. Formed in 1957 by Art, Bill, Walter, McCusker, and Carl. Operated under the mottos "One bad idea deserves another" and "Why open your chute that high? Are you planning to live forever?"

MIKE LUSSIER

Art's younger brother, one of the world's youngest parachuters at age thirteen and an early member of the MPC.

REGINA SCHNEIDEGGER

Walt's mother, widowed after her husband was electrocuted while their children were still young. Reluctantly "jumped" out of a plane in her forties with the MPC.

SANDRA "SANDY" (PECA)

Walt's younger sister and the mother of Lisa. Attended to Walt in his final days. Sandy also read Walt's confession at the same time that Lisa Story read it but didn't ask questions as Lisa did.

SINCLAIR

Friend of Art and Walt out West and a pioneer in parachuting cinematography. Lived in a trailer for seven years in Carl's front yard.

SISSLER

Member of the Air Force Reserves who jumped with the MPC. Joined the Army Rangers, went to Vietnam, and won a medal of honor.

SUICIDE SLIM

A member of the MPC; "not fearless, just stupid."

TINA MUCKLOW

Stewardess aboard hijacked Flight 305 who voluntarily stayed with the plane and was the go-between for the hijacker and the cockpit until D.B. Cooper's jump.

WALTER "WALT" R. RECA (PECA JR.)

a.k.a. "D.B. Cooper." Former military paratrooper, daredevil, and intelligence operative. Believed it was "better to be dead than poor." Polish heritage with Catholic roots. Former barber. Chain smoker. Born September 20, 1933. Spent more than fifteen years revealing the mysteries of his life to his best friend, Carl, but went to his grave with many secrets untold. Beloved and mourned by Carl.

WALTER "BIG WALT" PECA, SR.

Walt's father, killed by electrocution in a coal yard accident when Walt was just six years old. Big Walt was studying to be a doctor at the time of his death. How different would Walt's life have been if his father hadn't died?

WARD SEELEY

Airplane mechanic and pilot who sometimes flew for the MPC. A good pilot and the best mechanic Carl ever knew.

"FAT" WILLARD STAHL

A member of the MPC and one of Walt's closest friends. A former juvenile delinquent with a long rap sheet, which he was proud of. A "damn good fighter," too.

Condition noted
8-20-20
JC

CPSIA information can be obtained
at www.ICGtesting.com
Printed in the USA
BVHW01s2245310518
517946BV00018B/171/P

9 781614 853251